Finding the Middle Ground

Insights and Applications of the Value Orientations Method

Finding the Middle Ground

Insights and Applications of the Value Orientations Method

Edited by Kurt W. Russo

INTERCULTURAL PRESS, INC.

For information contact:
Intercultural Press, Inc.
PO Box 700
Yarmouth, ME 04096 USA
207-846-5168

Book and cover design and production: Patty J. Topel

Printed in the United States of America

03 02 01 00 99 1 2 3 4 5

Library of Congress Cataloging-in-Publication Data

Finding the middle ground: insights and applications of the Value Orientations Method/edited by Kurt W. Russo.
p. cm.
Includes bibliographical references
ISBN 1-877864-76-5 (alk. paper)
1. Values. 2. Kluckhohn, Florence Rockwood. Variations in value orientations. I. Russo, Kurt W.

BF778.F56 2000
303.3'72—dc21 99-048807

We dedicate this book to Florence Rockwood Kluckhohn and her grandchildren, Guilbert and Bruce, and to the memory of Dr. Fremont J. Lyden.

Table of Contents

Part 3: Value Orientations and Education

Part 4: Value Orientations and Conflict Resolution

Appendices

The Value of Values

George E. Taylor

My interest in understanding values began when I read a book by the Dutchman Gustaaf Johannes Renier called *The English: Are They Human?* There was also another book by a Spaniard, Salvador de Madariage, called *The English, the Germans and the French*. These were early attempts, in the thirties and forties, to get down to values. Then, when the war came, I found myself in the Office of War Information (OWI) in charge of psychological warfare against Japan. One of the first questions we raised was, Who are the Japanese? And nobody could tell us. There was no literature whatsoever on the basic values of the Japanese. One man in my office, Jeffrey Gorer, an English anthropologist, had written about Japanese toilet training, which, he said quite correctly, began early and was very severe, making the Japanese aggressive. We had no way of changing toilet training, so we parted company.

I turned then to Dr. Alexander H. Leighton. I had met him first in the Posten, Arizona, relocation camp, where I was gathering material on Japanese relocation. He had been sent there by the navy to study the Japanese from the point of view of governing them after the war during the occupation. I said, "Can you tell me who the Japanese are?" And he said, "No, but I can work on it." So we went to his admiral, and within five minutes we were out of the office and on our way back to the Office of War Information.

Dr. Leighton built a team. We did not invite Margaret Mead, because she belonged to a group, a large group I'm afraid, of psychologists and psychoanalysts who claimed that both the Japanese and the Germans were victims of cultural determinism and there was nothing you could do about it. Dr. Leighton put together a blue-ribbon group of social scientists, including Clyde Kluckhohn—almost thirty scholars in all. It was called the Foreign Morale Analysis Division (FMAD). We even talked Ruth Benedict into joining the group, and she used the material after the war to write *The Chrysanthemum and the Sword*.

Florence R. Kluckhohn came from Harvard to join FMAD and to be the liaison between Alexander Leighton's office and mine. In a very short time FMAD provided the psychological ammunition for the decision not to attack the Japanese Emperor. The United States was under great pressure to do so, but we explained that if we attacked him, we would not succeed in making any impression on the Japanese except to make them furious. And secondly, we would remove the only known institution that could bring about an organized surrender—this was the key point. Ambassador MacGrew agreed with this, fortunately, but a lot of people did not, including President Roosevelt.

Three times Elmer Davis, director of the OWI, called on President Roosevelt to request a modification of unconditional surrender and gave him the arguments for doing so. And three times Roosevelt said no, in no uncertain terms, using some of the strongest language Davis had ever heard. After Truman succeeded to the presidency, Davis went to see him. When he came back to the office, we asked, "Well, what did President Truman say?" According to Elmer, he said, "It makes sense to me" and then made it clear that he would in due course make a statement of Allied policy on the issue. But he instructed the OWI in the meantime to tell the Japanese via shortwave radio that we were not going to humiliate the Emperor and that we were not going to enslave the Japanese as a nation. In the Potsdam Declaration, however, Truman stated that the Japanese army *would* have to surrender unconditionally. But he made no mention of the Emperor or the Japanese people, except to say the United States would not enslave them. So we secured a modification of unconditional surrender. Our European team did not succeed in getting the same deal in Europe, a decision that cost a lot of lives, in my view. So the importance of values and the study of the values of other countries has never been shown more vividly than it was at that time. As far as I'm concerned, FMAD was the beginning of serious social science interest in the importance of values in international affairs.

Not long after the war was over, Harvard raised money for what became known as the Harvard Values Project. Harry Scarr worked with Florence Kluckhohn and Fred L. Strodtbeck on *Variations in Value Orientations*, which reported the results of the project.

Largely through the efforts of Kurt W. Russo, we have been able to continue working on the application of the Harvard theory of values to concrete situations and problems such as the use of natural resources involving the Lummi Nation and the organizations with which it has to interact.

I hope this volume of articles succeeds in reflecting the growing interest in the study of values. It is clear that few things are more important today—nationally and internationally—than understanding how values drive behavior in the real world.

Introduction

Kurt W. Russo

This book is concerned with the question of values and the concept of value orientations originally developed by Dr. Florence Rockwood Kluckhohn. It was my good fortune to have had the opportunity to work with Dr. Kluckhohn from 1982 until her death in January of 1986. Each week I drove from Bellingham, Washington, where I worked with the Lummi Indians, to her home in the Highlands District of Seattle. There, in a library filled with books that reflected a lifetime devoted to working across cultures, Dr. Kluckhohn tutored me in the use of the value orientations method. Unknown to either of us, these sessions were the beginning of a research and training program that has since expanded across the United States and has come to include the involvement of scholars and specialists now using the method to promote values-based understanding within and among diverse cultural groups and communities.

Dr. Kluckhohn began working on the theoretical and philosophical framework of the value orientations method as early as 1936. At the time, she was conducting field research for her doctoral thesis in a Spanish-speaking village in New Mexico. It was there, in the small community of Los Atarqueños, that she first developed the concept of the *general life situation*. Dr. Kluckhohn proposed that a group's orientation to life's most generalized situations was an outward manifestation of its inward belief about the nature of "what is" *best, right, and true*. For example, although groups may differ in how they bring order to human relations, the general life situation requires they resolve this problem or perish. How they resolve this problem must correspond to, and be meaningful in terms of, the groups' innermost belief about what is best, right, and true. Similarly, while groups may differ in their orientation to the natural world, the general life situation requires that they create for themselves a meaningful, coherent, and enduring relationship with nature (and supernature). Dr. Kluckhohn proposed that the group's orientation to these, and a finite number of other general life situations, would help to answer questions of fundamental interest to students of culture change, culture conflict, and cross-cultural communication.

Dr. Kluckhohn often recounted how important the development of this concept was to her later work and to the evolution of the value orientations method. Her experience in Los Atarqueños and her subsequent work at Harvard University led her to conclude that *there are a limited number of common human problems for which all societies at all times must find some solution.* She asserted that *how a group is predisposed to understand, give meaning to, and solve these common problems is an outward manifestation of its innermost values, its window on the world: its value orientations.* This critical insight would later prove to be a centerpiece in the classification of value orientations first presented by Dr. Kluckhohn in two articles published in 1950.

At approximately the same time as these articles were published, funds were made available by the Rockefeller Foundation to Harvard University for a large-scale and long-range study of values in the American Southwest. The site selected for the study was an area where five distinct cultural communities lived within a radius of forty miles. The five communities, located in an area referred to as the Rimrock, included a Texan homestead community, a Mormon village, a Mexican American village, a decentralized Navaho Indian band, and a centralized Zuni pueblo. The Rimrock area presented the Harvard team with a living laboratory in which they could conduct several kinds of research on the subject of values in this culturally diverse, and geographically confined, area.

The study became known as the Harvard Values Project. It was codirected by Dr. John Roberts and Dr. Evon Vogt and involved the work of a team of social scientists from Harvard University's Laboratory of Social Relations, among them Dr. Kluckhohn and Dr. Fred Strodtbeck. The results of this monumental project were published in the book *People of Rimrock: A Study of Values in Five Cultures* (Vogt and Albert 1966). This was, and remains, one of the most extensive and intensive studies of values in the history of cultural anthropology.

The Rimrock project provided Dr. Kluckhohn and her colleagues the perfect setting for refining and field testing the value orientations method.* Her first and most daunting task was to more fully develop the general life situations. In developing these situations she and her colleagues were guided by four major considerations. First, the general life situation had to be an expression of a single value dimension, uncontaminated by other "behavior spheres." The five value dimensions postulated by Dr. Kluckhohn included Human Relations, Activity, Person-Nature, Time, and Human Nature. These will be discussed at length in the first article, "Value Orientations Method." The difficulty of developing "uncontaminated" situations, however, prevented the team from developing general life situations for the Human Nature behavior sphere. Second in magnitude was the question of selecting situations that had a relatively equal degree of significance in communities that were culturally distinct. Third, the situation had to be structured to minimize the distorting effect of a respondent's defensive reaction. Fourth, the situation had to be designed in a manner that minimized "the purely idiosyncratic life experiences of particular individuals" (Kluckhohn and Strodtbeck 1961, 79).

The team spent countless hours developing the general life situations for use in a value orientations survey. The survey would eventually include twenty-two situations designed to elicit the individual's value orientations in the value dimensions of Human Relations, Activity, Person-Nature, and Time. Due to a shortage of time, however, the team did not develop situations for the Human Nature dimension, and, for similar reasons, elected to develop only two of the three alternative orientations in the Activity dimension. A few items were then field-tested in 1950–1951 in the Zuni and Navaho groups. The results of this initial field test were sufficiently interesting to warrant a large-scale project in all five of the communities. The results of this study would later be published in the volume *Variations in Value Orientations* (Kluckhohn and Strodtbeck 1961).

It was my good fortune in 1982 to learn of the value orientations method through the late Dr. Fremont Lyden, a professor at

* The value orientations method consists of two components: the value orientations framework (introduced in the first article in Part 1, page 3) and the research instrument (the value orientations survey, presented in Appendix A).

the Graduate School of Public Affairs at the University of Washington. I had been working for three years with the Lummi Indian Nation† in an effort to help it acquire a twelve-hundred-acre island located just off the southern tip of their reservation. After the Lummi Nation acquired the island, I began working with the community to develop a plan that would preserve the island's wilderness character. Several months into this project, however, it became clear that the term *wilderness* had many different, and often contradictory, meanings within the community. In order to make sense of this puzzle, I turned to Dr. Lyden, who had served on my graduate committee at the University of Washington. Drawing on over two decades of the study of values, he immediately recommended Dr. Kluckhohn's value orientations method as a means for understanding—and bridging—value-based differences within the Lummi Indian Nation.

What followed was a two-year research program, sponsored by the Tides Foundation of San Francisco, in which Kluckhohn's Value Orientations Survey was administered in the 2,800-member Lummi Indian Nation. Lummi tribal members who had been trained in the use of the Value Orientations Survey completed 115 interviews in the community—one of the largest random sample populations ever surveyed with the method. Dr. Kluckhohn, Dr. Lyden, an academic advisory board from the University of Washington, and designated tribal members provided invaluable assistance in identifying the sample population, administering the survey, and analyzing the findings. The resulting profile of variations in the orientations in the Lummi Indian community was successfully applied in recasting the meaning of wilderness and delineating the nature and scope of activities that could take place on the island. In addition, the results of the research were later used to evaluate the meaning of work and the workplace to the Lummi Indian community. The results provided a new mechanism for evaluating the impact of development and for designing projects that were compatible with the community's value orientations.

Just as significant, the Lummi program was a springboard for a much more ambitious endeavor—the Values Project Northwest:

† The Lummi Indians most often use the term *nation*, rather than *tribe*, as an expression of their political status as a sovereign government. While other native communities in the Pacific Northwest share this view on sovereignty, many of them still retain the use of tribe in referring to their community.

xwlemi.[†] The Lummi Nation must routinely consult with local and regional public and private sector groups that have little if any understanding of the tribe and its culture. These misunderstandings inevitably lead to mistrust and suspicion that amplify preexisting conflicts of interest.

In 1984 I was asked by the tribe to design and implement a project that would address this long-standing crisis in communication. The result was the Values Project Northwest, which would later evolve into the Florence R. Kluckhohn Center for the Study of Values. Over six hundred value orientations interviews were conducted in public and private sector groups whose decisions had a social, cultural, or economic impact on the Lummi Nation. Over a thirteen-year period, the Value Orientations Survey was administered in natural resource management groups (Weyerhaeuser Company, the United States Forest Service, and the Washington State Department of Natural Resources), energy and hydroelectric development organizations (the Northwest Power Planning Council, Tacoma City Light, Puget Sound Power and Light, the Washington State Department of Ecology, and Seattle City Light), financial and economic development interests (Rainier National Bank and Pacific International Terminals), and local government (Whatcom County Government).

The significance of this far-ranging project and the accompanying training programs is illustrated in the application of the Kluckhohn method to the relationship between the Washington State Department of Natural Resources and the Lummi Indians. This agency is responsible for managing all the state forestlands in the state of Washington, including old-growth forest areas in the aboriginal territory of the Lummi Indians. The agency's forest plans and programs had often brought the agency into conflict with the Lummi Nation, particularly over the use of state forestlands by members of the *seyown*.

The seyown is a Pacific Northwest aboriginal spiritual tradition in which individuals use the forest for spirit questing, spiritual cleansing, and fasting in order to obtain special powers. These powers and the practices associated with them embody aboriginal concepts of the natural world that date back hundreds, perhaps thou-

---

† *xwlemi* (qwha-lem-me) is a Lummi Indian term from which the word *Lummi* is derived.

sands, of years. The issue at hand was not just a matter of biology and board feet of lumber. Rather, it was a conflict of paradigms, of what is real and true in the natural world around us.

In 1987 this conflict led both parties to agree to take part in a project, designed and facilitated by the Values Project Northwest under the auspices of the newly formed Florence R. Kluckhohn Center for the Study of Values. The Center completed forty-four interviews in the Department of Natural Resources, administering the value orientation survey to individuals at every level of the organization. Center staff used this information, and the results of identical value orientations interviews previously completed in the Lummi Indian community, in the design of a series of workshops between the two groups. In retrospect, it is clear that the project with the Lummi Nation and the Washington State Department of Natural Resources was a watershed event. The eighteen-month project was the first time the value orientations method had been employed in a workshop setting to resolve a value-based conflict between two culturally distinct communities. The effort was, by measure of the outcomes and participant feedback, an unqualified success.

As a result of the project, the two parties reached a more basic understanding of how their groups' beliefs about what is "best, right, or true"—their worldview—compared to those of the cultural "other." They also learned, by virtue of the value orientations method, how their preconceptions of each other distorted patterns of communication. This understanding provided a foundation for true communication and meaningful consultation that has endured to this day. The reader is referred to a description of the structure and outcomes of the Values Project Northwest in two articles in Part 4 of the present volume, "A Sharing of Subjectivities" and "Value Orientations as a Tool for Cross-Cultural Understanding."

The project was living proof, if any was still needed, of the enduring value and significance of the value orientations method as a tool for promoting true communication. The persistence of the method can be attributed to four outstanding features: (1) the intellectual rigor of the method, (2) the relative ease of administering the Value Orientations Survey, (3) the universality and adaptability of the general life situations, and (4) the instrumental value of information generated by the method. The method not only provides a means for identifying and measuring value orientations but has also proven to be a highly effective and adaptive tool for characterizing and dispelling stereotypes that can exacerbate and prolong conflict between culturally diverse groups. Just as important, the method cultivates a "reflective capacity" in both the researcher and the participating groups, regardless of the cultural setting. The ability to reflect with understanding is the first, and most crucial, step in promoting trust and providing enduring solutions between groups in conflict.

The lasting relevance of Dr. Kluckhohn's method is also a tribute to her observation that cultural groups are mistakenly perceived by outsiders as homogeneous wholes guided by an all-inclusive set of norms, values, and beliefs. Dr. Kluckhohn asserted that, to the contrary, cultural groups were a rich tapestry of rank-ordered variations. This critical insight—that *each of the value orientations were found in all persons and all groups though differently preferred*—provides a guiding light for understanding the genius, ingenuity, and durability of the method.

There are those who insist that the notion of universal common human problems is contradictory to what we know of basic differences among cultural groups. Others contend that while humankind may face common problems, we can never know with sufficient certainty the true meaning of these problems to people in other cultural communities. Still others assert that core values of culturally diverse groups are either immeasurable or incommensurable.

Dr. Kluckhohn was aware of these and other criticisms of the method. She went to great pains in *Variations* to warn against the dangers in social science research of circular reasoning and was mindful of the ever-present danger of the illusion of technique. She was also among the first to insist that cultural groups are distinct in how they give meaning to the world of experience. Just as important, she was greatly concerned with the role of the participant-observer. By this, she was not only referring to an impartial and informed researcher. She was equally adamant in her belief that researchers and research subjects should together have a "dialogue with the data." A fact, she would argue, is one thing; its meaning is another. She often impressed upon me the importance of working hand in hand with respondents in the interpretation of their value orientation profile.

Dr. Kluckhohn could hardly have known, in the early years of her work, how extensively the method would be applied in the decades to follow. To date, it has been used in distinct ethnic and cultural communities in Puerto Rico, Canada, Mexico, Colombia, Scotland, Palestine, Uganda, South Africa, Japan, Vietnam, South Korea, New Zealand, and Polynesia. The Kluckhohn Center and its Associate Scholars in the United States are currently employing the method in research, training, and conflict resolution programs in the African American, Native American, Asian American, white ethnic, and Latino American communities as well as business groups, public agencies, and colleges and universities. This range of applications is a testimony to Dr. Kluckhohn and to the insight of skilled scholars and practitioners throughout the world now using the method to resolve conflict between distinct cultural groups and communities.

All too often, cross-cultural research methods are developed that never see the light of day in real-life situations. At the other extreme, ad hoc or highly limited cross-cultural communication tools are employed that lack a broad-based theoretical foundation. The Center and its Associate Scholars are committed to the use of the value orientations method and uniting the two domains of theory and practice in the design and implementation of values-based research programs, cross-cultural training workshops, educational seminars, and scholarly symposia both in the United States and abroad. The Center is also designed to serve as a clearinghouse for ideas and information for scholars and practitioners now using the Kluckhohn method. A critical component of the Center's role as a clearinghouse is its Values Symposium series. The symposia, sponsored and coordinated by the Center, bring together values scholars and cross-cultural specialists from a variety of fields to refine the value orientations method and promote the development of other cross-cultural tools and techniques.

The present volume contains a selection of the articles presented by Kluckhohn scholars at two of the Center's Values Symposia, 1993 and 1997. In selecting these articles, it was our intent to introduce the reader to the theoretical framework of the Kluckhohn method and to present applications of the method in the fields of mental health care, education, and conflict resolution. Each of the articles is a response to a central question that was also of primary concern to Dr. Kluckhohn: how can we best understand why people from diverse cultural and ethnic backgrounds think and act as they do?

This volume begins with a foreword by George E. Taylor on the meaning and importance today of the study of values. The first article in Part 1, by the editor, introduces the reader to the philosophical underpinnings and conceptual framework of the value orientations method. This is followed by a contribution from Dr. Alexander H. Leighton that provides a historical overview of the science of values as it relates to the development of the value orientations method. Dr. Richard D. Robinson's article surveys and critiques a number of values-assessment tools and techniques, including the value orientations method, and explains how they can be related to perceptions of reality and the modernizing process. The section concludes with a portrait of the woman behind the work, written by Dorothy Caplow. It is only fitting that in a volume dedicated to the value orientations method the reader understand how Dr. Kluckhohn arrived at this most ingenious tool for promoting intercultural understanding.

Part 2 takes the reader into the field of mental health care and how the Kluckhohn method has been used in a clinical setting. John P. Spiegel and John Papajohn, who have employed the method for over thirty years, present a portion of their work in immigrant communities in the Boston area of northeastern United States. Danilo E. Ponce describes how he has utilized the method in the mental health field among diverse ethnic and cultural communities in Hawaii. Pamela J. Brink takes us to Canada in her discussion of the importance of the method in providing culturally appropriate health care for indigenous peoples.

Part 3 shifts to the field of education. L. Robert Kohls offers his reflections on the challenges and opportunities of using the value orientations method to compare and contrast core values among diverse cultural groups in his book, *Survival Kit for Overseas Living* (1996), written to prepare those who plan to live and work abroad. The utility of the method in the multicultural and foreign language college classrooms is then explored by Marian M. Ortuño and Ann D. Chapman. The implications of their work extend beyond the college classroom to the general area of multicultural curriculum design.

Part 4 evaluates the use of the method as a tool for resolving conflicts between diverse cultural groups and communities. The articles by the editor and Bill Wallace take the reader into a workshop setting and show how the method was used to promote understanding and cooperation between an Indian tribe and a public agency in the management of sites and areas held sacred by the native community. The section concludes with the reflections of

Dr. Thomas J. Gallagher on the more general implications of value-based differences between the native community and resource agencies in Alaska.

Dr. Kluckhohn would, I think, be pleased with this volume and with the work of the Center. In our fast-paced world, where crisis management is often the rule, it is all too tempting to seek remedial, patchwork solutions to those problems that require time, patience, effort, and reflection. These articles drive home the point that enduring solutions require that we take the time to go beneath the surface of the issue at hand to the undercurrent of core values and perceptions that guide and direct behavior.

There will, of course, always be conflicts of interest. In and of themselves, these conflicts are not the problem—resolving them is. Seemingly, there are two ways to go about conflict resolution. One is on an issue-by-issue basis, the more common approach. The other way is to forge an understanding between contending parties. Though it may not eliminate the conflicts, it will perhaps lead to more fruitful and enduring solutions. It certainly has the best chance, for while understanding doesn't always guarantee cooperation, cooperation is impossible without it.

References

Kluckhohn, Florence R., and Fred L. Strodtbeck. *Variations in Value Orientations,* 1961. Evanston, IL: Row, Peterson, 1961.

Kohls, L. Robert. *Survival Kit for Overseas Living.* 3d ed. Yarmouth, ME: Intercultural Press, 1996.

Vogt, Evon, and Ethel Albert. *People of Rimrock: A Study of Values in Five Cultures.* Cambridge, MA: Harvard University Press, 1966.

Part 1

Reflections on the Value Orientations Method

Value Orientations Method: The Conceptual Framework

Kurt W. Russo

Truth. What is the meaning and measure of truth?

Different cultures conceive of truth in their own particular way. Moreover, variation in the experience of truth is not an insulated or isolated event. Rather, conceptions such as truth or honor or the virtuous life are an outward expression of innermost beliefs about the nature of what is real, best, right, and proper.

How do we—individually and collectively—arrive at our concept of truth? Some conceive of it as universal and constant. Others believe that truth is in each case relative to the situation and the overall cultural context. Whether it is revealed or discovered, implicit or explicit, conscious or subconscious, our conception of truth is, at the very least, relative to the needs, experiences, aspirations, and overarching worldview of the cultural collective.

In the context of the Kluckhohn value orientations method, truth, like other general life concepts, is an expression of individual and group value orientations. In this chapter, we will explore the concept of value orientations and the theoretical foundation and framework of the value orientations method. We will also examine the Kluckhohn survey, which is used to elicit individual and group value orientation profiles. Finally, we will look into the interpretation of these profiles and how to relate them to different types of role settings.

The Value Orientations Concept

Value orientations are guiding principles or premises—the *predispositions of belief*—that direct how we organize and integrate our life experience. How we are oriented to the world of experience around us as well as within us is not a random event, nor is, strictly, the exercise of free will or conscious choice. Instead, the value orientations concept assumes that the principles that guide our behavior result from the transactional interplay of three key elements of the evaluative process: the cognitive element (how we think), the affective element (how we feel), and the directive element (biologically determined disposition). These guiding principles are subject to varying degrees of awareness that "give order and direction to the ever-flowing stream of human acts and thoughts as these relate to the solutions of common human problems" (Kluckhohn and Strodtbeck 1961, 4).

In describing this "transactional" process, Dr. Kluckhohn made a critical distinction between the *content* and the *direction* of a value system. The content of a value system consists of the normative assumptions about what is proper and right, as well as existential premises about what is believed to be true. It is the directive element which is of primary significance to the value orientations method as an integral part of the evaluative process. In the most general sense, directiveness refers to a biologically determined disposition to seek and maintain a meaningful order as part of the human life process. This innate human quality is a central feature of the evaluative process, informing our thoughts, actions, and behavior and integrating experience in every life situation. This aspect of directiveness is crucial for the understanding of both the integration of the total value system and its continuity through time.

Dr. Kluckhohn repeatedly stressed the importance of value orientations to the evaluative process, or what she termed the phenomenon of *selectivity*. Each of us is faced, daily, with situations in which we employ value orientations. In each case we evaluate and make sense of situations based on what we know and believe to be best, right, proper, and true. Moreover, we espouse ideals such as fairness, decency, equity, or honesty and assume that they have similar meanings to others around us. Yet hidden from view are our value orientations, which shape and give meaning to the reality of these value-laden concepts. Perhaps an example drawn from real life will illustrate this point.

A Question of Honor

Several years ago a Canadian doctor working in sub-Saharan Africa was tending to a young girl from a nearby village whose leg had been severely injured by a land mine. After examining the girl, the doctor informed the parents that she would most likely die unless the mangled leg was immediately amputated. The parents thanked him for his advice, then took the young girl home, where she passed away a few days later. Shocked by the unnecessary and tragic death, the doctor turned to a colleague who had been raised in a nearby village. How, he asked, could the parents be so insensitive to their daughter's situation? To his colleague, however, it was not a matter of sensitivity but a question of honor. The role of women in the tribe was to farm the fields, gather wood and water, and bear children. To her parents, saving the young girl would dishonor her, her family, and the traditional beliefs of the tribe by the fact that she would be condemned to a life devoid of all meaning.

A few years after leaving the village, the doctor returned home to Canada, accompanied by his African colleague. After several days in the city, the African asked the doctor about the number of homeless persons. Why is it, he asked, that some people can be so wealthy while others must live on the streets? Why don't people share what they have with others in their community? Is there no sense of honor in the community?

The question in each case was one of honor. And in each case, the meaning of honor was conditioned by an understanding of what was real, best, right, and proper. To the girl's parents, the Collateral bond within a community of interrelated families, the emphasis on Human Relations over other value dimensions, and the guiding light of tradition (the Past orientation) were underlying factors in selecting the honorable course of action. Contrariwise, in Canada honor does not mean people must, or should, take responsibility for the lives of people around them. Instead, whether a person succeeds or fails in his or her battle with reality is largely a personal matter. Honoring others in this sense is guided by the belief that people are expected to look after their own personal well-being and that of their immediate family (the Individualistic orientation), even if this means leaving the past behind. In these instances, as in so many others, value orientations not only invest meaning in a situation but also serve as cues or mechanisms we employ to select from a limited range of possibilities a fair, reasonable, and realistic solution.

Theoretical Framework of the Value Orientations Method

The value orientations method consists of a theoretical framework (the classification of value dimensions and range of value orientations) linked to a research instrument (the Value Orientations Survey). The framework rests upon three primary assumptions that are basic to both the classification of value orientations and the treatment of the types of variations in orientations. The first assumption is that *there is a limited number of common human problems for which all peoples at all times must find solutions*. These problems are presented below in the form of questions, followed in parentheses by the corresponding *value orientation dimension*:

What is the character of innate human nature? (*Human Nature*)
What is the relationship of people to nature? (*Person-Nature*)*
What is the temporal focus of human life? (*Time*)
What is the modality of human activity? (*Activity*)
What is the modality of a person's relationship to others in the group? (*Human Relations*)

Second is the assumption that while there is variability in solutions to all of these problems, the *solutions* are neither limitless nor random but *vary within a range of possible alternatives*, or *value orientations*. The third assumption is that *each of the value orientations is present in all persons and all societies at all times but is differentially preferred*. This rank ordering of preferred solutions gives expression to the dominant and subdominant value orientations profiles for the individual and his or her group.

Classification of Value Dimensions and Range of Value Orientations

The classification and range of value orientations are based on the five common human problems represented by the value dimensions of Human Nature, Person-Nature, Time, Activity, and Human Relations. It should first be noted that these dimensions are highly interactive and that a change in an orientation in one dimension can affect the rank ordering of orientations in one or more of the other dimensions. Also, different groups in different situations may

* In Dr. Kluckhohn's framework, she refers to the value dimension Man-Nature. We have elected to change the name of this dimension to Person-Nature.

vary in how they rank the dimensions as a whole. Thus, in certain situations, or among certain cultural groups, the Human Relations dimension might be of greatest importance, while in other situations the Activity dimension takes precedence, and so on. How the dimensions themselves are ranked is critical to the meaning of any of the individual value orientation profiles.

Human Nature. The first dimension to be discussed, Human Nature, is concerned with the inherent quality of human beings. In a scale noticeably more complex than any of the other dimensions, the Human Nature orientations range from Good to Neutral or Mixed to Evil and include the variables of mutability and immutability. These Human Nature value orientation preferences are set forth in Table 1.

Table 1
Human Nature Value Orientation Preferences

Evil (mutable or immutable): Human nature is viewed as inherently bad and is either fixed (immutable) or subject to change (mutable).

Neutral or Mixed (mutable or immutable): Human nature is viewed as either neutral or mixed and is either fixed or changeable.

Good (mutable or immutable): Human nature is viewed as inherently good and is either fixed or subject to change.

A classic example of human nature as Evil and immutable is the Calvinists, who believed that humankind was inevitably depraved and, except for a chosen elite, beyond redemption. Some would consider this view profoundly pessimistic. Certainly, a Tibetan Buddhist monk would. The monk, in contrast, would maintain that Human Nature is Good and proclaim the power of enlightenment once we are freed from negative impulses and emotions. In the middle ground is the secular humanist, who holds the Neutral or Mixed view that people are born the product of both nurture and nature and are simply hosts to the contradictions of the human heart.

In a group where people view Human Nature as inherently Evil (and if not Evil, then Neutral), the pattern would appear as follows: *Evil > Neutral > Good.* (The " > " sign indicates that the orientation to the left of the symbol is preferred to each of the others that follow it.) Drs. Kluckhohn and Strodtbeck and their colleagues were not able to develop situations for this dimension, as I mentioned in the Introduction. Commenting on this gap in the method, Dr. Strodtbeck recalled how the team was unable to develop situations that were distinct and separate ("uncontaminated") from the other value dimensions. Situations for this dimension are, however, being field-tested by the Center and its Associate Scholars.

Person-Nature. The second value dimension, Person-Nature, focuses on our relationship to natural forces within and around us. Do we control them (Mastery over)? Do they control us (Subject to)? Or is life really a matter of balance (Harmony with)? This continuum of control is presented in the value orientation preferences in Table 2.

Table 2
Person-Nature Value Orientation Preferences

Mastery over Nature: **Human beings can, and should, exercise total control over the forces of nature within and around them.**

Harmony with Nature: **Human beings can, and should, seek a balance of control with the forces of nature within and around them.**

Subject to Nature: **Human beings have little or no control over the forces of nature within and around them.**

In the Old Testament, God instructs humankind to "multiply and subdue the earth." This admonition most clearly expresses the value orientation preference of Mastery over Nature. This orientation is also embedded in the scientific ethos and the belief that it is the destiny of humankind to identify and apply universal natural laws. In this dimension, the "middle way" is represented by the Harmony with Nature orientation. Balance is the centerpiece of this orientation, which mediates between the extremes of Mastery over and Subject to Nature orientations, while receiving influences from both. At the far end of the spectrum is the Subject to Nature orientation in which the forces of nature are largely beyond our control or understanding. The best we can do, from this point of view, is roll with the punches, placing our fate in the hands of unknown and unknowable forces within and around us.

An example may shed light on these value orientation preferences. In a project conducted by the Kluckhohn Center, value orientation interviews were conducted in a Pacific Northwest tribal community. The overall pattern for the community was *Mastery over* > *Subject to* > *Harmony with*. However, for one subgroup of fishers in the community, we found the following variation: *Mastery over* = *Subject to* > *Harmony with*. (The "=" sign indicates that the orientations to either side of the symbol are equivalent in preference.) The fishers, in other words, were even less inclined than the community as a whole to believe people can, or should, control impersonal life forces that occur within and around them. From the fishers' point of view, these forces, as often as not, control us despite our best efforts. It doesn't mean we shouldn't try, and try our very best; rather it implies a sense of humility among women and men who are daily exposed to the elemental forces of nature and an understanding that people can try to ride on the waves, but they'll never control the tides. This variation on the common cultural theme has consequences that bridge over into issues as diverse as negotiation styles, community governance, and undertaking large-scale, long-range economic development projects.

Activity. The Human Activity dimension is concerned with the locus of meaning in activity such as work. It brings into play the issues of intrinsic versus extrinsic rewards and why we find meaning in the things that we do. The range of orientations is presented in Table 3. As noted in the Introduction, the situations for the Being-in-Becoming orientation were not developed by Dr. Kluckhohn, nor have any been developed and field-tested in subsequent years.

Table 3
Activity Value Orientation Preferences

Doing: **Greatest meaning is found in activities that result in tangible, concrete rewards valued both by the individual and others in the group.**

Being-in-Becoming: **Emphasizes the kind of activity which has as its goal the development of all aspects of self (intrinsic and extrinsic) as an integrated whole.**

Being: **Greatest meaning is found in activities that offer intrinsic or intangible rewards that gratify the individual or group need for spontaneous expression of impulse and desire.**

One outstanding example of the Doing orientation is the oft-cited ideal of the Puritan work ethic, which stresses the importance of staying busy and accomplishing concrete, tangible tasks that conform to the expectations of the group or community. The Being orientation, on the other hand, is more inward and introspective. It places greatest emphasis on rewards that are intrinsically meaningful to the person, regardless of how much or how little those rewards conform to the expectations of others around us.

In a surprising turnaround, Kluckhohn Center research has found that public-sector groups have a tendency to prefer the Being orientation more often than private-sector organizations or the tribal community. In discussing the results in workshops within these public groups, participants often stressed their belief that work was a means, not an end in itself. A high quality of life was not only, even primarily, measured by career advancement. Instead, participants referred to the importance of personal growth and development: the intrinsic rewards characterized by the Being orientation. On the other hand, most members of the Lummi Nation had a strong preference for the more enterprising and outward-oriented Doing alternative, with fewer than one in three persons selecting the Being orientation. Reflecting on their choice of orientation, Lummi community members would return to their view that life is hard and requires that people stay busy and work hard if they are to succeed. Beyond this, or beneath it, is the importance to tribal members of doing things that are meaningful and important, not only to the individual but to the group as a whole: the family, the clan, the community. Interestingly, the actual profiles for these groups defied their stated preconceptions of each other in most cases.

Human Relations. The Human Relations dimension is concerned with the individual's relationship to his or her group or community. Every human group must organize itself if it is to survive. The question is not whether but how groups will organize to solve common problems. The value orientation preferences for this dimension are presented in Table 4.

Table 4
Human Relations Value Orientation Preferences

Collaterality: **Emphasis is placed on consensus, reciprocity, and participation in decisions that have an impact on the group.**

Lineality: **Emphasis is placed on hierarchical principles and deferring to higher authority or authorities within the group.**

Individualism: **Emphasis is placed on independent action and making decisions separate from others in the group.**

All organizations advocate teamwork and team building. The word *team*, however, is semantically very ambiguous. In groups whose members share, and remain true to, the Collateral orientation, for example, meaningful and fulfilling teamwork will involve full and equal participation, reciprocity, and the achievement of a consensus on issues of common concern. Teamwork will have a somewhat different meaning for individuals or groups that are Lineal in their orientation. In this case, they will place less emphasis on reciprocity and consensus. Instead, they will be most comfortable and productive if they know they can ultimately rely on, and defer to, those in the group with the greatest age or experience and who are the ultimate decision makers. For groups with an Individualistic orientation, teamwork will more resemble a confederation of interests and abilities. Decisions will be based on the principle of majority rule, where team members are expected to argue for and stand behind their point of view.

Problems can occur, however, when the value orientations of an organization conflict with the orientations of its members. Such was the case in a private timber company in the Pacific Northwest. When interviewed (via the Kluckhohn survey), respondents often described the organization as one that followed without question the direction set by its chief executive officer. The employees' orientations, however, told a different story. The employees' value orientation profile was first-order Collateral, with Lineality the least preferred of the three alternatives (*Collaterality* > *Individualism* > *Lineality*). This conflict between the perceived (Lineal) value environment of the company and the actual (Collateral) orientation of its members served to undermine and subvert organizational effectiveness, efficiency, and morale and disrupt patterns of communication throughout the organization. Other symptoms of this conflict in the company included an increase in personnel turnover among young mid-level managers and a general decline in the ability of the organization as a whole to respond to rapid and unprecedented changes in the forest industry in the Pacific Northwest.

Time. The fifth and final value dimension in the Kluckhohn framework is Time. This dimension is concerned with a group's temporal focus, that is, how it conceives of time as measured by its orientation to the Past, the Present, or the Future. The framework was designed to be sensitive to different time modalities. For example, Dr. Kluckhohn was aware that not all groups experience time as a linear progression, a grand march leading from the past through the present to the future. She understood that for some groups time is a cycle, a rhythmic repetition where change is timeless, and more apparent than real. The value orientation preferences of the Time dimension are presented in Table 5.

Table 5
Time Value Orientation Preferences

Past: Focus on the way things were, on maintaining, or restoring, traditions from the past.

Present: Focus on what is happening now, on accommodating change.

Future: Focus on the time to come, on seeking out change and finding new ways of doing things to replace the old.

The Time dimension provides a window for understanding how a person or group conceives of, and is predisposed to respond to, such time-related issues as progress and change. Does the group resist change (Past), accommodate it (Present), or actively seek it out (Future)? Examples of variations in this temporal focus are easily found.

One example of this variation was uncovered in a project conducted by the Center among the members of an Indian tribe and the employees in a public resource management agency in the Pacific Northwest. The tribe's overall orientation profile (*Past = Present > Future*) placed much greater emphasis on the past than did that of the agency (*Present > Future > Past).* Indeed, most of the tribal members who were interviewed expressed the belief that time was a cycle, with a coexistent past and present. Just as important were the strong variations within the tribe, particularly among the fishers, who placed less emphasis on the past and more on the future than did the community as a whole. This value orientation profile was expressed in the fishers' pattern of *Present > Future > Past*.

As a result of these variations, the agency faced a twofold challenge. First, it had to work with a community for whom the past and traditional beliefs about what is real and true were ever-present. Second, the agency needed to understand the nature and range of variations within the community. For example, representatives from the agency at times engage in consultation with the tribe's Natural Resource Commission, most of whom were full-time fishers. At other times, the agency would meet with the tribe's Cultural Committee, drawn from the community as a whole. To their dismay, the agency representatives would find that natural resource solutions acceptable to the Commission members were rejected out of hand by the more Past-oriented Cultural Committee members. Unfortunately, this behavior was often perceived as a sign of the tribe's unwillingness to consult in good faith, as an inability to make a decision, or as part of a larger strategy of veiled environmentalism.

In fact, the tribe was acting in good faith and, like the agency, was most concerned with coming to a reasonable and appropriate solution to the problem. In reality, the Commission and the Committee had differing views on the meaning of change, or of the values at risk, due to their variations in value orientations. Failure to understand the content and consequences of these variations can, and often has, led to false starts and dead ends in negotiations between the tribe and the agency.

Space. Late in her life, Dr. Kluckhohn proposed a sixth dimension for incorporation into the classification schema: Space. Although she did not develop the Space situations for the Value Orientations Survey, she did outline three primary Space orientations: Personal Space, Social Space, and Universal Space. Space and perspective have long been subjects of discussion among social scientists. In an example drawn from his experience in Africa, Colin Turnbull described a forest Pygmy's bewilderment in distance perception when there were no trees and a consequent loss of perspective. Taken to the open grasslands to observe a herd of buffaloes grazing several miles away, Turnbull's Pygmy informant, Kenge, asked, "What kind of insects are these?" This critical dimension of space, and spatial cues for perspective, are currently under consideration by Kluckhohn Center staff and its Associate Scholars.

Value Orientations Survey

The Survey Instrument

The Value Orientations Survey was developed over a period of years by Dr. Kluckhohn and others to attempt to measure the value orientations dimensions of various groups. It consists of twenty-three general life situations and poses alternative responses to these situations in terms of four of the five value orientations dimensions: Activity (6 situations), Person-Nature (5 situations), Human Relations (7 situations), and Time (5 situations). A listing of these situations is presented in Table 6 (see Appendix A for the complete survey instrument).

Table 6: Survey Items

Item #	Item	Number in Schedule
Activity Dimension		
A1:	Job Choice (a)	(1)
A2:	Job Choice (b)	(2)
A3:	Ways of Living*	(16)
A4:	Care of Fields*	(19)
A5:	Housework	(22)
A6:	Nonworking Time	(23)
Person-Nature Dimension		
PN1:	Livestock Dying	(5)
PN2:	Facing Conditions*	(7)
PN3:	Use of Fields*	(11)
PN4:	Belief in Control*	(14)
PN5:	Length of Life*	(20)
Human Relations Dimension		
R1:	Well Arrangements*	(3)
R2:	Help in Misfortune*	(8)
R3:	Family Work Relations*	(9)
R4:	Choice of a Delegate*	(10)
R5:	Wage Work*	(13)
R6:	Livestock Inheritance*	(17)
R7:	Land Inheritance*	(18)
Time Dimension		
T1:	Child Training	(4)
T2:	Expectations about Change	(6)
T3:	Philosophy of Life*	(12)
T4:	Ceremonial Innovation*	(15)
T5:	Water Allocation	(20)

*Situation measures self "Actual" as well as "Ideal"

Each survey item is considered to be a situation that the respondent can visualize herself or himself encountering, although perhaps in a somewhat different context. The situation is not peculiar to one culture, nor is it one that will elicit a defensive response from the person being questioned. Finally, the situation is not one that calls forth the strictly idiosyncratic life experiences of particular individuals.

In reacting to each situation, respondents are asked to select which orientation they believe to be best, right, or true. In situations where there are three possible orientations (Human Relations, Person-Nature, Time), the respondent is also asked which of the other two possible choices is second best. If respondents feel that they really cannot choose, equal weight (=) can be given to two or even three choices (Kluckhohn and Strodtbeck 1961, 78). The intent, though, is to encourage the respondent to come to a conclusion that one choice is preferable to the other one or two and that "don't know" is not an available option.

In many of the situations the respondent is also asked the question, which of these choices best describes how you *actually* are (see starred items in Table 6)? This measurement provides important insight into dissonance between the individuals' *ideal* self-concept and how they perceive their *actual* behavior. The respondent is also asked which one of the choices "other persons" would most prefer (and, optionally, at the researcher's discretion, the second most preferred). The other persons can be either an outside group (such as the other party in a collective bargaining relationship or the cultural "other") or an inside group (other members of one's own group). These questions provide the researcher with information on the perceptual diversity of the group and how well individuals in it understand the orientations of others inside or outside their group.

The situations listed in Table 6 are drawn from the original schedule developed by Dr. Kluckhohn. Modified surveys have been developed by a number of Kluckhohn scholars over the years. For example, a slightly revised schedule was developed by Dr. Carolyn Attneave for use among urban-based groups. A more radical revision of the survey was developed by Dr. Robert Carter for work in white and in African American communities. In a third instance a research team from the University of Virginia and the University of Western Ontario developed and field-tested a modified survey for use among business groups. It should be noted, however, that the Kluckhohn Center has successfully employed the original Kluckhohn survey in rural settings and in public- and private-sector groups both in the United States and abroad.

Administering the Survey

Experience has shown that the most reliable data is gathered in one-on-one oral interviews in which the respondents are individually encouraged to openly reflect on their choices. This format is time-consuming but provides the interviewer with invaluable information on how the respondents arrived at their choice of orientation. This information is crucial for both interpreting the value orientation profile and applying the results in a workshop or seminar setting. A more detailed discussion of how to administer and modify the Kluckhohn survey is presented in Appendix C.

Analysis and Interpretation of the Value Orientation Profiles

Analysis and interpretation of the data typically take place in two phases. In the first phase the analyst is looking for statistically significant variations in value orientation profiles that cast light on inter- or intragroup behaviors. In brief, the first phase employs an eight-step process: an analysis of (1) overall patterns, or sums, for each of the four dimensions, (2) an evaluation of individual situations within each dimension, (3) variations in orientations between situations but across dimensions within the group, (4) role-related situations across dimensions, (5) the degree of divergence between self "actual" and self "ideal," (6) variations across dimensions but between groups, (7) intra- and intergroup perceptions, and (8) cumulative data. The reader is encouraged to turn to Appendix B for a more detailed discussion of this analytical process.

The second phase of analysis and interpretation involves a dialogue with individuals from the participating group(s). In this phase, results are shared with the respondents to provide them the opportunity to observe their value orientation profiles and to comment on the possible meaning and implications of the data. Their comments combined with the respondents' reflections during the interviews are critical to both the interpretation of the data and its use in intra- or intergroup workshops or seminars.

Sample Situation: Ceremonial Innovation

How does this information translate to everyday situations we are likely to encounter? We have selected one of the five situations in the Time dimension survey to illustrate how orientations can be expressed and experienced. Like each of the other general life situations in the Time dimension, this situation, Ceremonial Innovation, is concerned with change in relation to what was (the Past), what is (the Present), and what might be (the Future). It is important to note, however, that each situation is interdependent with each of the others in the survey. Understanding this complex "tapestry" effect is crucial to unlocking the deeper significance of the orientations in each situation.

Some people in a community like your own saw that the religious ceremonies were changing from what they used to be.

1. Some people were really pleased because of the changes in religious ceremonies. They felt that new ways are usually better than old ones, and they like to keep everything—even ceremonies—moving ahead (Future orientation).
2. Some people were unhappy because of the change. They felt that religious ceremonies should be kept exactly—in every way—as they had been in the past (Past orientation).
3. Some people felt that the old ways for religious ceremonies were best, but you just can't hang on to them. It makes life easier just to accept some changes as they come along (Present orientation).

First Order:	**Which of these persons expressed most nearly what you believe to be *best*?**
Second Order:	**Which of the other two choices is *second best*?**
Self "Actual":	**Which of all three alternatives best describes how you *actually* behave?**
Intragroup:	**Which of all three choices would *most other people* in your group say is best?**
Intergroup:	**Which of all three choices would most people (*in the other group*) say is best?**

We often read of conflicts within as well as between groups over the rate and direction of change. A particularly bitter conflict may ensue when the issue embraces basic change in religious traditions. Predictably, those with a more orthodox view would likely prefer the Past in this situation, perhaps characterizing those who do not share this orientation as lacking any sense of value or respect for tradition. At the other extreme are the Future-oriented "progressives." In their view, those oriented to the Past might be seen as intractable and irrational, living in the past. Standing between these two extremes is the Present orientation with its emphasis on borrowing from, but not necessarily adhering to, practices and beliefs that come from the past. In situations where *basic change* is the issue, these moderates would be in the best position to understand the situation from both points of view.

Beneath the apparent differences between the orthodox and the progressive, however, may be common ground in participants' *second-order* preference. The opposing factions might, for example, select the Present orientation as the second-best solution. Armed with this knowledge, both sides would be in a better position to uncover new and innovative approaches that both maintain tradition and allow the group to move forward. Just as important, foreknowledge of this hidden commonality could greatly assist Present-oriented individuals to moderate and facilitate the dialogue.

What is at play in such cases are variations in value orientations, the nature of which may not be understood by either party. Whether at the bargaining table, in the boardroom, or in the multicultural classroom, it behooves us to make a good-faith effort to understand others' points of view. Entering into the subjectivity of others who are different from us not only breaks down false stereotypes but also serves to humanize a situation by encouraging each side to stretch its view to see from within the orientation of the other. For groups in conflict, this process can elevate the discussion to higher common ground and can replace reflexivity with reasoned, open dialogue.

Role Settings

A final consideration, one that was not developed in the initial Kluckhohn and Strodtbeck study, is the different way respondents may behave in different role settings. Respondents may view the roles they play, for example, in family, work, and community from different perspectives. Thus a husband's or father's role in the family may be authoritarian in relation to his wife and children, but his work role as an accountant may be submissive in relation to a supervisor who is an engineer. And in his community role the same man may be egalitarian when voting as a citizen. Here his family role may well be serving as an emotional release from the frustration of the role he must play in the work situation. Examining responses for all role sets allows one to determine whether a composite role orientation assigned to a respondent really reflects a homogeneous response.

Concluding Remarks

The value orientations method is not the first attempt, nor will it be the last, to understand why people tend to think and act as they do.

However, the durability and adaptability of the method are tributes to the breadth and depth of the value orientations concept, the range and scope of the value dimension schema, and the intersubjectivity of the general life situations in the Kluckhohn survey. The method provides a framework for identifying differences that make a difference in how groups interact.

While it may be true that understanding does not always lead to agreement, cooperation is impossible without it. And where there is not understanding, there is misunderstanding, which is one source of enmity. Inspired by Dr. Kluckhohn's lifelong interest in why people speak past each other, the Kluckhohn method provides common ground for overcoming differences and uncovering similarities to forge lasting understandings.

Reference

Kluckhohn, Florence R., and Fred L. Strodtbeck. *Variations in Value Orientations*. Evanston, IL: Row, Peterson, 1961.

Science and Values: A Historical Perspective

Alexander H. Leighton

People are always interested in values. The problem is to make that interest useful and enlightening. In order to achieve this goal, one has to carry out scientific studies of how values arise and what they consist of as well as how people share and make them work. One of the central problems has to do with why it is that some values can be easily and reasonably altered, while others, which we call prejudices, have astonishing persistency despite manifest destructiveness. The importance of a basic systematic understanding of values was the heart of the conception of *value orientations* as set forth by Florence R. Kluckhohn.

What I hope to do is to point out that today new opportunities are emerging for progress along lines she had in mind. This constitutes good news after more than three decades (roughly 1958–1988) during which academic, political, and other diverse winds have been blowing with considerable strength against the notion of applying scientific concepts and methods to the betterment of human relations.

The Favorable Climate for Values Study Pre-1960

From the perspective of today, it is evident that in 1948, when the Harvard Values Project, of which Florence Kluckhohn was a member, was taking shape, the circumstances were unusually favorable to such an enterprise, provided it was scientific as well as caring in its orientation. It was a period when expectations were high on the part of many institutions and governments (and in the population generally) that the cultural, psychological, social, and behavioral sciences were going to achieve major advances, the results of which would be applied to the promotion of peace and understanding among peoples. This spirit was exemplified in the founding of the Department of Social Relations at Harvard and the Ford Foundation's creation of the Center for Advanced Study in the Behavioral Sciences near Stanford.

It happened that at the same time as the beginning of the Harvard Values Project at Rimrock in New Mexico, colleagues and I were taking advantage of the same favorable climate and launching what in some ways was a "sister" project, 2,500 miles away in Eastern Canada. This we called the Stirling County Study and we focused it on two contrasting rural populations, rather than on five as at Rimrock. One of the two was Anglophone and the other, Francophone. A major goal of the project was to discover whether and how variation in cultural and socioeconomic values in the populations related to variations in the prevalence and incidence in clinical anxiety, depression, and other mental illnesses. We were concerned, in short, with how values influence mental health.

Some of the main participants in both projects had done fieldwork at Rimrock before the war. Then later, during the war, we were enabled by the foresight of George E. Taylor, at that time head of the Far Eastern Branch in the Office of War Information, to do further work together in the Foreign Morale Analysis Division (FMAD) on developing methods for the analysis of Japanese military and home-front morale through the use of data collected from war-zone and home-front sources (Leighton 1949). This pragmatically oriented charge required us to develop objective methods for describing certain patterns of human behavior, detecting changes in these patterns, identifying the factors responsible for the changes, and then testing hypotheses by making predictions. It was at this time, as part of the morale studies, that Florence Kluckhohn laid the foundations of her conception of value orientations.

To a major degree, all of us in FMAD jointly hammered out and shared notions with regard to the applicability of scientific methods to human behavior—as well as with regard to the nature of culture and certain universalities in the psychology of individuals. Serving as guides and advisers were Sam A. Stouffer, Talcott Parsons, and Harry Murray. By the end of the war, most of us had come to believe that the application of empirical methods to human behavior in natural settings could lead to major improvements in health and education and to community development in underdeveloped areas, such as became envisioned in Truman's foreign aid program, which was called "Point Four."

What I should like to do now is to outline some of the major changes which began to occur in the values of American society itself after midcentury, changes that created enormous difficulties for projects like Rimrock and the Stirling County Study. It is my hope that doing so will highlight the importance of other changes taking place on the more recent scene, changes that constitute new opportunities for advancing research in the use of value orientations. I will use my experiences as director of Rimrock's sister project, the Stirling County Study, in this historical summary, because the study has been in existence since 1948, although at times very much diminished in scope and on occasion forced by circumstances to modify its aims.

As a point of departure, let us first note that the favorable circumstances mentioned as existing in 1948 were the cumulative product of national reactions to two great upheavals. The first was the economic depression of the 1930s, which led the U.S. government under Franklin Roosevelt to consult with university economists on a scale that was unprecedented. This was followed by additional calls to other kinds of social scientists because jump-starting the economy turned out to have many ramifications requiring assistance from sociologists, cultural anthropologists, and psychologists. One problem, for example, was the question of how to free individuals from counterproductive states of reactive mental depression and how to elevate the morale of communities and other collectivities that had been overcome by that state of paralysis known as anomie. Efforts to investigate and remedy such problems were illuminated by a number of what were regarded as successes in large and small programs such as the Tennessee Valley Authority and the efforts of the Indian Services under John Collier Sr. to promote self-government and self-respect among Indian peoples. Members of academia were also moved to examine pragmatic problems of these kinds, as illustrated in W. Lloyd Warner and colleagues' important study of Yankee City and its failing industries (1963). It was at this time also that the Society for Applied Anthropology was formed, with membership coming from several different disciplines.

The second upheaval was World War II and its aftermath, when there was further expansion of involvement of social and behavioral scientists into work on problems of human relations. A major example consisted of the studies conducted in the army, led by sociologist Sam Stouffer (Stouffer, et al. 1949).

A feature of these efforts to deal more effectively with difficulties in human relations was an orientation that played down heavy commitment to sweeping theoretical systems such as psychoanalysis and cultural determinism. The climate of opinion favored a tentative attitude toward the implications of such large theories and a preference for trying out short-range hypotheses that could in some sense be tested against factual evidence and so lead to predictions that were reliable, valid, and useful. Although cultural determinism and cultural relativity were in the air, so to speak, and very much pushed by Margaret Mead and Ruth Benedict, some social and behavioral scientists thought it important to be cautious. Florence Kluckhohn was one of these, and she drew our attention to this need in the first paragraph of the first chapter in the book she wrote with Fred L. Strodtbeck, *Variations in Value Orientations*. She says, "...the theory of cultural relativity has at times threatened to override all conceptions of universals and has thus become, when taken too literally, almost as restrictive to an understanding of human behavior as the naive forms of evolutionism or economic determinism" (Kluckhohn and Strodtbeck 1961).

Post-1960 Antiempiricism

Turning now to the changes after midcentury, one of the first to affect us in the Stirling County Study was a progressive decline in concern among cultural anthropologists for empirical data. *Empiricism* shifted from being a discussable concept to being a bad word, while *cultural determinism* and *cultural relativity* shifted from being theory to being doctrine supported by strong values of moral correctness.

At about the same time in psychiatry, the empirical and multidisciplinary approach to problems represented by psychobiology (Lazardsfeld and Rosenberg 1955), which had been dominant in North America and Britain for the previous thirty years, became submerged by psychoanalysis and its emphasis on metapsychological theory. On the heels of this, there followed a breakup of psychoanalysis itself—as so often happens to theories unconstrained by systematic evidence—and the spread of many derivative theories and practices. One result of this, in turn, was the growth of uncertainty and lack of consensus about how psychiatric disorders should be defined, identified, and systematically classified—or whether there was in fact any such phenomenon as a mental illness. This latter perspective created serious doubts about the possibility of doing psychiatric epidemiology.

Sociology took a course parallel to that of anthropology and psychiatry by stepping away from the kind of empiricism and "middle range" theorizing and hypothesis testing recommended by Robert K. Merton (1968) and Paul F. Lazersfeldt (1955). Instead, many scholars, followed by political decision makers, came to believe in the validity of various speculative systems, such as Thomas J. Scheff's theory of labeling (1966).

I am sure you will recognize that what I am touching upon is, in a larger frame of reference, the widespread revolt against positivism, which not only condemned the philosophy of the logical positivists who made up the Vienna Circle, but also the whole notion of empiricism in science, including the idea that scientific methods have any special advantage as approaches to a valid understanding of nature, much less human behavior and values. All this was, of course, embedded in a still larger movement that was opposed to the power structures of Western societies and all the values supporting their major institutions, a movement that in France has been called *le nihilisme moderne* and that had invaded campuses everywhere, producing much uncertainty among educators, policy makers, planners, and administrators.

I would not like you to think that I saw no benefits to humanity in what was happening, because in fact I saw many, and some of profoundly positive significance, such as the rise of women in educational attainment and positions of influence. I must confess, however, to being bewildered by the extremism also evident and to having had to take refuge often in Josh Billing's peerless aphorism, "It ain't so much ignorance that hurts folks, as it is knowing so dern many things that ain't so."

Sound work in the social and behavioral sciences was not abolished by the growth of the antiscience ethos, but it was diminished by the consequent reduction in funding and popular support. The Ford Foundation, for example, dropped its Center for Advanced Study in the Behavioral Sciences, while at Harvard the new Social Relations Department was like a child who failed to thrive.

That the Stirling County Study was able to continue was very largely because its scientific emphasis and practical usefulness proved interesting to medical schools, to schools of public health, and to government agencies concerned with the improvement of human services.

Had our work been focused only on the study of values, I doubt very much that it would have continued. This is based on the suspicion that the biologically oriented sources of funding would have turned us down because of their disenchantment with the possibility of there being anything worth calling science in the social sciences, while the social and culturally oriented sources of funding would have been repelled by our empiricism.

The cutting back on what we had hoped to do in the study of values, however, was also due to difficulties in recruiting staff with the requisite training. It became progressively more and more difficult to find anthropologists, sociologists, and even psychologists with an interest in values and also trained in relevant scientific methods. Most of those who had an interest in values seemed to feel that the only important questions had to do with persuasion and action, not scientific inquiry.

The Return of Optimism Regarding Values Research

Turning now finally to the emerging good news of today, it may be said that this optimism has two components, one old and one new. The older has been from the start inherent in the analytic structure of the conception of value orientations, while the new one lies in the scientific advances made in recent years by sciences cognate with this analytic structure. It is the possibility of bringing these advances into contact with the analytic structures of value orientations and with the development of value-adjusting programs that constitutes the basis for the optimism to which I referred in my opening remarks.

Florence Kluckhohn defined value orientations as composed of three distinguishable interacting elements: cognitive, affective, and directive. *Cognitive* and *affective* are familiar enough terms, but let us pause on *directive*. What she meant by this was "a biologically determined predisposition," in other words an instinct or drive.

It is of interest to note that in the psychology subfield of personality, there is a concept of "sentiment" that had its origins early in this century and with which the names of W. H. R. Rivers and William McDougall are associated. McDougall (1921) was a clinical psychologist, while Rivers (1922) made noteworthy contributions not only to anthropology but also to neurophysiology and psychiatry. A "sentiment," according to this theoretical frame, anticipated "values" by being defined as a composite of three interacting elements: cognition, affect, and "conation," which is similar if not identical to what Florence Kluckhohn meant by "biologically determined predisposition" (Leighton 1959).

I mention the concept of sentiment in order to bring forward the fact that the notion of values as developed by Kluckhohn and Strodtbeck has all along been something of a doppelgänger, or double, in psychology and psychiatry, going under a different name in each. Sentiment played a significant part in the psychobiological approach of Adolf Meyer to psychiatric diagnosis (Lief 1948) and to the study of personality—and, like values, has been largely ignored since the 1950s. In the Stirling County Study we employed the term *sentiments* as the equivalent of *values*.

This brings us to the advances in the sciences cognate with the analytic structure of value orientations. Progress since midcentury in *cognitive* studies has resulted from a major movement in psychology, while at the same time new work on *affect* has come largely out of psychiatry and psychopharmacology. Much of the focus here has been on how episodes of fear and sadness can achieve dominance and destructiveness in the lives of individuals, and also how such states may be reversed or prevented.

Cognitive and affective studies have also begun to be in touch with studies of *brain function*. Much has been learned in this domain, so that we no longer think in terms of brain centers but rather in terms of patterns of interactions among many parts of the brain, some of them functioning in parallel and some of them in cascading sequences.

Systematic understanding of the third analytic element, *directive* or *biological predisposition*, has received a considerable boost from genetic studies, especially those focused on families and on twins. Given the hostility to genetics expressed by many social scientists of the past, it is a little ironic to note that some of the strongest evidence we have regarding the causal influence of the environment in human behavior now comes from genetics, particularly twin studies. It seems fairly sure, for example, that in the disorder schizophrenia, about half of the causal factors are not genetic and so must be in some way environmental.

Of all the investigative work now going on with regard to cognition, affect, and biological predispositions, it seems possible that the type most immediately relevant to value studies is the work on *temperament*. While there is no standard definition for the term, one proposed by Jerome Kagan (1994) gives the central idea. He suggests that temperament is a quality of personality that varies among individuals, is stable in a given individual across time and situations, is under genetic influence, and, for the most part, appears early in life. What makes temperament, so defined, pertinent for those of us interested in values is the fact that scientific investigators of temperament give much attention to the integration of findings derived from cognition, affect, and biological predisposition. Such are the kinds of syntheses that hold promise of opening doors with regard to the nature of values. They are directly concerned with all three of the analytic elements that Florence Kluckhohn identified as basic to the notion of values and value orientations.

A Call for Caution

Even though there have been advances in empirically oriented research in fields relevant to values, nevertheless we have to recognize that attacks on science continue, albeit with signs of weakening. The hoax on relativistic metaphysics perpetrated by the theoretical physicist Alan Sokal in 1994 by way of the journal *Social Text* (Boghossian 1966) has apparently had widespread effect and persuaded many people that they really should look more carefully to see whether or not the emperor of postmodernism is wearing clothes. In a recent article, Stein Ringen, professor of sociology and social policy at Oxford, was apparently speaking for many when he said, "If values, facts and truths are (entirely) relative, then there is no fact and no truth...there are no things to investigate, only constructions to contemplate. The relativists may believe in absolute relativism, but empiricists cannot accept more than relative relativism" (Ringen 1997).

What I should like to emphasize in drawing to a close is, once more, the long-term importance of striving for scientific soundness in the conduct of values research and of not getting drawn into metaphysical games. The recent history of the changing values exhibited by our society makes it clear that rhetorical skill applied to metaphysical questions can get you much attention and even fame. What it does not advance is knowledge about the nature of nature, including human nature. Sooner or later, the crowds who confer fame discover this and then turn away toward something else.

References

Boghossian, P. "What the Sokal Hoax Ought to Teach Us." *Times Literary Supplement*. 13 December 1966, 14–15.

Kagan, Jerome. *Galen's Prophecy: Temperament in Human Nature*. New York: Basic Books, 1994.

Kluckhohn, Florence R., and Fred L. Strodtbeck. *Variations in Value Orientations*. Evanston, IL: Row, Peterson, 1961.

Lazardsfeld, Paul F., and M. Rosenberg, eds. *The Language of Social Research*. New York: The Free Press, 1955.

Leighton, Alexander H. *My Name Is Legion: The Stirling County Study of Psychiatric Disorder and Sociocultural Environment*. New York: Basic Books, 1959.

———. *Human Relations in a Changing World*. New York: E. P. Dutton, 1949.

Lief, A., ed. *The Commonsense Psychiatry of Dr. Adolf Meyer: Fifty-two Selected Papers Edited with Biographic Narrative*. New York: McGraw-Hill, 1948.

McDougall, William. *An Introduction to Social Psychology*. London: Methuen, 1921.

Merton, Robert K. *Social Theory and Social Structure*. New York: The Free Press, 1968.

Ringen, Stein. "The Open Society and the Closed Mind." *Times Literary Supplement,* 24 January 1997, 6.

Rivers, W. H. R. "The Relations of Complex and Sentiments." *British Journal of Psychology* 13, no. 2 (1922): 107–48.

Scheff, Thomas J. *Being Mentally Ill: A Sociological Theory*. Chicago: Aldine Publishing, 1966.

Stouffer, Sam A., A. A. Lumsdaine, M. H. Lumsdaine, R. M. Williams, M. B. Smith, I. L. Janis, S. A. Star, and L. S. Cottrell. *The American Soldier: Combat and Its Aftermath*. Princeton, NJ: Princeton University Press, 1949.

Warner, W. Lloyd, J. D. Low, P. S. Lunt, and L. Srole. *Yankee City*. New Haven, CT: Yale University Press, 1963.

Perceptions of Reality and the Modernizing Process: A Critique of the Kluckhohn-Strodtbeck Value Orientations Model

Richard D. Robinson

Much behavior, we know, is culturally determined, not idiosyncratic to the individual. Indeed, the ratio of the truly idiosyncratic to the culturally determined may be an important differentiator between cultures. So far as I know, no one has researched this point directly. It may be significant.

Examples of culturally determined behavior abound, though we are not always aware of such. Take silence. Maintaining silence in social situations conveys a message, but one that can vary greatly from culture to culture. In many situations in American culture—though not in all—silence is felt to be unfriendly, cold, inappropriate. It often seems to compel people to start talking, sometimes about things they really wished they had not. I have tried this out in classes by entering a classroom, sitting down, and not speaking for several moments. Eventually, the pressure and the tension are such that someone feels compelled to talk about something. The same occurs in interview situations. In some other societies that may not be the case. In Central Anatolian village society, where people are quite accustomed to sitting around of an evening and absorbing long periods of silence, nobody feels compelled to break it.

Another aspect of culturally induced behavior has to do with gift giving. The rules associated with such are particularly troublesome while traveling and living abroad. When is a gift appropriate? When is a gift likely to be considered a bribe, an act of charity (and, hence, possibly demeaning to the recipient and arousing resentment), a part of a quid pro quo, a form of sexual harassment, or simply a token of friendship or of love?

Perceptions of what constitutes appropriate behavior relate to one's beliefs about what constitutes reality—reality in respect to the assumptions one makes about social relationships, time, the quality of human nature, the individual's position in nature, the definition of the individual, the cultural context of communication, spatial relationships, and so on.

In Turkey there is told a story of an old Sufi teacher named Nostradin Hodja, who gained fame because he used to ride about the countryside facing the hind end of his donkey. He insisted that it was much more worthwhile to view where one had been than to see where one was going—past-oriented, we might say. The story is told that one day he met the ruler of a great city, who observed with much regret, "My people rarely tell the truth, and that is bothering me a great deal." Nostradin Hodja responded that it really did not matter if something were absolutely true or not; what mattered was if something were true in relation to other things. The ruler thought for a moment and said, "That is one of your Sufi tricks; something is either true or false, it can be no other way." The more he thought about the matter, the more the ruler wanted his people to be truthful. At last he felt that he had found a way to make them so. One morning, when the city gates were opened, the people saw that a gallows had been constructed within. An official proclamation was posted that if anyone wanted to enter the city, he or she must first answer some questions. If the answers were later found to be false, that person would be hanged until dead. Nostradin Hodja stepped up and announced that he would enter the city. "Why do you wish to do so?" the Captain of the Guard asked. "To be hanged on yonder gallows until I am dead," he responded. "I don't believe you," said the Captain of the Guard. "Very well," said Nostradin, "if I am not telling the truth, then you must hang me." The Captain of the Guard thought a moment and then said, "But, I cannot hang you because that would make your statement true, and if you're telling the truth, you have entry to the city." "Right," said Nostradin. "Which truth is the real truth?" So, what is the reality? That which is perceived. But by whom?

In that my academic and professional background is at considerable variance from that of most of the other contributors to this volume, I confess that I add my comments with considerable trepidation. My point of departure is international management and economics, although within the purview of my academic interest there has been strong concern with the social, psychological, and anthropological dimensions of the global marketplace. Indeed, I have used the Kluckhohn-Strodtbeck paradigm in my management classes for many years to provide students with analytical insights into the nature of possibly significant cultural differences, which may under some circumstances erupt into conflict, enough to subject any international business relationship to great peril and needless cost.

The Nature of Modernization

For several decades my central thesis in teaching and writing has been that the business function may interfere seriously with what I call the *modernizing* process. In so doing, the institutions of business are at risk, a fact that the international executive should understand. The term *modernization,* as I use it, describes in a nonjudgmental sense an ongoing evolutionary process, one that is fundamentally social and psychological in nature, not economic. Of course, to a considerable extent, these three aspects cannot be separated. To some, it may seem that I am referring simply to social change, but the problem is, that phrase implies no direction. To me, the essence of modernization—which may be perceived as good, bad, or indifferent—is, first, a growing awareness of alternative values and worldviews. Second, there is an increasing acceptance of change as possibly being desirable under certain circumstances. And, finally, modernization is identified with increasing the general satisfaction of felt needs of a group or society. All three elements—the growing awareness of alternatives, increasing acceptance of change, and increasing the satisfaction of felt needs—are culturally determined in that they are the product of particular worldviews (value orientations) and underlying values; that is, perceptions of reality, of what really counts.

The question I would pose here is this: Can instruments thus far developed be used to reliably measure cultural or social change in the modernizing sense—that is, a shift in values and/or worldviews? Although there is some discussion of this issue elsewhere in this volume, the question remains: Does a cultural confrontation that is resolved to some degree by the utilization of one or more of the methods described (and in particular the Kluckhohn-Strodtbeck approach) to measure and articulate value orientations result in any sort of *permanent* change as people are made aware of their own cultural orientations and the cultural orientations of the others involved in a confrontation? Surely, the persons involved become more aware of alternative ways of perceiving reality, but in response to such change in perceptions, is the process of modernization advanced? If that awareness of alternatives is actually internalized, such that the idea of change is accepted as possibly desirable, do different values and worldviews emerge within the social units, whatever they may be? We have no clear answers.

Some Definitions

It seems useful to break the flow of my article here to introduce some definitions. The nuances of words vary from person to person. In this discussion, I differentiate needs, values, and worldviews. *Need*, as the term is used here, refers to an inner tendency to organize perceptions and reactions in certain directions, which results in a feeling of satisfaction if one acts accordingly. *Value* refers to that which determines where and how an individual finds it satisfying to express his or her needs, that is, the selection of a satisfying object or type of action. In contrast, a *worldview* relates to one's perceptions—or assumptions—about the true nature of oneself and of one's environment, that is, of general reality. A worldview is a product of both the individual's (and society's) needs and values. S. G. Redding (1978) describes worldviews in terms of six forms of cognition: (1) *linearity* (that is, whether time is perceived to be linear or circular; whether events are linked by straight-line causality or exist within an interactive system—the "field of force" notion); (2) *universality* (how and the degree to which things and observed phenomena are placed in general classifications); (3) *definition of personality* (how one perceives the self and others, the importance of personality); (4) *probability* (whether events are seen as fatalistic or subject to logical prediction); (5) *relativity* (whether events or things are seen as separate from the observer); and (6) *morality* (what system is used to differentiate "right" from "wrong," to define guilt or shame). Although the above may provide insight, I find it possibly more useful to think of *worldview* as being defined by the following matrix (Figure 1) suggested by Everett E. Hagen in private conversation (1962).

Figure 1
A Classification of Worldviews
(a product of needs and values)

The world is seen as	Friendly	Orderly	Manageable	Dynamic	Durable	Continuous
Threatening	XX					
Chaotic		XX				
Uncontrollable			XX			
Static				XX		
Transient					XX	
Episodic (discontinuous)						XX

Florence R. Kluckhohn and Fred L. Strodtbeck (1961) defined reality in terms of Human Nature (Evil, Neutral or Mixed, Good; immutable or mutable), Person-Nature relationship (Subject to, Harmony with, Mastery over), Time (Past, Present, Future), Activity (Being, Being-in-Becoming, Doing), and Human Relations (Lineality, Collaterality, Individualism). What is the reality? What is assumed to be the appropriate (relevant?) worldview? What needs are thereby generated?

One cannot really discuss needs without reference to Abraham H. Maslow's hierarchy of needs (1943). The hierarchy ascends from intrinsic or physiological need (for food, shelter, security), extrinsic or social need (for affiliation, belonging, social esteem, prestige), and finally to self-actualization (need for self-esteem and a sense of competence, power, and achievement). Maslow's system is a dynamic one in that common sense and some empirical research suggest that basic physiological needs must be satisfied to a tolerable level before the individual is concerned with longer-term safety, which, when satisfied in some sense, activates—indeed, perhaps requires—the satisfaction of certain social needs. In turn, these social needs must be satisfied to some degree before the self-actualization needs are engaged. Change, then, is driven by changing need, but what drives that changing need?

Psychological Development

The degree to which a lower-order need must be satisfied before a higher-order need is engaged is, to a degree, culturally determined, and just how a need is satisfied is also culture-specific. Therefore, the theory begs a myriad of questions, not the least of which is this: What motivates individuals—and through them, society as a whole—to change, once the self-actualization need has been achieved by a critical portion of that society? Does everything then come to a screeching halt? What is next?

In further defining needs, one moves into the area of socio-psychology, where need is identified as an inner tendency to organize perceptions and reactions in certain ways. These needs are often presented as a function of parental behavior (and/or behavior of admired models) and of social norms, also possibly of health, degree of affluence, age, gender, and other idiosyncratic factors. These needs are sometimes classified into (1) *manipulative needs* (such as the need for achievement, autonomy, order, and understanding—where satisfaction rests on the behavior or responses of others); (2) *aggressive needs* (such as the need for aggression-out [aggression to another], aggression-in [agression to self], guilt, dominance, or power); and (3) *passive needs* (such as the need for dependence, submission, affiliation, succor—i.e., the need to receive sympathy and help—and nurture—i.e., the need to give sympathy and help). Each individual possibly feels all of these needs, but their relative strength or priority varies (Murray 1938). The question then arises as to which mix of needs, internalized by a critical mass of individuals within a society, renders that society more "modern" in the sense *modern* is used here?

Approaches to a More Dynamic Model of Change

Erik H. Erikson (1950) proposed a model of change on the individual level. He defined the eight crises each individual faces within his or her lifetime, all of which, he argued, contribute to the formation of something called "personality." The resolution of each of these crises may be reinforcing, or in conflict. In each case, the development of a well-adjusted, creative individual is associated with the outcomes in the right-hand column in Figure 2. Maladjustment and asocial or antisocial behavior is associated with a mix of resolutions from the right- and left-hand columns of the eight crises. The model is driven by the passage of time, or maturation of the individual.

Figure 2
Erikson's Eight Stages of Adult Adjustment

			Rough Age Categories (differs with sex)
1. Basic Mistrust vs. Basic Trust			
Crisis of Infancy	Distrusts self and doubts the world. Feels that others "get you into trouble."	Confident in self and in the world. Trusts associates. Feels optimistic about people's motives.	0-1
2. Shame and Doubt vs. Autonomy			
Crisis of Self-Awareness	Awkwardly self-conscious of own ideas. Stays within familiar ways; needs the approval of others and avoids asserting self against group.	Confident to hold own opinions and to do what he or she feels is best.	2-4
3. Guilt vs. Initiative			
Crisis of Childhood	Lets others initiate action; plays down success or accomplishment.	Takes pleasure in planning and initiating action; plans ahead and designs own schedule.	5-7
4. Inferiority vs. Industry			
Crisis of Self-Esteem (puberty)	Is passive; leaves things undone; feels inadequate about ability to do things. Feels that one's product is unsatisfactory.	Likes to make things and carry them to completion; strives to master skills. Feels proud of one's product.	8-11
5. Role Diffusion vs. Ego Identity			
Crisis of Identity	Ill at ease and lacking conviction in roles; lost in groups and affiliations; may abruptly switch work, residence, or marriage [in the upper end of the age range]; without meaning or purpose.	Is definite about self and enjoys work, family, and affiliations; has sense of belonging; feels continuity with past and present.	12-20

Figure 2—Cont.

			Rough Age Categories (differs with sex)
	6. Isolation vs. Intimacy		
Crisis of Intimacy	Lives relatively isolated from spouse, children; avoids intimate contact with others. Either absorbed in self or indiscriminately sociable, in a stereotyped manner.	Has close intimate relationships with spouse and friends; enjoys sharing thoughts, spending time with them, and expressing warm feelings for them.	21-30
	7. Stagnation vs. Generativity		
Crisis of Middle Age	Seems to be vegetating; does nothing more than routines of work and necessary daily activities; is preoccupied with self.	Plans for future with sustained application of skills and abilities; invests energy in exploring new ideas; senses continuity with future generations.	31-65
	8. Despair vs. Integrity		
Crisis of Old Age	Depressed and morose about life, emphasizes failures; would change life or career if had another chance; fears getting older and dying.	Happy and content with life, work accomplishments; accepts responsibility for life; maximizes success.	66-

If a group, or a society as a whole, tends to encourage resolution of each crisis in such a way that the outcomes of the right-hand columns are achieved consistently, then individuals by and large will be trusting, have a high need for autonomy and achievement, and be well disciplined and highly motivated. In general, society will produce a large number of creative individuals, which presumably leads to modernization. If, for some reason, the way in which individuals tend to resolve these eight crises shifts in a society, then the type of individuals generated by that society likewise alters. This schema approaches a dynamic analysis in that it purports to explain at the individual level why certain personality types are produced and why the outcomes might change over time. But what influences individuals to resolve crises in particular ways?

Further insight into the nature of social change is that suggested by Talcott Parsons' "pattern variables" (Parsons 1951), which can be capsulized in five choices confronting an individual and from which five continua can be derived, as is shown in Figure 3.

Figure 3
A Summarized Version of Parsons' Pattern Variables

Choice 1: Is one motivated by the gratification of immediate impulses or by evaluation of the effects of one's acts?
Affectivity (i.e., emotional) ~ effective neutrality (i.e., logical or rational)

Choice 2: If one decides to evaluate, should the primary concern be given to interests and values shared by others or to one's own?
Collectively oriented ~ self-oriented

Choice 3: In either case, does one treat persons or objects in a situation on the basis of one's personal relationship with them or in accord with a general norm covering all objects in a class (e.g., members of a group)?
Particularism ~ universalism

Choice 4: Does one treat a person or object on the basis of some quality that person or object is perceived to have (e.g., age, kinship, gender, etc.) or on the basis of the results expected to flow from that person's actions?
Ascription ~ achievement

Choice 5: Is one concerned with all aspects of another person or object or does one restrict involvement to specific aspects?
Functional diffuseness ~ functional specificity

One is left with the impression that the more "modern" folk are characterized by responses which tend toward the right side of each of these continua. It is not clear, however, just how or why individuals move from the left (the more traditional) to the right (the more modern) nor how many within a society must so move before the character of that society changes—the critical-mass problem.

One can use Parsons' "pattern variables" in describing (but not really explaining) the development of a political culture from "primitive" to "modern" by tracking the eight political functions constituting such cultures. These functions, according to some political theorists (Almond and Coleman 1960) are as follows (Figure 4).

Figure 4
The Eight Functions of Political Culture according to Almond

Input Functions

1. Political socialization: the manner and degree to which the members of a society identify with a political culture
2. Political recruitment: the manner and degree to which a society participates in legitimizing the exercise of political authority
3. Articulation of interests: the manner and degree to which a population makes known its demands for the exercise of political authority
4. Aggregation of interests: the manner and degree to which interests relating to political authority are aggregated
5. Communication of interest: the manner and degree to which political interests are communicated to the political authority

Output Functions

6. Rule making: the manner in which decisions are made by the political authority and the degree of their inclusiveness (i.e., geographical, social, temporal, content)
7. Rule enforcement: the manner in which political decisions are enforced and the degree to which enforcement is achieved
8. Rule adjudication: the manner in which conflicts among rules and between rules and enforcement are resolved and the degree to which such judgments are enforced

The idealized political culture (the most modern) is presumed to be one in which all political functions are (1) affectively neutral (i.e., are governed by expected results, not by immediate impulses or emotion); (2) individual-oriented (i.e., tend to value the individual rather than the collective); (3) universalistic (affect all members of the political culture similarly); (4) specific (are differentiated from other functions, not diffuse); and (5) achievement-oriented (treat persons or objects on the basis of ability to accomplish a given task or end, not on the basis of qualities unrelated to this ability).

Some years ago, I observed that

> One of the earliest moves toward the modern is perhaps the differentiation of the political culture itself from the religious. Generally, a somewhat later development is the relating of the

> dominant political culture to all individuals within a given geographical area—that is, the establishment of a universal political authority admitting of no racial or religious bars. Following such expansion and intensification of the political socialization process may be a movement to extend the political culture impartially to all citizens and to define political roles on the basis of ability rather than various ascriptive norms. Often accompanying these developments is a broadening of the process of political recruitment, which tends to generate a different manner and intensity of interest articulation. Another characteristic of political development is the formation of specialized interest-aggregating and communicating functions and of differentiated rule-enforcing and rule-adjudicating agencies—that is, differentiated from the rule making. At some point during this whole process a differentiation of the economic or business culture from the political will usually appear. There is possibly a tendency for the two to remain largely undifferentiated until the business culture becomes so highly specialized and professionalized as to adopt substantially different values and roles from those associated with the political. Business then tends to be blocked from the performance of any significant political function other than aggregating and communicating its own interests. (Robinson 1964)

Still, the underlying dynamics driving a society to change are unclear.

A contribution to an understanding of the *process* of change was suggested by sociologist Daniel Lerner (1958). He hypothesized—and set about proving to his satisfaction—that individuals move out of a static traditionalist mode toward the more modern dynamic mode via a set of external influences. Although the optimum sequence is open to some debate, Lerner himself believed that the path to modernity begins with the physical movement of the individual (most frequently, a move toward urbanization) and proceeds via the achievement of literacy (enhanced psychic mobility) to mass-media participation (the "mobility multiplier"), and finally to the development of a capacity for empathy, which to Lerner was the hallmark of the modern person. His schema is presented below as Figure 5.

Figure 5
Lerner's Schema of Social Transition

	Urbanization *	Literacy	Media Participation	Empathy
Traditionalists	-	-	-	-
Transitionalists	A+ B+ C+	- + +	- - +	- - -
Moderns	+	+	+	+

*Geographic mobility ~ New experience ~ Literacy ~ Psychic mobility
"-" = Quality absent "+" = Quality present

Lerner certainly defines a dynamic system, although possibly overly simplistic. His paradigm also begs the question as to what percentage of a society needs to achieve the capacity to empathize, (i.e., become modern, according to his definition) before general *social* change is induced (modernization). Perhaps the now-empathetic modern individuals either flee their host society, which they may find intolerably traditionalist, or are encapsulated by it as a socially separate minority, so that their influence is minimal.

Some writers (Lerner; McClelland 1961; Hagen 1962) have argued that a *modern* society is one in which a critical mass of individuals possess creative personalities, characterized by relatively high manipulative needs and, particularly, by a high need for achievement. McClelland and Winter (1969) even went so far as to claim that individuals could be induced to be achievement-oriented by training. They postulated that if individuals were induced for a time to behave as though they were high-need achievers, a high need for achievement would be internalized and they would, in fact, become high-need achievers—that is, modern, creative individuals. However, the evidence for success of this artificially induced process, largely derived from experience in India, is hardly convincing.

Renegade economist Everett Hagen offered a sociopsychological theory for the conversion of individuals (and hence, of societies) from the traditionalist to the modern mode, which has perhaps more appeal. His analysis rests on the idea that if an individual suffers a denial of expected status (or status denigration) and if that denial continues for long, a certain pattern of behavior emerges. Figure 6 below gives an overly simplistic rendition of Hagen's notion.

Figure 6
Hagen's Model of Personality Transition

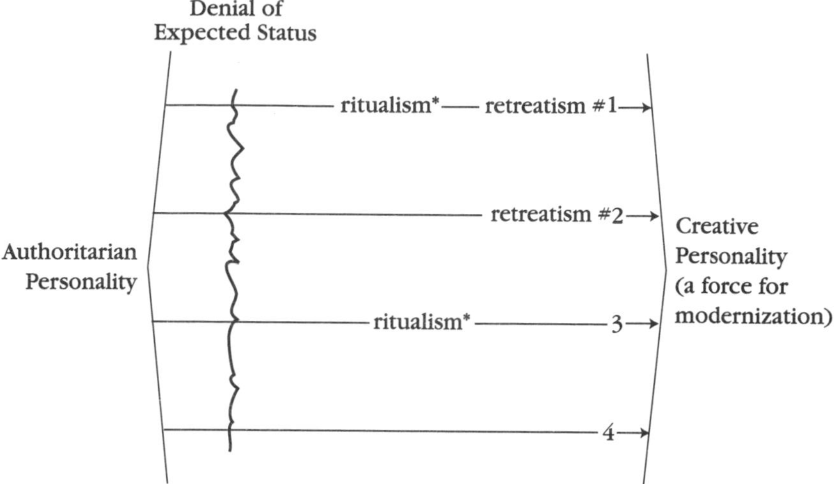

1 is the most likely path; 4 is the least likely path
*Characterized by institutional conformity
(appearance of "Uncle Toms," bureaucrats, collaborators).
#Characterized by hopelessness and despair.

It should be borne in mind that a denigration or denial of expected status may occur for many reasons, some externally induced (such as a war or natural disaster, which results in the oppression of an ethnic or religious group, or the denigration of an entire society) or internally generated, as by revolution or civil war, which causes denigration of the status of a certain group relative to others, or by population explosion, which pushes rural traditionalists into an urban environment. The expectation of higher status within the larger society is an essential part of the theory. So long as African Americans accepted second-class status in U.S. society, the process of modernizing did not operate, but once they began to develop a self-consciousness as a group possessed of inherent equality, change occurred. Perhaps at first there appeared a certain number of individuals mimicking the larger society and trying to become part of it, the "ritualists" or "Uncle Toms" in the African American case. Sooner or later that behavior can lead to retreatism based on despair or helplessness when it is perceived that joining the larger society is neither a feasible nor a desirable option. Eventually, however, Hagen postulates, a certain number of highly creative individuals appear who learn how to achieve status within the reference society. According to Hagen's theory, within a generation or two a large number of African Americans will appear who feel a high need for achievement and will attain high levels of creativity—in a socially constructive way—if the larger society permits; socially destructive, if it does not. We are seeing the results. Hagen's predictions are being borne out in contemporary reality. An increasing number of African Americans are perceiving alternative ways of life, accepting change as possibly desirable, and attempting to satisfy felt needs through either socially constructive or destructive ways.

For Chinese Americans and Japanese Americans, the process has been much more rapid, for they perceived themselves early on as inherently equal to everybody else, and their emphasis on discipline, industry, and self-improvement (long embedded in their Confucian culture) pushed them into the larger society which, over time, grudgingly recognized the value of their full participation.

Many examples of the process can be cited. The denial to the entire nation of Japan, as a result of its World War II defeat, of expected status in the world society has surely driven the Japanese to extraordinary levels of achievement to prove themselves the equal of other modern societies. Having achieved that target and in the absence of stimulation from large immigrant groups, Japan's modernizing push may well stall in neotraditionalism. It may already have done so.

The children and grandchildren of U.S. clergy are said to be heavily overrepresented in the *Who's Who of America*. The point is that the relative status of the U.S. clergy has declined dramatically over the past three or so generations. And immigrant minorities everywhere—be they overseas Chinese, Italian Americans, Jews, or whatever—tend to produce an extraordinary number of high-need achievers. At first, they are denied their expected status by the host society. Members of second and third generations find themselves psychologically driven to devise ways in which to create the status they feel is rightfully theirs. There seems to be a good bit of plausibility in Hagen's theory, which would explain the drive toward modernity.

Some years ago, I worked out a further application of the Hagen thesis in reference to a society's class structure. Assuming that membership in a given social class is determined by the scope of influence one has within society—whether by reason of wealth, age, religious piety, learning, occupation, or whatever—it would appear that each class contains those who are members by reason of certain ascribed characteristics (age, kinship, gender, inherited wealth, etc.) and others who are members by reason of achieved characteristics (learning, earned wealth, personal skills, etc.). The former might be called "traditionalists"; the latter, "climbers." There are, of course, some "fall-outs," who fail in their effort to seek lost status. Some may find antisocial alternatives (such as lawlessness, violence, or criminal activity). The model can be represented thus (Figure 7).

Figure 7
A Model of the Dynamics of Class Structure of a Society

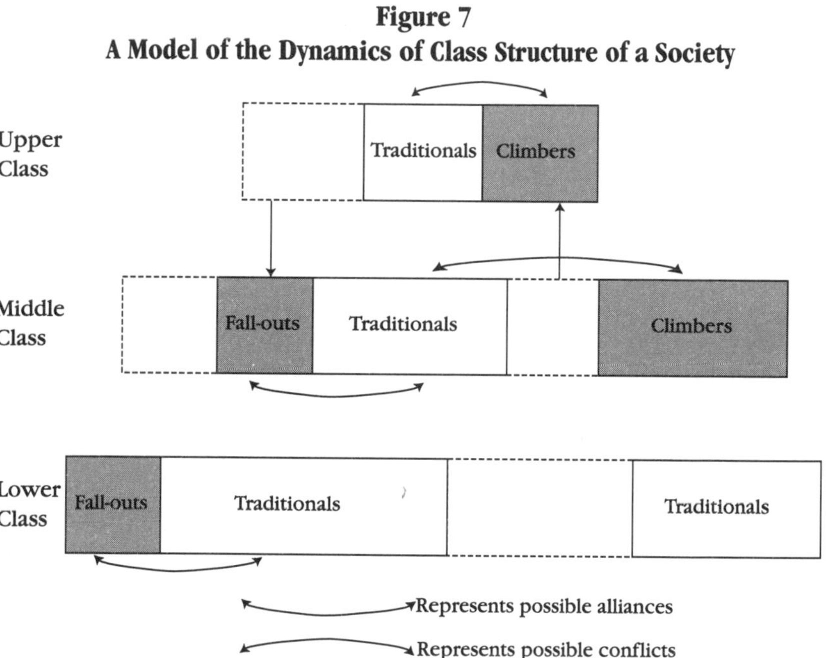

The relative strength of the various groups in each class, and the strength of the alliances and conflicts among them, presumably determine the extent to which a society will be dynamic. The larger the traditionalist group at each level, the less dynamic the society is likely to be; the larger the fall-outs and climbers groups, the more dynamic. Climbers tend to see the system as satisfying; fall-outs, as dissatisfying. The *level* of dynamism of a society—that is, its propensity for its members to be aware of alternatives and to see change as possibly desirable, as opposed to those who do not—may thus influence the speed of the modernizing process. However, if the system is overheated by change, the level of disorganization is likely to be so great as to inhibit the third element of modernization—an increasing satisfaction of felt needs. Upheaval, disorganization, and backsliding may be the result. If the system is static or regressive in the modernizing sense, a significant number of its participants must either be unaware of alternatives and/or do not perceive change as possibly desirable, perhaps because such is against their own perceived best interests. Such a society may become neotraditionalist.

Merely because a society has moved to the forefront of modernity, as we have defined it, does not mean that the process will continue forever. Some observers, for example, have opined that U.S. society—or at least a certain portion of the formal leadership elite—is becoming neotraditionalist and the process of modernization thereby slowed. The path to modernity has many curves and switchbacks.

Perhaps the system most utilized for analyzing cultural differences within the international business context is that developed by Geert Hofstede (1980). He proposed a four-factor analytical scheme—power distance, uncertainty avoidance, individualism, and masculinity. Later, he added time orientation. The first relates to the degree to which individuals in a hierarchical situation perceive greater or lesser ability to control each other's behavior. One measure is the perception of inequality between superior and subordinates. Hofstede observes that inequality can occur in reference to prestige, wealth, and power and that different societies place different weight on status within these categories.

Uncertainty avoidance, or tolerance of uncertainty, Hofstede observes, likewise varies among societies. The three indicators he uses to measure this aspect are rule orientation, employment stability, and stress. The third dimension of national culture used by Hofstede is individualism, the relationship between an individual and the collectivity to which he or she belongs. His fourth dimension relates to what he calls masculinity, the degree to which aggressive (male) and nurturing (female) roles are clearly distinguished.

Some years later, Hofstede (1988) added a time orientation to these four dimensions, which he defined in a way very similar to the Kluckhohn-Strodtbeck time orientation.

Hofstede, and subsequent researchers following his definitions and utilizing similar research techniques, developed some agreement as to how different national societies are classified along these five dimensions. Unlike some typologists, he speculated as to how societies might change over time, and why. Among other things, he notes a steady erosion in the legitimacy accorded social inequality, that inequality is no longer accepted generally as part of the natural order. In general, Hofstede seems to imply that the more "modern" or "advanced" societies exhibit a relatively high level of tolerance for uncertainty, greater emphasis on the individual, a blurring of masculine and feminine roles, lower inequality, and a relatively long time horizon.

Further Critique of the Kluckhohn-Strodtbeck Method of Analysis

As valuable as the Kluckhohn-Strodtbeck paradigm (and the instruments developed to make it operational) is in providing insight into cultural differences, it is nonetheless essentially descriptive. It does not address *why* these differences exist. Admittedly, the paradigm does not really purport to do so. For example, whether on the level of the individual or of a collectivity, why should the dominant values orientation be past, present, or future? Apparently, it just is. Given the situation, the orientation must be satisfying to a critical mass.

Somehow, we are left with the impression that the right side of each of the five values-orientation continua are characterized as the most modern, the most advanced. That is, a modern society is dominated by the following orientations: (1) people as basically "Good" (Human Nature), (2) Mastery over Nature (Person-Nature), (3) Future orientation (Time), (4) the Doing mode (Activity), and (5) Individualism (Human Relations). Is this really true? In all circumstances, is such a society more likely to generate and support an ongoing modernization process? One could argue otherwise—that the most modern (in a sustainable sense) is one characterized by a strong Harmony-with-Nature orientation, a Present orientation, a Being-in-Becoming orientation, and a Collateral orientation in Human Relations. Are assumptions about Human Nature (Evil, Neutral or Mixed, Good) really relevant? If human nature is seen as truly mutable (or adjustable), perhaps that is all that is necessary for the modernizing process. It is either subject to change or it is not.

If a particular configuration of value orientations (or worldviews—this phrase seems to me to be more descriptive of what is involved) dominates a society, the surrounding social system must continue to induce individuals within the system to perceive that configuration of value orientations (or worldviews) to be functional within that system. It must be satisfying in some sense to the inhabitants of that system. So, in order to understand the system, one must understand the relationships and dynamics within that system. The word *patterns* does not quite capture what I have in mind, but it is close. What it seems to me we have to deal with is an *interactive dynamic system,* a dynamic set of interrelated patterns that exist because they are satisfying to at least a critical number of those inhabiting the system.

Nor does it seem to me that the Kluckhohn-Strodtbeck approach really explains the *process* or direction of change. Perhaps their analytical scheme needs to be married with one or more of the dynamic models of change discussed previously. For example, the element of *expectations* (and their frustration?) should be taken into consideration in the Hagen sense. The element of *empathy* as a separate variable should likewise be measured (Lerner), also the degree of *masculinity/femininity* and the willingness to tolerate *uncertainty* (Hofstede). It should also be noted that if there exist substantial differences in the needs (Maslow) of two cultural groups involved in a confrontation, a simple measure of cultural differences à la Kluckhohn-Strodtbeck may be, at best, misleading. The same could well be true if one were measuring cultural differences between two groups of disparate average age; that is, the Parsons' schema may be relevant. The differences may be due to difference in maturation and are not reflective of deeper-lying cultural disparity.

One should bear in mind that change in values on both the individual and collective levels is not necessarily slow. It can happen quite rapidly under certain circumstances. The interesting question is, under what circumstances? Value changes may be part of the social/political crises currently observed in rapidly modernizing societies. I have lived in one such country—Turkey—and have observed the enormous individual identity crises that accompany accelerated change (the "big bang") as various pressures build to a breaking point, where long-held values are suddenly no longer satisfying. They become dysfunctional in the newly emerging system. The cause? An explosion of population, urbanization, external threat, environmental pressure, international competition, growth of the mass media, geographical mobility, technological innovation—one could go on. Many or all of these pressures now tend to converge in time, thereby accelerating social change to a degree never before witnessed.

I suspect that right now the so-called dominant American values, whatever they may be, are shifting quite rapidly, or have already done so. A Mastery-over-Nature mode may be giving way to a Harmony-with-Nature orientation; Individual to a Collateral orientation; Future to a Present orientation. I do not *know* that to be the case, but I hypothesize that it may well be. The point is that, increasingly, the past profile of individual value orientations becomes dysfunctional within the larger American culture. They are no longer satisfying to the individual American in that one cannot lead a satisfying life guided by outmoded value orientations. For example, it may be possible that the Time dimension in personal decision making is such as to render the future less relevant, in part because it is so uncertain. I would argue that all persistent values and worldviews are rational—that is, satisfying within the system that generates them.

This brings us to another question: Can the Kluckhohn-Strodtbeck methodology be used effectively in the resolution of conflict? It would seem that the evidence is really not complete. If, for example, there is a change induced on both sides of a cultural frontier, however defined, such as to reduce the level of tension and make possible the resolution of a specific issue in a manner tolerable to both groups, is a more generalized change in values and worldviews thereby generated? Is the resolution of successive intercultural conflict through this method (or any method) thereby facilitated? Again, one does not know, though there is some highly suggestive anecdotal evidence that such is true. These questions seem to me to be terribly relevant in the contemporary world as ethnic and religious nationalism becomes increasingly confrontational, whether within or between nation-states.

At a more personal level, I have a problem in responding to a lot of the situations described in the Kluckhohn instrument. I have thought about this problem on and off for a long time, and there appears to be a possible explanation. Perhaps the paradigm is not complete. For example, conceptually, what could lie beyond what appear to be terminal points on the five continua: Innate goodness of the individual, Future time orientation, Mastery-over-Nature orientation, Doing orientation, and Individualism?

In respect to the Future orientation, what of a cyclical view of time, which is embedded in some of the Asian Time orientations?

One's orientation is neither Past, Present, nor Future; it is all of these simultaneously, depending upon the situation. Which one(s) do you engage? All? In respect to the Individual orientation, what of a voluntary cooperative mode? That seems to be different from the Collateral or collective as discussed in the literature, because it implies that one is cooperating with a group with which one may have no direct relationship. In fact, this mode seems to be developing in some societies and under certain circumstances.

I also have a problem with the Mastery-over-Nature orientation. What of a sustainable optimizing relationship with nature? I realize that is not very catchy phraseology for what seems to me to be quite a different category. In respect to Being and Doing, I would propose "self- fulfillment" and "being self-fulfilled." What constitutes self-fulfillment is, of course, culturally determined. In respect to the man-is-good mode, what of the man-is-flexible mode? Let us say that man is generally good, but vulnerable, which is more situationally determined, or perhaps the Human Nature dimension should be eliminated entirely. (Indeed, its possible irrelevance here may explain the alleged difficulty that Florence Kluckhohn had in framing situations with which to identify assumptions as to human nature, a difficulty shared by subsequent researchers.)

The upshot of my concerns is that I have a very difficult time answering many of the Kluckhohn questions, perhaps because the options are incomplete. One has to be wary of forcing people to respond in ways they don't believe in simply because of the limited nature of the instruments used. Perhaps there is another set of concepts out there, another column which should be articulated, other possible responses to the situations postulated.

One final point: in respect to specific applications in my own field, international business and economics, I have used the idea of self-perceived and other-perceived values since 1976 in analyzing international joint ventures. Done on a cost-benefit basis, one works out one's own self-perceived benefits and costs and what one perceives the proposed partner would gain and lose in the arrangement. Then the two parties exchange the "other" perceptions. The degree to which those are not congruent with one's own perceptions implies conflict down the track. At that point, one can lay the differences in perception on the table and talk about them. It is often hard to put these differences into dollars-and-cents terms, but sometimes it can be done. I am convinced that the value orientations analysis could play an important role in trying to understand another party, whether the situation be a marriage, a joint business venture, or a strategic business alliance, but I worry about forcing people to think and respond in categories too rigidly drawn. Nostradin Hodja would have asked, "So what is the reality, yours or mine?"

References

Almond, Gabriel A., and James S. Coleman, eds. *The Politics of the Developing Areas.* Princeton, NJ: Princeton University Press, 1960. See particularly the "Introduction by Almond."

Erikson, Erik H. *Childhood and Society.* New York: W. W. Norton, 1950.

Hagen, Everett E. *On the Theory of Social Change.* Homewood, IL: Dorsey Press, 1962.

Hofstede, Geert. *Culture's Consequence, International Differences in Work-Related Values.* Beverly Hills, CA: Sage, 1980.

Hofstede, Geert, and Michael Harris Bond. "The Confucius Connection: From Cultural Roots to Economic Growth." *Organization Dynamics* 16 (1988).

Kluckhohn, Florence R., and Fred L. Strodtbeck, *Variations in Value Orientations.* Evanston, IL: Row, Peterson, 1961.

Lerner, Daniel. *The Passing of Traditional Society.* Glencoe, IL: Free Press, 1958.

Maslow, Abraham H. "The Theory of Human Motivation." *Psychological Review* (5 July 1943): 370–96.

McClelland, David C. *The Achieving Society.* Princeton, NJ: D. Van Norstrand, 1961.

McClelland, David C., and David G. Winter. *Motivating Economic Achievement.* New York: The Free Press, 1969.

Murray, Henry A., et al. *Explorations in Personality.* New York: Oxford University Press, 1938.

Parsons, Talcott. *The Social System.* Glencoe, IL: Free Press, 1951.

Redding, S. G. "Cognition as an Aspect of Culture and Its Relation to Management Processes: An Exploratory View of the Chinese Case." Paper, Academy of International Business, Manchester, UK, November 1978.

Robinson, Richard D. *High-Level Manpower in Economic Development—The Turkish Case.* Cambridge: Harvard University Press, 1967.

———. *International Business Policy.* New York: Holt, Rinehart and Winston, 1964.

Staking Out the Middle Ground: Florence Kluckhohn's Early Work

Dorothy Caplow

A crucial question in both general social analysis and specific conflict resolution is, what kind of change is likely or possible, in this situation, for these people, given their values? Florence R. Kluckhohn's work, throughout her life, addresses both the scholarly and the practical aspects of this question. As a researcher, Kluckhohn was a genuine diagnostician. Never working in a tower or a vacuum, she saw the depth of her scholarship as a very real response to the depth of the problem, both in its academic sense (How does it work?) and in its political sense (How can we make it work?) Unusually sensitive to input from a variety of academic disciplines—sociology, anthropology, psychology, cultural history, and philosophy—and to her own experience and common sense, Kluckhohn had that rare gift of discovering the "middle position" in almost any sensitive discussion.

Few people in the 1950s ever thought that the problem confronting the "social fabric" was the diversity of the cultural orientations it was trying to assimilate, but Florence Kluckhohn started with the assumption that the equilibrium of culture actually depends upon the dynamic interactions of diverse orientations. In a time when *deviant* was a word still used by serious social scientists, Kluckhohn developed the idea of "cultural ecology," which not only embraced but demanded different species of values. The Kluckhohn model and method is in one sense the language she invented to universalize (and supplement) her own ability to intuit the motivations and worldviews of others.

Kluckhohn's model provides a global framework of cultural variation, yet seeks to describe that variation in value-neutral terms. Its blend of relativism and scientific replicability has proved to be remarkably well suited to the demands of workable conflict negotiation as well as to the requirements of scientific research. Anthropologists and other social scientists have used the method for years to explore the value systems of other cultures. Nurses, clinical psychologists, and resource managers have found Kluckhohn's model useful as a means of displacing stereotypes and fine-tuning cultural awareness. Conflict resolution specialists have used the method to explore deeper, less obvious sources of miscommunication and chronic tension between cultural groups. These social applications arise naturally out of Kluckhohn's distinctive approach to cultural values and cultural conflicts.

Like many social scientists, Kluckhohn hoped that a better understanding of social dynamics would create the potential for greater social harmony. But to an unusual extent, her respect for the autonomy and value of different values systems allowed her to make serious political suggestions without, at the same time, making accusations or moral judgments. A true democrat, she was able to hear many voices without prejudice, while striving continually for deeper and more universal insight. Her lifelong work reveals the tenor of her thoughts and efforts clearly.

While most who use the method are familiar with Kluckhohn and Strodtbeck's 1961 book, *Variations in Value Orientations,* very few are familiar with her earlier work. The several papers she published prior to the publication of *Variations* (in one of which she first introduced the value orientations schema to the world), paint a rich portrait of her intellectual and political development. In several she discusses the nature of academic inquiry; in two she raises class issues; and in the following three she intently explores the role of women and the family in America. These early writings provide a unique opportunity to observe Kluckhohn applying the concepts of her theory to social problems, both to analyze them and to frame suggestions for their amelioration.

Even as a graduate student at Radcliffe College, Florence Kluckhohn was interested in problems of cultural definition. In 1936 she lived in and studied a small Spanish-speaking village in New Mexico. She submitted her study of the community, Los Atarqueños, as her Ph.D. thesis in 1941. She also published a portion of the project in the *American Journal of Sociology* in 1940. This paper,

"The Participant-Observer Technique in Small Communities," is one of Florence Kluckhohn's earliest published works and shows her already strongly engaged with basic questions about how cultural anthropology should be conducted.

"The Participant-Observer Technique in Small Communities"

While participant observation is fairly commonplace among field researchers these days, it was much less so at the time of Kluckhohn's study, and she takes pains to describe it and explain its advantages. As she defines the technique,

> Participant observation is conscious and systematic sharing, in so far as circumstances permit, in the life-activities and on occasion, in the interests and affects of a group of persons. Its purpose is to obtain data about behavior...in which the distortion that results from the investigator's being an outside agent is reduced to a minimum. (Kluckhohn 1940, 331)

Kluckhohn used in her own study what would probably be known today as "covert participant observation": the villagers did not know that she was researching them.[1]

She practiced covert observation in the guise of a housewife, waiting each day for her husband, Clyde, to return, as did all the other women in the village. This natural role made it easy for her to blend into the community. Clyde at the time was engaged in his studies among the Navajo; he was also already much better known than she was.

Describing the degree to which her interests merged with those of the community, Kluckhohn says, "My participation was in most respects hypocritical," but adds that in some instances, "I found myself a more or less genuine participant" (341–42). She relates an incident in which a visitor from another village asked her to dance more times than was strictly proper by the community's standards. Her ensuing nervousness betrayed the extent to which she had adopted community mores, as did her accompanying strong feeling (which proved to be correct) that the community would act without her asking to take care of the problem. One of the men did indeed speak to the visitor, and he apologized. She admits that such experiences represent at least a momentary loss of objectivity, of scientific distance; however, she asserts definitively that after the fact she could always return to her objective analysis. Though careful to avoid misinterpretation, she is not shy about the advantages of her method: "In my opinion I gained understanding and insight by such experiences. I think I gained more than I lost by the temporary lapses of cold objectivity" (343).

Kluckhohn describes the balance between emotional identification and scientific distance, which she believes produces the most accurate cultural information. On no account does she wish to be confused with those anthropologists who have "gone native." She explicitly cautions against intimate liaisons with researchees. On the other hand, purely observational studies—what she calls "behavioristic" studies—are "products of a sustained aloofness from the interests and emotional life" (342).

Although Kluckhohn seems almost morally offended by this aloofness, she argues against it on scientific grounds. Some of her contemporaries, she says, claim that the status of investigator/outsider actually helped in the collection of data, because people, when flattered by outside attention, tend to talk more than they would ordinarily. Kluckhohn points out that this only applies to a certain type of person, and wonders pointedly whether such a technique does not often attract less valuable informants: "Is it not often the person with exhibitionist tendencies or the person who is maladjusted whose vanity and desire for gain or recognition are most easily appealed to" (341)?

She points out that all people...have "egos" and not necessarily ones that are stimulated by condescension (342). One wonders if there is not a slight personal tinge to this statement, coming as it does from a young female academic in 1940. Regardless, the necessary coupling of accuracy and courtesy is a distinctive feature of Kluckhohn's approach, one that in many ways is still revolutionary.

Kluckhohn's originality emerges strongly in this early paper and seems somewhat frustrated by the limits of the language available to her. She has already discovered concepts she wants to describe—for instance, the effect that a method of observation has upon interview subjects—that do not fit easily into accepted terms of either emotional or intellectual appeals. While obviously proficient in the rigorous methods of scientific academic inquiry, she betrays some uneasiness with the whole business. She stations herself very consciously between objectivity, the stance of normative academic anthropologists of the time, and subjectivity, the stance available to anyone who develops special relationships with the people he or she studies. She takes considerable pains to appreciate the advantages of both approaches.

"American Culture: Generalized Orientations and Class Patterns"

Another paper, written with her husband Clyde after the war, in the mid- to late 1940s, expresses more openly a sense of political and social responsibility that finds itself at odds with the slow pace and structure of research. Frustrated by sheer academic study, the Kluckhohns wished to use their training in precise observation, together with their common sense, to come up with a model of American value orientations.

The paper, entitled "American Culture: Generalized Orientations and Class Patterns," was never published, but it was presented at the Seventh Conference on Science, Philosophy, and Religion. Unfortunately, the New York Public Library's special edition—the only known copy—is missing a few final pages.* From the sixteen intact pages, however, it is possible to educe the Kluckhohns' intent to show (1) that interclass stress and conflict can be traced to an underlying difference in value orientations (although they do not, at this point, use the word); (2) that the middle-class orientations that dominate society differ predictably from lower-class orientations; and (3) that general dissemination and understanding of these differences may, they hope, ease class tension. This last idea, that understanding differences leads to a reduction in conflict, is a theme that surfaces in Florence Kluckhohn's work again and again.

Very early in the paper, the Kluckhohns stress that the paper is not scientific in the proper sense but is based on shared experience. Together they present and discuss an outline of the main American orientations for people of all classes and then delve into class differences. They point out that the middle class in the United States is very large and really sets the pace, in a values sense, for the entire country. Effectively, middle-class orientations are American orientations.

The Kluckhohns find that lower- and middle-class institutions start from the outset with different sets of priorities and proceed naturally to inculcate different orientations. These value patterns

* The actual date of the Seventh Conference is unknown.

put lower-class people at odds with those of the general American middle class. The Kluckhohns suggest that many of the stresses and strains in the American social fabric could be relieved if a greater understanding of these differing orientations were widespread.

The Kluckhohns ask themselves the question, "What values, what life goals do Americans, of every region and of all social classes, tend to share?" (Kluckhohn, Seventh Conference, 2). They come up with this schema, or view of life (3).

1. Effort and optimism
    a. Moral purpose
    b. Rationalism—the individual in life
2. Romantic individualism
    a. Cult of the average man[2]
    b. Tendency to personalize the individual and social values
3. Change a value in itself
4. Pleasure principle
5. Externalism
6. Simple answers
7. Humor
8. Generosity

The Kluckhohns go on to describe what is particularly American about all these orientations and suborientations to life.[3] A portrait of middle-class society, the demographically and ideologically dominant culture group in the United States in the 1940s, emerges from the Kluckhohns' analysis. Middle-class America is a society composed of small, strong, isolated, child-centered nuclear families possessing financial security and further structured into organizations that command wider social recognition. Furthermore, the general goals of these organizations, (e.g., Elks, Boy Scouts, etc.) are closely aligned with those of American schools. In order to prepare children for a middle-class lifestyle, parents lay great stress on property and respect for ownership, work for work's sake, cleanliness, emotional control, good manners, the inevitable positive relationship between education and success, a good marriage, and strong nuclear family relations (though not especially strong extended family relations). Children in such families are encouraged to seek the approval of adults, are given long-term rewards for good behavior, are monitored in their choice of friends and encouraged to seek "suitable" ones, and are supervised with regard to commercial recreation (movies, gambling).

The Kluckhohns present a companion portrait of lower-class society, having made it clear that they are drawing their conclusions from anecdote and experience. They caution that, since 90 percent of Americans consider themselves to be middle class, for the most part the classes they describe "were defined by social science analysis rather than in the minds of the people in the society" (11). The goals of lower-class families are different from those of middle-class families because they find themselves in different circumstances. Most lower-class families are financially unstable, one-parent families, extended along the maternal line and not child-centered. Typically, lower-class people belong to few organizations outside their churches except for ones, such as gangs, that do not receive positive recognition from the wider community and whose goals are in opposition to the goals of the schools. Most money in the family is spent on the immediate needs of food and shelter. Since saving is usually impossible, parents are not able to give children long-term rewards. Children are encouraged to achieve independence quickly and to work as soon as possible. They are allowed to choose their own friends, and their access to commercial forms of entertainment is not closely guarded. Sexual and aggressive prowess contributes directly to community standing, and education is linked only hazily to improving one's status.

The Kluckhohns stress that the difference in orientations between the middle class and the lower class is not a qualitative one. They point out that a child raised in a lower-class family does gain something from the experience. They note that such a child is encouraged to be more self-sufficient than his or her middle-class counterpart and "more often escapes quasi-neurotic dependence on his mother's approval." Of course, "he also tends to lack that reward as an enduring stimulus to socially useful behavior" (16). In methods of punishment, the middle class "tends to stress deprivations of things or activities, of love and affection, and of praise rather than physical punishment" (16). And while the Kluckhohns acknowledge that lower-class parents lack the ability to give their children long-term rewards and so encourage thriftiness and future-orientedness, it is clear that they are already thinking in variational terms. For instance, even if most Americans value a Future orientation, it is no better than any other orientation to time. Even though the Kluckhohns do not use terms such as "Future orientation" in this paper, the drift of Florence Kluckhohn's later thoughts is already evident.

One note toward the end of the existing pages reveals the general direction of the Kluckhohns' thoughts. They mention that many teachers are frustrated with some aspects of lower-class children's performance in school and think that the children are purposely and stubbornly misbehaving. The Kluckhohns suggest that if more teachers were generally aware of the value differences involved, they would be better able both to understand the children's existing behavior and to motivate them toward changing their behavior. They hope their paper will go some way toward accomplishing this end.

"Dominant and Substitute Profiles"

In another paper, written a few years later, Florence Kluckhohn takes a more determinedly scholarly tack. In this paper, "Dominant and Substitute Profiles," published in 1950 by *Social Forces*, she first presents the complete value orientations schema. If the Seventh Conference paper shows her at the height of her annoyance with traditional scholarship, the paper in *Social Forces* reveals, in contrast, the strength of her commitment to academic procedure.

In "The Participant-Observer Technique," Kluckhohn locates herself between two different techniques of practical anthropology: scientific objectivism and "going native." In the *Social Forces* paper, Kluckhohn locates herself between the two disciplines of anthropology and sociology. She lays out the necessity for her new, more rigorous model, capable of distinguishing not only American value orientations but those of other societies as well. She then presents the five common human problems as she sees them: (1) What are the innate predispositions of men? (2) What is the relation of man to nature? (3) What is the significant time dimension? or What is the direction in time of the action process? (4) What type of personality is to be most valued? (5) What is the dominant modality of relationships? She explains her rationale for each category. The questions of innate human nature and of people's relation to nature she regards as familiar and needing little clarification. She also believes the language of the personality types—Being, Being-in-Becoming, Doing—is quite familiar from the works of various philosophers and cultural historians.

She explores her rationale for the Time dimension more thoroughly: "Far too little attention has been given to this problem and its phrasings" (Kluckhohn 1950b, 379). Too often, she says, the distinction has been drawn between a supposed ahistorical "timeless" attitude of folk and rural peoples in contrast with the time-aware, future-oriented lives of urban industrialists. She explains that she herself became interested in the problem of time when studying the Spanish-speaking New Mexicans. She noticed that their concept of time was very different from that of most other Americans but was not content to explain the difference she observed in terms of an ahistorical/historical dichotomy. In her opinion, the "clocklessness" of a culture, or the presence or absence of recording historians, does not in itself determine that culture's relationship to time. Instead, she extends the range of the question—peoples may be oriented to the past, present, or future in Kluckhohn's schema—and draws no a priori distinctions between modernized city peoples and their rural counterparts.

The thread of her thought here is interesting in light of some current criticisms of the Kluckhohn model. Frequently the schema is criticized for its very linear view of time: What about sacred time? What about circular time? ask the postmodern anthropologists. Isn't Kluckhohn's model hopelessly Eurocentric? The fact that she was, in 1950, working quite consciously against just that sort of dichotomy, perceiving it as romantic and possibly prejudicial, is instructive. Kluckhohn's model, albeit strongly informed by her Western tradition, allows for counterintuitive discoveries. For instance, several Native American tribes tested with Kluckhohn's survey instrument appear to be more Future-oriented than ordinary dominant-culture Americans.[4] Some very modern societies, such as Japan, appear to lean strongly toward the past.

The Human Relations orientation deals with human beings as social organisms and "is, therefore, the orientation which phrases, in the most general way, to be sure, the character of the social solidarity" (381). Kluckhohn notes that sociologists are for the most part familiar with binary distinctions, for example, between gemeinschaft and gesellschaft or between mechanical and organic solidarity. Anthropologists, for their part, are accustomed to the language of lineage and collaterality but tend to focus on family and kinship communities (gemeinschaft) rather than on broad systems of social structure (gesellschaft). Kluckhohn wants to combine these insights and examine the Human Relations orientation that underlies the structuring of both companies and families in terms of three facets of biological relatedness, which all societies share but prioritize differently. A social focus on parentage and generational difference is Lineality; on siblings and peer groups, Collaterality; and on individual differentiation and one's being as a single organism, Individualism.

Kluckhohn explains dominant American values in terms of the schema (Future, Doing, Individualism, Mastery, Evil)[5] and then asserts that

> we are, whether social scientists or laymen, more or less self-consciously aware of some or all of the dominant orientations. We are much less aware of the alternative ones, or their importance, and too often tend to view them, when recognized at all, simply as contradictions that threaten integration. Such a view would seem to indicate a general tendency to think in static rather than dynamic terms. (383)

Kluckhohn hopes that the successful communication of difference—and of its necessity—in an atmosphere of mutual respect will work to ease what she calls the "strains" in the social fabric.

Toward that end she specifically desires in this paper to refute some well-known studies of social class in the United States. These studies, by W. Lloyd Warner, et al., are of a small town called Jonesville, which, they claim, is a microcosm of American society. They find in Jonesville a much more rigid and definite class structure (they divided the town into nine levels of class) than most Americans at the time liked to think was possible.

Kluckhohn does not dispute that the society of Jonesville exists as it has been described, but she suggests that it represents a pocket of alternatively oriented folk who put more emphasis on the Lineal principle, on Being, and on the Past than do the majority of Americans. She claims that dominant American values—Future, Mastery, Doing—can only exist in an expanding community. She produces census figures and other statistics that demonstrate that "The towns studied thus far by Warner and his co-workers are not expanding communities" (387).

Then Kluckhohn draws her own peculiar lesson from what she sees as Warner's misguided analysis:

> Although a Jonesville is clearly not America in microcosm, it remains a fact that millions of Americans do live in Jonesvilles. Millions more, who live in still other kinds of communities...

> give expression in their behavior to orientations other than those of the dominant cultural profile. (391)

With a prescience and insight astonishing in 1950, Kluckhohn follows a line of thinking which is still fresh today:

> One important question relative to the situation as thus pictured for America, and one which is seldom asked (for the reason, perhaps, that the tendency has not been to consider alternative orientations as always present in the system) is this one: Is the patterning of the American social system, inclusive of stratification, in its dominant emphasis actually dependent upon the continued existence of some total groups and some segments of groups which are structured according to alternative orientations? Is this perhaps a feature of social structuring in general which is more evident with some kinds of cultural profiles than others? (391)

She asks not whether diversity potentially enriches a society, but whether or not diversity is actually necessary for that society's dynamic stability.[6]

Kluckhohn insists, disarmingly and repeatedly, that greater and more accurate intellectual understanding of difference will improve society. Those used to hearing diversity preached as an unquestionable good might be almost surprised at the way in which she offers to prove its merit. She does so in a truly democratic fashion: by trying to explain herself and open her discourse to as many people as possible. Her papers stand as she says societies do: their themes formed from the dynamic equilibrium between several alternative points of view.

The Role of Women in American Society

Nowhere are these alternative points of view more beautifully illustrated than in her treatment of the question of women in American society.[7] There are three papers in which Kluckhohn discusses the role of women in American society. One is a lecture entitled "What Education for Women?" and the other two comprise a book (really, two papers under one cover) called *The American Family, Past and Present and America's Women*. In them she describes the American family and the social role of the American woman of the 1950s.

She outlines the conceptual and practical challenges facing American society in defining (or redefining) these social creations.

Her ideas on the subject might be briefly summarized in two problem statements. First, the role of women is the most important stress point in the American social fabric, and it is where we should turn our attention. Second, there are two related problems in the roles of women: (1) the domestic role receives no significant social rewards in our society and (2) the economic role, which women historically have been barred from sharing, receives a disproportionate share of the rewards. One suggestion for resolving these problems is placing a greater social value on the domestic role as an intellectual and creative endeavor and providing more specific training for it. A second solution is the widespread creation of serious part-time jobs for most women (and fully equal pay and treatment for those women who choose to work full-time all their lives). Kluckhohn also urges more involvement of American men in the lives of their families and communities, with less focus in society in general on the achievements of the occupational/economic sphere alone and more focus on relational and domestic or recreationally artistic pursuits.

With characteristic intellectual frankness, Kluckhohn begins her consideration in *America's Women* with the question of the distinction between men and women. "Few problems," she says, "other than that of the creation or the fact of life itself, have so plagued the mind[s] of men and women of all periods in history as has this one of the differences between the male and the female." Few discussions of the problem are poised as shrewdly and as fairly as Kluckhohn's, though. Her tone is interesting.

> **Not infrequently the question has been argued on the basis of inferiority or superiority. More often it becomes a disagreement over sex-determined attributes of mind and matter. But let that disagreement become sufficiently bitter, and the competitive issue of superiority and inferiority again emerges. In fact, something of the issue is almost always present whether explicitly stated or not. (Kluckhohn 1952, 71)**

Throughout her discussion, Kluckhohn attempts to avoid that competition without sidestepping any issues. She steers her argument delicately between various extremes. At times, she consciously addresses those who might be called traditionalists; at other times she consciously addresses progressives.

Americans opposed to feminism and its effects on the role of women often express concern lest differences between men and women be obscured. Kluckhohn addresses these concerns by acknowledging the social inevitability of distinguishing somehow between men and women. All societies, she points out, seem to create separate roles for men and women. She exhibits a kind of biological functionalism by assuming that anything so universal as the family or the differentiation of sex roles must be serving a very useful purpose or it wouldn't be so persistent. Most societies need some kind of regulation of the sex drive, she argues, and also some system for delivering care and nurture to the young. Child rearing and the management of the home in which the children are reared constitute what Kluckhohn calls "the domestic aspect of the feminine role." She lays out the social necessity behind this role because she feels that

> there is some danger...that we are irreparably warping this aspect of the role by means of our continuous demeaning of its significance.This is especially true of those who urge so strongly the equality of the sexes with small or no regard of even biologically known differences. (79)

Despite this domestic focus, however, Kluckhohn insists throughout on the necessity of equal social rewards for both men and women. She reassures feminist fears of limitation and confinement by making it clear that, though gender distinctions are always made in every society, they are by no means always the same distinctions. The crucial question for American society, Kluckhohn argues, is the particular shape of the American version of the female role vis-à-vis the family. This shape depends very much on American value orientations, which she describes in terms of the five orientations.

To bring out the way in which American family relationships are shaped by a basic value orientation to Individualism, Kluckhohn contrasts family relationships in American and Mexican society. She points out that the Mexican orientations toward Being, the Present, and Collaterality and Lineality sustain and structure a society that, in contrast to American society, is extremely "familistic."[8] In fact, "the family of the Mexican society...really is the whole society. The whole society is formed by an extension of family relationships both up and down and sideways" (42).

In contrast, Kluckhohn says, American society is not family-centered, even though we are very attached to our notions of family. The nuclear family, says Kluckhohn, is distinctively and appropriately American.

> If we are to produce achievement-minded, future-oriented independent individuals, we must have the kind of family which permits individualistic expression and allows its members to go free of bonds that would tie them to particular people and places. (60)

She points out that the business world plays more of a role in determination of social status in American society than the family: "In many—even in most—societies of the world, family or other hereditary traditions govern occupations. To a very marked degree we have reversed this order of affairs" (61–62).

But even if the nuclear family is the most suitable for America, says Kluckhohn, it is not perfect. There are strains in the nuclear family, which she attributes to the imperfect way in which it fits with our cultural orientations. Kluckhohn describes the historical processes that gave rise to American value orientations and, concomitantly, to those strains. The American orientation to Individualism, she argues, made gender-based economic exclusion particularly unsatisfying. The language of value orientations provides her with a means of analyzing and approaching the history of the American family, and of women's role within it, in a language remarkably unburdened by partisan terms. Rather than labeling the traditional family structure as backward or oppressive, for instance, she points out that it does not offer much challenge or opportunity for the American woman.

She notes that early colonial families were strongly patriarchal, a Lineal orientation, which, combined with a religious belief in the innate Evil character of human nature, gave rise to strict child-rearing practices and a generalized suspicion of women's characters. But,

> even stronger in our value system, however, have been those other orientations which we have designated as individualism, the stress on future time, the belief in overcoming obstacles, and making a prime virtue of achievement. Both because the germs of these values were present very early and because of the vast resources offered by the natural environment it was

> almost inevitable that there would develop an emphasis upon the achievement of all individuals. It was...simply not possible, in this vast country, to hold and develop values of this kind and still keep them applicable to only a part of the population—that is, to the adult males. The so-called emancipation of both women and children from the kind of authoritarian ties common in colonial families was certain to occur. (52)

Next she describes the reinforcing presence of industrialism and middle-class dominance and the changes in the last fifty years because of increasing urbanization. She explains that the isolation of the small nuclear family, the ideal American "good family" (56), brings particular pressures to bear on its members. Fathers generally have the sole financial responsibility for the family. Mothers do not have relatives to call on to help with housework and child rearing. These pressures take their toll. As an indicator of the severity of the current problems, Kluckhohn points naturally to divorce. American men and women are not as happy with each other as they could be, she feels. While acknowledging the changes in the role of women and children and the greater democratization of the family, Kluckhohn suggests that the father's role is still too autonomous, the mother's role not autonomous enough.

In contrast, she mentions the security Mexican women have in their family-oriented society. They expect marriage to be permanent, and they know what is expected of them. American women have more choice, mobility, and independence—all things we prize—but also more uncertainty.

In addition to her use of the value orientations model, Kluckhohn's concentration on roles gives her—just as it did in her study of participant observation—a neutral point of entry. To say that men and women are in doubt about who women are, or to say that women themselves are experiencing a lot of strain, would be to cast the question in a different light. It would be a discussion at once less accessible to disagreement and at the same time more restricted in its sense of who women are and with what voices they speak.

She delineates this problem in "What Education for Women?". American women, she explains, are encouraged to seek success in at least four different roles, which she labels domestic (subdivided into housewife and mother), career woman, culture bearer, and glamour girl. Proficiency in the domestic sphere is expected, especially with regard to motherhood, yet there is very little systematic training for that role. Instead, says Kluckhohn, women are educated along exactly the same lines as men, but in their case it is a "contingency education," not really meant to be deployed in a full-time career.

The result, says Kluckhohn, is that although American women enjoy a comparatively high degree of legal and educational parity as compared with women in other cultures, they remain confused and dissatisfied. While they do not yet have occupational parity with men, the relatively low social importance of family in American society provides relatively few rewards for family-centeredness. American women, she says, will not settle for less than an equal share or less than direct representation. As America has always been a theoretically classless society in which those who wish to get ahead, can, women will continue to fight for social recognition and reward wherever it is available. In a society structured such as ours, with all social rewards accruing to the professional work world, women will naturally want more and more entree to that world: "They know that success in it is the only kind of success for which most Americans give unqualified respect. Thus, what they are trying to claim for themselves is the opportunity to participate in the total society as man's equal rather than as his symbol" (Kluckhohn 1952, 115–16). But at the same time Kluckhohn worries that

> anything like a full-time participation of women in the occupations will so diminish what is left in the domestic component of the feminine role that it will become truly negligible. And, as it shrinks down into nothingness, the frustrations in the mother role will mount accordingly. There is, in other words, small chance that very many women can be both successful mothers and successful job or career women on a full-time basis. Yet, this is precisely what many women are already trying to do and what even more of them show signs of wanting to do. (116–17)

Kluckhohn proposes that what most women really want is an expanded opportunity to compete for social rewards in the economic sphere, coupled with a more artistic and valued domestic role. She notes, however, that while she was teaching at a women's college, she observed that none of her students professed interest in things like cooking, the rearing of children, marketing, or household management. Almost universally they felt those subjects beneath their notice: "I will do all that when I have to" (Kluckhohn 1950a, 100). This is a direct result, she feels, of the hollowness and low status of the domestic role as it is currently advertised in America.

Kluckhohn points out that there will, of course, be women who want full-time careers as well as those who wish to be full-time homemakers, and she insists that they must be fully supported and encouraged. But she thinks that the majority of women would prefer an integrated role and that the education of both men and women should be restructured so as to prepare society for a new attitude toward the role of women. She hopes that in the future, Americans will not, as they tend to now, "put all of their first-grade 'value eggs' in the one basket of the economic" (127). And yet, since we currently do exactly that, she insists, "The goal of interesting women in their homes and training them for their work...must coincide [with], perhaps even follow, a recognition of women's right to have a defined place in the economic structure for which she is also trained" (16).

Kluckhohn's structured gender roles and her feeling that women are the natural inhabiters of the domestic role appears dated and uncomfortable today. Perhaps she did not take American individualism seriously enough! Both her concerns and her manner of expressing them are, however, provocative, as well as prescient. The domestic role does appear to be slowly regaining stature in American society, although in a slightly less gendered sense than Kluckhohn imagined. Martha Stewart's popularity and the growing interest in simple living, to name just two examples, reflect a growing feeling that the art of domestic living rewards creative industry. Certainly, few college students today consider cooking an automatic skill that requires no training. And as the social value of cooking rises, more and more men enter the kitchen. Many men are also openly interested in, and proud of, their ability to parent and to enter into and sustain intimate relationships. Women, for their part, clearly no longer go to school for "contingency educations"; they hold positions of greater responsibility, populate the occupations more densely, and receive more equitable pay and treatment. And while the sixty-hour workweek is an economic and social necessity for many young professionals, a number of others, both men and women, look for jobs that provide extended paternity and maternity leave, flexible hours, and satisfying and challenging part-time work. The integrated role Kluckhohn says most women want may turn out to be what many men want, too. Few people would have thought so in 1950.

Not only Kluckhohn's ideas but also her dialectical means compel attention. She carefully situates her suggestions for thinking about American women as a kind of conflict resolution. She wishes her proposals to be accepted by both "camps" and is acutely aware of the language and values important to each. Yet, she does not sidestep difficult issues; on the contrary, she faces them frankly. Her desire to avoid driving negotiators away from the table is less political in the pejorative sense than it is profoundly democratic. In a characteristic gesture at the end of her book on family and women, she appeals for more input: "Here again what is needed is the thought of many persons. Our main goal at present has been mainly that of posing the problem" (Kluckhohn 1952, 135).

Kluckhohn writes as she does, apparently, because she hopes to help create real social consensus on necessary social change. Partly, this is sensible social science: significant change is unlikely to occur in the absence of significant consensus. But partly this hope reflects the same visionary intellectual courtesy that distinguishes all her work. Kluckhohn's solid confidence that greater understanding will produce greater harmony makes her generous and fearless in welcoming diverse opinions for balanced consideration. This rare approach of hers must account, at least in part, for the well-deserved renaissance of scholarly interest in her work. We are, in our present contentious and uncommunicative society, rather desperately in need of Florence Kluckhohn's intellectual attitude.

---

[1] Obviously covert observation raises tricky ethical and philosophical issues. Elsewhere, Kluckhohn mentions,

> There are in all groups certain kinds of data that are guarded more closely than other types. Direct questions regarding such information may be met with evasions if not outright misinterpretations. Indirect questions may also fail. Simulation of behavior made possible by participation may, however, open the door to this guarded realm. Space does not permit illustration of this point, but to indicate what is meant: It was through a gradual simulation of the Spanish-American woman's fear that I obtained most of my information about witchcraft and other beliefs that are jealously guarded by the Spanish-Americans. (Kluckhohn 1940, 338)

It would be easy to argue today that her covert observation of these "jealously guarded beliefs" amounted to an invasion of privacy, although almost certainly she did not see it in those terms. In her mind, caution and subterfuge were necessary for unnatural reasons: "It was not advisable to approach this community—whose population is a part of a strong minority element that none-too-scrupulous politicians have kept inflamed on ethnic issues—through direct methods" (331). Against the suggestion, though, that she was innately insensitive to the privacy of the villagers should be set her continual insistence on human-centered interaction and interviewing. She stresses that "Obsession with one's own interests should never be such that an informant is pushed beyond his desire to speak," and apparently finds in participant observation an antidote to the dehumanizing character of research:

> Participant observation increases in many instances the desire of informants to speak because the interviewer is an apprentice who is learning, not an all-seeing demigod who has come to question coldly and record. A stick or stone has no curiosity, no sensitivity, no desire for ego expression, but human beings have, and to ignore these by appealing solely to vanity, local pride, and economic advantage or by depending upon personality attraction is to my mind a serious mistake. (339)

2 The age of this article, from the late 1940s, must be taken into consideration vis-à-vis the use of the male gender to represent both men and women.

3 In certain passages, one can see a foreshadowing of the complete value orientations schema. In discussing the American belief in rationalism, the Kluckhohns say,

> Mysticism and supernaturalism have been very minor themes in American life. Our glorification of "science" and our faith in what can be accomplished through "education," are two striking aspects of our generalized conviction that secular, humanistic effort will improve the world in a series of changes, all or mainly for the better. We further tend to believe that morality and reason must coincide. Fatalism is generally repudiated, and even acceptance seems to be uncongenial. (4)

Part of a concept of man's relation to nature (supernature)—as master of it—emerges here. Similarly, when discussing the subcategory "change, a value in itself," the Kluckhohns demonstrate temporal imagination: "faith in progress" became entrenched.... "America's golden age has been located mainly in the future rather than in the past. To some extent, to be sure, the future has been brought into the present by installment plan buying...." (8). This is an impressionistic version of the method's sensitivity to cultural variations in the orientation to Time. Another intimation of future categories comes during comparison of middle-class family structure with lower-class family structure; the authors explain that the middle-class family is "ideally an isolated conjugal unit made up of the father, mother and children. The relatives usually do not live with the family and relatives who are considered undesirable are disregarded" (12). In lower-class families "Members of extended family groups aid each other and all relatives are recognized. The independence of the conjugal unit is not as great as in the middle class" (15). Although the words are never mentioned, this is a pretty succinct account of Individualism vs. Collateralism.

[4] One Native American culture that is Future-oriented and has been evaluated by researchers using the Kluckhohn model is the Hupa. See Louise M. Bachtold and Karin L. Eckvall, "Current Value Orientations of American Indians in Northern California: The Hupa," *Journal of Cross-Cultural Psychology* 9, no.3 (September 1978).

[5] At this point, in 1950, Kluckhohn had not yet developed the interview instrument, and so she arrived at her conclusions about the dominant orientations of any particular society through educated guesswork. Her plans for such a method were well under way, however. She mentions the Ramah Values Project as a possible testing ground for the schema.

[6] She also goes on to wonder

> whether the American system as a whole is in the process of real change in spite of the evidence of some national trends to the contrary. Is it, perhaps, changing—not in the direction suggested by the alternatively oriented behavior of the people of a Jonesville—but rather towards the stressing of some version of the collateral principle and a concomitant reduction of emphasis upon both achievement and future time? (392)

We do not yet have general agreement, although we may have our strong opinions, on the answer to Kluckhohn's first question. But the evidence of those who have tested recently for dominant American value orientations using Kluckhohn's model definitely does suggest a change in those orientations along the lines she predicted.

[7] These three papers were written in the 1950s, predating the women's movement in the United States and therefore quite radical and prescient for the times.

[8] Kluckhohn draws a complicated interrelation between value orientations and what she calls "behavior spheres" in order to explain this dynamic interdependence. Unfortunately, she discusses this only fleetingly.

References

Bachtold, Louise M., and Karin L. Eckvall. "Current Value Orientations of American Indians in Northern California: The Hupa." *Journal of Cross-Cultural Psychology* 9, no. 3, September 1978.

Hollingshead, A. B. *Elmtown's Youth.* New York: John Wiley, 1949.

Kluckhohn, Florence R., and Clyde Kluckhohn. "American Culture: Generalized Orientations and Class Patterns." Paper presented at the Seventh Conference on Science, Philosophy, and Religion, date unknown.

Kluckhohn, Florence R. *The American Family: Past and Present & America's Women.* N.p.: The Delphian Society, 1952.

———. "What Education for Women?" Isabel Bever Memorial Lecture, University of Illinois, 1950a.

———. "Dominant and Substitute Profiles." *Social Forces* xxviii, 4 (May 1950b).

———. "The Participant-Observer Technique in Small Communities." *American Journal of Sociology* XLVI: 1940.

Warner, W. Lloyd, et al., *Democracy in Jonesville.* New York: Harper, 1949.

Part 2

Value Orientations, Ethnicity, and Mental Health Care

Training Program in Ethnicity and Mental Health

John P. Spiegel and John Papajohn

The Ethnicity Training Program was devised for an interdisciplinary team of nonindigenous mental health professionals in the later stages of their initial clinical training. The choice of "nonindigenous" personnel was based on the assumption that there were already in existence a number of "indigenous" training programs in which African Americans were being trained to deal with black populations; Latinos with Latin American populations; and Asians with Chinese, Japanese, Koreans, and the newcomers from Southeast Asia. Under an affirmative action ideology, the needs of the "official" minorities were being addressed—although perhaps not perfectly in all instances—while the needs of the so-called "white ethnics," such as Irish Americans or Portuguese Americans, were being overlooked. In addition, we assumed that it would take a long time before there existed a sufficient number of well-trained African Americans, Latinos, Asians, Native Americans, and so on to meet the needs of the "official" minorities wherever they happened to be living. In the meantime, such ethnic populations were receiving mental health services from mainstream mental health professionals who lacked the cross-cultural perspective and the skills to provide culturally relevant services. Accordingly, we visualized our program as one model of a much-needed corrective measure in the context of the pluralistic and diverse character of the "unmelted" structure of American society.

The approach governing our design of the training program utilized the epistemological and theoretical perspectives that constituted the framework that we intended to teach to the trainees.

Transactional systems theory and cultural value orientations theory were the two conceptual mainstays guiding us in considering modes of intervening in the two training sites where our work was to be done. These training sites were both Harvard-affiliated teaching institutions: the Cambridge/Somerville Hospital and Community Health Center and the Erich Lindemann Community Mental Health Center. We perceived these sites as being systems characterized by discrete cultures, each having a social role structure where relationships among the staff and other personnel were patterned in a consistent manner that reflected the cultural values of the "system" as well as those of individuals, each with his or her idiosyncratic personality structure. Thus, culture, social roles, and individual psychological organization constituted the three foci in a transacting system of events that would have to be considered if we were to be effective in organizing a successful program for teaching concepts of disordered behavior related to the ethnic backgrounds of individuals who are receiving mental health services in traditional psychiatric settings.

Our target sample of trainees was to consist of two psychiatric residents, two clinical psychology interns, and two psychiatric social work students who were working in the clinical settings of university hospitals, outpatient clinics, and community mental health centers. They were selected from the general population of trainees already accepted into these programs because of their high motivation for and interest in cross-cultural work. We considered it important to introduce these trainees to the cross-cultural and ethnic perspective at a relatively early stage of their professional experiences, before their ideas of how to deliver services had become too fixed in mainstream patterns, which are constructed, for the most part, for urban, middle-class, acculturated populations.

A formal program of this kind almost always develops out of a background of experiences that generates ideas that seem useful for educational purposes. For many years we had been engaged in extensive research with several different ethnic groups on the relationship between subculture values and perceptions, family interaction styles, and mental illness (Papajohn and Spiegel 1975). Although our interest in research of this sort continued, when we first submitted a grant proposal to the National Institute of Mental Health (NIMH) in 1976, we had arrived at the opinion that the time had come to translate our accumulated knowledge base and skills into a training procedure. Because of this opinion we had spent the previous year testing out the feasibility of such a transmission of knowledge and skill by means of a small pilot project conducted at the Cambridge/Somerville Hospital and Community Health Center, funded by the Marcus Foundation of Chicago. During this pilot year we made ourselves available for consultation on "difficult" ethnic cases in the various components of the Department of Psychiatry and in the Emergency Service. During the course of the experimental year we managed to prove to ourselves and to members of the staff that we had something of value to offer. Enough support emerged to encourage us to plan a program to be submitted to NIMH for funding.

In addition, the pilot year had made us acutely aware of some hazards and obstacles that would have to be taken into consideration in order for such a training program to have a reasonable chance of success in the departments of psychiatry of major medical schools. These obstacles were understandable from a systems point of view, and we summarized them as deriving from three sources.

The first of these sources was implicit forms of resistance to a new theoretical approach, that is, cultural value orientations theory, which, in some of its underlying assumptions, could be construed as inconsistent with psychoanalytic theory. Psychoanalysis constitutes the main theoretical basis on which these traditional training programs are structured (in a very real way psychoanalysis serves as the ideological or cultural foundation of these training programs). Its tenets are shared by the training directors and have both a direct patterning effect on the content of the formal teaching inputs and an indirect effect by mediating the epistemological assumptions on which it is based. Psychoanalytic theory assumes a shared genetic (biological) heritage that characterizes human development wherein individuation becomes the goal of therapy. This is a process of continuing differentiation and reintegration through progressive stages of development. Cultural value orientations theory assumes a shared sociocultural heritage where individual modes of thinking, feeling, and acting are shaped by common environmental (ecological) experiences and are necessary for effective functioning within that cultural system.

The second obstacle we anticipated was how to accommodate our entrance into these two training institutions to the extant role structure. We needed to be allied with and validated both by the senior administrators, who could facilitate our entrance into their systems, and by the line clinical workers, who provided direct services to the clients. We had to earn the latter's support by demonstrating that we could be useful to them in alleviating their burden in treating difficult, that is, restive, ethnic patients.

The third obstacle to be overcome was covert ethnocentricity; that is, the lack of awareness on the part of mental health professionals of their own "learned" tendencies to value patients who shared characteristics common to themselves: white, educated, attractive, middle class. This denial of cultural bias allows professionals to see patients as "untreatable" because they are viewed as lacking intelligence, motivation, and other such characteristics associated with their own social class background.

At this juncture it should be noted that while we were able to meet our training objectives more or less successfully during the three years of the program, in the end we made very little impact on the overall "culture"—the ideological assumptions—that undergirds these teaching centers. Indeed, we were able to engage the system, to effect a balanced role for ourselves that assured the support of both the power structure and the line clinical workers, to carry out our specific teaching and training roles, and to earn the respect of the staffs in both institutions. Nevertheless, when we had completed our assignment, there was little interest in incorporating this ethnocultural dimension as a permanent component of the training capabilities of the two training sites.

Theoretical Concepts

We have made it clear that we attach a great deal of importance to theory and conceptualization as aids to appropriate service delivery and to training procedures. Clinicians need to internalize a frame of reference that equips them to order cultural variables in a useful way in diagnosis and treatment. Next we will elaborate the theoretical constructs that are central to our approach to training.

Transactional Field Theory

Most of us have learned to order events in cause-and-effect terms, which reflect the Aristotelian assumptions of linear causality. This position is the essence of the scientific method, and it delimits the range of variables that can be examined at one time. A person's neurotic reaction, for example, may be conceptualized as caused by a disturbed relationship to the mother (lack of physical and psychological nurturance, overcontrol, and overinvolvement). The cause of the dysfunctional behavior can be understood as the relationship between a "dependent variable" (a symptom or problematic behavior) and an "independent variable," or cause. This search is limited, furthermore, to the psychological aspects of the individual. An exception will be found in cases of schizophrenia, where biological or genetic causes are also presumed to be present and may interact with psychological stress. Even then the causal relationships are conceptualized in a linear fashion.

Transactional systems theory is based on a very different conceptual assumption; that is, that events constitute a field of transaction processes in which change in one part is related to change in all the other parts (see Figure 1).

Figure 1

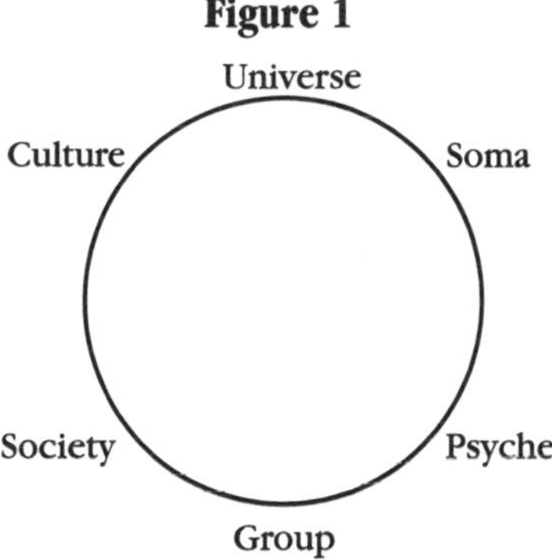

An individual's neurosis can be understood as reflecting a transactional interplay of psychological, cultural, social, and biological events. The disturbed behavior (for example, a symbiotic bond to the mother) is not explained solely as a fixation in psychological development but rather as being related concomitantly to cultural conflict, social dislocation, biological events, and so forth. Events in any one of these domains, then, transact with each other domain to produce a neurotic reaction in the individual. Ordinarily, these events are not included in a differential diagnosis. Although they may be noted in the history taking, they are not viewed as significant data that need to be utilized in the treatment planning. From a transactional systems perspective, the treatment objective is to address the disequilibrium in the field of events that is impinging on the individual to bring about a new and more functional balance.

Value Orientations Theory and Its Applications

In the context of the transactional systems approach, culture is the focus from which to begin the inquiry into families undergoing acculturation, since we are dealing with a clash of cultural understandings and norms. For this purpose we need a map. The map we have been using is the theory of variation in cultural value orientations prepared by Florence R. Kluckhohn. She defines value orientation as follows: A value orientation is a generalized and organized conception of time, of nature, of one's place in it, of one's relation to others, and of the desirable and nondesirable aspects of the human environment and transactions among people, all of which influence behavior (Kluckhohn and Strodtbeck 1961). In addition, value orientations have a directional, a cognitive, and an affective function. These three functions constitute the "program" for selecting between more- or less-favored choices of alternative behaviors for individuals within a particular culture. Furthermore, communication among individuals within a particular culture is contingent on their shared value orientations.

Kluckhohn postulated five common human problems for which all peoples in all places must find some solution. They are: Time, which is the temporal focus of human life; Activity, the preferred pattern of action in daily living; Human Relations, which is the preferred way of relating interpersonally; Person-Nature, which defines the way one relates to the natural or the supernatural environment, however conceptualized; and Human Nature, concerned with conceptions of innate good and evil in human behavior. This last modality, however was not systematically researched by Kluckhohn.

The theory assumes three possible solutions for each of these common human problems, and the variation among and within cultures is based on the rank ordering (pattern of preferences) of these solutions in a dominant-substitute profile of values. It is important to underscore here a central feature of Kluckhohn's theory. Each of the orientations is present in all societies; it is the particular rank ordering that differentiates one culture from another. In Table 1 the patterning of preferences for mainstream American lifestyles (American middle class) is compared with profiles characteristic of rural southern Italian and rural southern Irish families drawn from our work with these migrant groups.

Table 1: Comparison of Value Orientations Profiles

	American Middle Class	Italian	Irish
Time	Future > Present > Past	Present > Past > Future	Present > Past > Future
Activity	Doing > Being	Being > Doing	Being > Doing
Human Relations	Individual > Collateral > Lineal	Collateral > Lineal > Individual	Lineal > Collateral > Individual
Person-Nature	Mastery over > Subjugation to > Harmony with	Subjugation to > Harmony with > Mastery over	Subjugation to > Harmony with > Mastery over

Let us first examine the American middle-class value orientations patterns (see Interpretive Key on pages 84–85). It readily becomes evident that there is a functional relationship between the value orientations profiles or patterns in the different problem areas or modalities and the adaptational demands of a technologically advanced society like that of the United States. The first-order Future orientation of a Time area, for example, is a critical one in our society where planning for the future is a necessary condition for effectively carrying on the functions required for maintaining a technologically advanced system. In the Activity area, the first-order Doing orientation reflects the achievement orientation of this society which is shared by other Western cultures. The opportunities for upward social mobility place demands on individuals to achieve economically and socially. The evaluation of one's individual worth is based on the degree to which one has been able to compete successfully. The first-order Individual preference in the Human Relations area reflects the lifelong thrust toward "individuation" and independence and is consistent with the Doing orientation in the Activity area. The first-order positioning of the Mastery over Nature preference in the Person-Nature modality is correlated with our assumption that given enough time, money, and technology, most problems between humans and nature can be solved in the name of "progress." Child-rearing practices in the United States are geared to preparing children for successful functioning in this society. Developmental stages such as weaning and toilet training are traversed at earlier ages than is the case in other cultures such as rural Italy and rural Ireland from which a significant portion of the American population has emigrated.

Value Orientations Interpretive Key

Time Modality

Future

The temporal focus is based on the future. The major emphasis, therefore, is on planning for change at points in time extending from the present into the future.

Example: American middle-class society

Present

The present is the major focus of time. Little attention is paid to the past, and the future is perceived as vague and unpredictable.

Example: Rural societies in Latin America and Italy

Past

The past is the major time focus. Tradition is of central importance in the life of the people.

Example: Traditional Chinese society

Activity Modality

Doing

Major emphasis is on the kind of activity which results in economic and social accomplishments that are measurable by standards conceived to be external to the acting individual, in other words, achievement. Individual worth is based on one's ability to compete successfully.

Example: American middle-class society

Being

The kind of activity that is a spontaneous expression of what is conceived to be "given" in the human personality—the spontaneous expression of impulses and desires.

Example: Mexican rural society

Human Relations Modality

Individual

Individual autonomy characterizes the relationships of humans to each other. Individual goals have primacy over the goals of the group. Reciprocal role relationships are characterized by a recognition of the independence of interrelating individuals. Group goals are attained through the realization of autonomous goals of individual members.

Example: American middle-class family

Collateral
The primacy of the goals of the laterally extended group determines the relationships of people to each other. Individual autonomous goals are subordinated to the goals of the group. Relationships are ordered on a horizontal, egalitarian dimension. Reciprocal role relationships are characterized by the "one for all and all for one" principle.

Example: Italian extended family

Lineal
Group goals again have primacy over individual goals. Relationships, however, on a vertical dimension are patterned by the hierarchically ordered positions that individuals hold in the group. Reciprocal role relationships within the group hierarchy are characterized by a dominance-submission mode of interrelationship.

Example: British upper-class family; the Irish family

Person-Nature Modality

Mastery over Nature
Natural forces of all kinds are to be overcome and harnessed for human purpose, in the name of progress.

Example: American society, with its emphasis on technology to solve all kinds of problems

Harmony with Nature
The sense of wholeness in the individual is based on continual communion with nature and the supernatural.

Example: Japanese society; Navaho Indian society

Subjugation to Nature
The human is subjugated to the forces of nature and does little to counteract them.

Example: Spanish rural society

In rural Ireland and rural Italy the first-order Time orientation is the Present. In rural societies individuals are rooted existentially in the present, since the future cannot be controlled or predicted and little change is expected. Daily life is modulated by the forces of nature, which also control the economic realities that are encountered. The seasons of the year determine what one does—planting, harvesting, and so on. The planning of activities in accordance with a changing future makes no sense in situations where life goes in cycles the same way every year.

Irish and Italians are "Being" oriented in the Activity dimension. The Being orientation places high value on "being oneself," in the sense of the spontaneous expression of inner feelings in given situations. Satisfaction is derived from experiencing—here and now—each other, food, and pleasures of the senses. While this does not imply an uncontrolled, hedonistic orientation, it is contrasted with the "Doing" orientation, where immediate pleasure is forfeited for the satisfaction of achievement in the future.

In the Human Relations area the Italians and Irish differ in the rank ordering of the three value orientations preferences. Italians are Collateral > Lineal > Individual, while the Irish are Lineal > Collateral > Individual. In both cultures, it should be noted, the individualistic orientation, which is the most preferred in American culture, is positioned last in the profiles of these two agrarian societies.

The first-order Collaterality in the Italian pattern reflects the interdependence among family members that is characteristic of the Italian family structure. Individuals in this society are socialized for interdependence, since the survival of the family is contingent on everyone collaborating in common, often agrarian, pursuits. Traditionally, Italians have never trusted agencies outside the family to protect them or provide for them.

The first-order Lineal preference in the Irish value orientations profile represents the essentially matriarchal character of the Irish family. The dominance of the wife and mother derives from a long history of political oppression and economic hardship in Ireland. Chronic unemployment relegated the male to a secondary, almost powerless role within the family, despite the wife's attempts to make her husband look good in the eyes of the public.

The "Subjugation to Nature" first-order preference in the Person-Nature dimension in both Irish and Italian cultures is consistent with the Present, Being, and Collateral and Lineal orientations. Man and woman are controlled either by the forces of nature or by a powerful deity. People cannot expect, as in technologically advanced societies, to harness the forces of nature to serve them. The farmer feels helpless and powerless in confronting physical forces beyond his control. This orientation, of course, generalizes to other areas of one's life. One is rooted in a present condition with no avenues available in order to plan for future achievement or upward social mobility. The alternative is emigration.

The value orientations framework makes it possible to conceptualize the strain that is experienced by Italian Americans and Irish Americans as they confront the American social system. There is an inconsistency in all five modalities between the internalized value orientations of the subculture in which they were socialized with that of the American mainstream social system to which they need to adapt. The strain of "acculturation stress" becomes evident in all domains of adaptation, such as occupational, recreational, and social. The clinician who has internalized our frame of reference can include this cultural understanding in assessing the specific psychological issues that confront his or her patient. He or she is not limited to a psychological theory that is designed to conceptualize developmental and characterological variables only.

The Program

NIMH approved our proposal on an experimental basis and provided funding through the Florence Heller Graduate School for Advanced Studies in Social Welfare at Brandeis University. The Ethnicity Training Program was launched.

Program Objectives

The program objectives are summarized as follows:

a. To provide the interdisciplinary staff and students operating clinical services in community mental health centers with insight into the effects of ethnicity on patients and families in treatment.
b. To differentiate these effects for the different ethnic groups to which the patients belong.
c. To provide staff and students with more effective tools for delivering services with respect to (1) diagnosis where distinguishing between subculture practices and psychopathology is a problem; (2) establishing a therapeutic alliance where social distance or ethnocentricity is the problem; and (3) assessing psychodynamic formulations where variant or deviant child-rearing customs, marital or parental relations, or extended family transactions are the problem.

Training Sites

John P. Spiegel, program director, and John Papajohn, associate program director, spent a year exploring potential field settings for the training program. In the end, as we mentioned much earlier, we settled on two Harvard Medical School-affiliated training facilities: the Cambridge/Somerville Hospital and Community Health Center, where the Department of Psychiatry is based at the Cambridge City Hospital, and the Erich Lindemann Community Mental Health Center, an affiliate of the Massachusetts General Hospital Department of Psychiatry, which serves the Harbor Area catchment zone.

Our engagement with the Cambridge/Somerville and the Lindemann Centers involved several meetings with the respective directors, whom we knew personally, as well as a protracted twelve-month period of providing consultation to the staff regarding ethnic cases. Dr. Racquel Cohen, the Lindemann Community Mental Health Center director, and Dr. Lee Macht, the Cambridge/Somerville Hospital chairperson in the department of psychiatry, knew of our research work on ethnic families and were committed to a cultural perspective. Dr. Cohen worked in the area of community psychiatry with Dr. Gerald Caplan at the Harvard Laboratory of Community Psychiatry, and Dr. Macht's work in community mental health was nationally recognized.

The communities for which the Lindemann Center was responsible included Boston's North End (almost 100 percent Italian American), East Boston (largely Italian), and the suburbs of Chelsea (30 percent Spanish-speaking, 60 percent traditional Jewish), Revere, and Charlestown. At Dr. Cohen's suggestion, we confined ourselves to the North End and to Chelsea. The reason for beginning in this fashion was the need to determine which ethnic group in which community should be the choice for the "intensive" part of the trainees' experiences. The decision to concentrate on Latinos in Chelsea was determined by the fact that they were being serviced by the Chelsea Community Counseling Center under the direction of Dr. Matthew Dumont, a psychiatrist dedicated to community psychiatry. He was also familiar with our approach and supportive of it. While Latinos comprised only 30 percent of the Chelsea population and only 10 percent of the Center's clientele, the numbers in both instances were rapidly rising. Chelsea also contained small percentages of blacks, Canadians, Irish, and Italians. Most of the Spanish-speaking residents were Puerto Rican.

The Cambridge/Somerville Hospital and Community Mental Health Center served a large geographical area that corresponded to the boundaries of these two cities. These are multiethnic, essentially working-class communities with a mixture of Irish, Italian,

Portuguese, black, Latino, Greek, and Haitian subgroups. The neighborhoods are ethnically mixed, except for North Cambridge, location of a housing project occupied mainly by African Americans, and the neighborhood close to the Cambridge City Hospital, home to a preponderance of Azorean-Portuguese people. The Greek and Azorean-Portuguese populations are composed of relatively newly arrived immigrants who left their homelands after 1965, when the immigration law was changed to allow immigrants from parts of Southern Europe with low quotas to emigrate in larger numbers. The Italians and the Irish are the children and the grandchildren of the first-generation immigrants who established themselves in these communities during the large wave of immigration that occurred at the turn of the century.

We decided to focus on the Azorean-Portuguese population as the group our trainees might learn to understand in greater depth. The presence of the Egas Moniz Clinic, a health center for Portuguese people nearby, facilitated this effort, since it provided a natural site where our trainees could gain experience with Portuguese patients seen in the mental health division.

Program Planning

Two quarter-time program coordinators were recruited from the staffs of the two training sites. Both were psychologists who had earned a considerable amount of credibility within their respective organizations and could therefore serve as mediators for the training program. The Cambridge/Somerville program coordinator was a black female psychologist; her Lindemann counterpart was a bilingual, Latino male. They interpreted and advocated for us among their colleagues. An advisory committee made up of senior members of these two training-site staffs was created to monitor the program, especially in the difficult initial phases. In addition, the program directors and the program coordinators met with the heads of the different clinical services to acquaint them with the program objectives and contemplated procedures. The directors of training for psychiatry, psychology, and social work were also members of the advisory committee. We negotiated with them the criteria for selection of recruits for our program that would satisfy their own independent training program guidelines. We examined with them the various clinical placements within their mental health centers where the trainees could get the appropriate experiences to satisfy both the hospital training objectives and those of the Ethnicity Training Program. We negotiated for blocks of time when the Ethnicity Training Program trainees would be free to attend the formal teaching seminars and clinical conferences that we had designed to be part of the specialized training we were providing. Our effort, in summary, was to integrate our training learnings with those extant forms that constitute the training format in traditional training programs for psychiatry, psychology, and social work.

The Training Program

The Ethnicity Training Program consisted of five components.

1. A one-semester course, "Social Aspects of Mental Health and Illness," offered by John Spiegel at the Heller School, was required of all trainees. This course was designed to provide the trainees with a macroscopic overview of social psychiatry; issues such as epidemiology from a cross-cultural perspective, social class and mental illness, and labeling theory were reviewed.
2. A one-semester course entitled "Ethnicity and Mental Health," offered at the Heller School by John Spiegel and John Papajohn, constituted the second major academic offering. It was in this course that transactional systems theory and cultural value orientations theory were reviewed with special reference to diagnosis and treatment.
3. A weekly ethnic clinical teaching conference was held on alternate weeks at each of the two training sites wherein cases seen by the trainees in their respective clinical placements were presented in the traditional mode. Spiegel and Papajohn alternated chairing these conferences. Guest consultants with special knowledge of different ethnic groups were invited for some of the conferences.
4. Ethnic cases seen by the trainees were supervised individually by Spiegel and Papajohn. These were structured in the traditional way, with the trainee presenting the case and describing the process of treatment and the supervisor providing suggestions and interpretations where appropriate. It was here the trainees could discuss their ideas, questions, and doubts about the differential effect of cultural and psychological factors in the clinical process of his or her own individual patient.
5. In the second year of the program we instituted an additional seminar, "Ethnocultural Factors in Diagnosis and Treat-

ment." This was a one-semester, weekly, two-hour seminar that focused specifically on the application of cultural theory to the clinical process. Formal presentations on different subcultures, including Irish, Puerto Rican, Japanese, and Haitian, were made by clinicians with special knowledge of these subcultures.

The Recruitment Process

We employed both formal (advertising in professional publications) and informal methods of recruiting candidates for the NIMH-funded traineeships who met our criteria and those of the training directors in the three disciplines. We wanted individuals who were highly motivated to work with poor ethnic populations and who could also meet the criteria for acceptance into the training slots of the Cambridge/Somerville and Lindemann Centers. The mental health center training directors themselves were motivated in this recruitment effort by the fact that each could expect to acquire two additional individuals for training in their programs who were funded by the Ethnicity Training Program.

In the end two major sources for recruits for our program emerged. The first was the mental health center training directors, Drs. Cohen and Macht, themselves. In reviewing candidates for their own traineeships, they introduced the availability of a conjoint program to those who met, in their views, criteria for both programs. In the first year, the two psychiatric residents and one of the clinical psychology interns were recruited in this way. The second psychology intern was recruited by word-of-mouth—a colleague with strong interests in ethnicity introduced to us an associate of his who was in the last stage of completing his doctorate in clinical psychology.

The two psychiatric social work trainees were recruited from the Smith College School of Social Work. There was already in existence a liaison between this school and the Department of Psychiatric Social Work at the Cambridge Hospital. In addition, we had personal contacts with the new administration of this institution that further facilitated our collaboration.

In the second year the recruitment process followed a course similar to the first year with one important exception; we were unable to recruit a psychiatric resident for either the Cambridge/Somerville Hospital or the Lindemann Center sites. We substituted two psychologists in their places: a Ph.D. from the Department of

Social Relations at Harvard University and an Ed.D. who wanted to do a postdoctoral internship in clinical psychology at Cambridge Hospital.

As regards ethnic background over the two years, the twelve trainees were almost evenly divided between those whose backgrounds were representative of mainstream American middle-class culture (WASP) and those whose parents or grandparents had emigrated from another country. Of the trainees, six derived from mainstream tradition; three were Jewish American with very weak ties to Judaism—either second- or third-generation American; one was of Azorean-Portuguese parentage, and one was born and raised in a Slavic country. With the exception of the Portuguese American, all of the trainees came from predominantly middle-class and professional backgrounds with strong liberal ideological traditions.

Ethnicity of Cases Seen by Trainees

The trainees were rotated through the customary sequence of placements in the mental health center system, which was designed to provide them with a broad range of experience with a variety of different patients. These included the inpatient/outpatient units as well as placements in the satellite clinics, where the major portion of patients were of ethnic origin. In Cambridge this was the Egas Moniz Mental Health Clinic, which serves the Portuguese, and in Chelsea the Community Counseling Center, which serves predominantly the Puerto Rican, low-income population. The experiences of our trainees, however, were not uniform regarding the number of ethnic patients they saw. This was a function of where they were placed, for how long, and what experiences their supervisors (from the mental health centers) determined they needed to have. At the end of the first training year the trainees were asked to provide a record of the ethnicity, age, and sex of patients they were seeing (see Table 2).

At least 25 of these cases involved more than one family member; hence, the total number of persons seen by trainees at this time was actually greater than 92. Some degree of family therapy took place with most of the 25 "family" cases. A correlation of the incidence of family therapy and ethnicity (Table 3) reveals the following:

Table 2

Ethnicity	Total	Chelsea	Cambridge
Puerto Rican	13	13	0
Irish	13	6	7
Portuguese	12	0	12
Jewish	7	4	3
Italian	6	3	3
Caribbean	3	0	3
Other	24	5	19
Unknown or "American"	14	12	2
Total	92	43	49

Table 3

Ethnicity	Number of Cases Involving Family Therapy
Puerto Rican	7
Irish	5
Portuguese	7
Jewish	4
Other	2
Total	25

Program Evaluation

The program evaluator, a doctoral student at the Heller School, was present at all of the meetings and conferences, and he continually monitored the progress of the program over the course of the two training years. He also scheduled an individual conference with each of the trainees twice during their twelve-month tenure in each of the two years. He inquired into the trainees' views on the relevance of the training format, the degree of satisfaction and dissatisfaction they derived, and their future plans as regards working with ethnic populations. At the end of the first training year the program evaluator's report highlighted the following outcomes of the program.

General Strengths of the Program. Trainees identified several components of the program that they considered strong points:

1. the general opportunity to treat ethnic patients in a systematic fashion;
2. the clinical case conferences, in which specific trainee cases were discussed; and
3. the course held at the Heller School on ethnicity and mental health.

These components were considered strengths because they served a consciousness-raising function that sensitized trainees to the problems of cross-cultural psychotherapy and the problems of making mental health systems responsive to the needs of ethnic patients. Thus, trainees typically commented that *before* entering the program they knew that ethnics experienced problems getting appropriate clinical services, but *now* they understood just how serious and complicated the problems really were. They now also understood the subtleties and complexities of cross-cultural psychotherapy and the difficulties in enabling mental health agencies to respond to needs of ethnics.

These observations are not intended to downplay the acquisition of substantive knowledge on the part of trainees concerning specific ethnic groups and related issues, as this was a significant gain. But, in a general sense, it seems that the primary impact of the program was in moving trainees from the position of knowing, in the abstract sense, that ethnic patients present unique problems to the clinician to understanding in a personal and deeper way *why* this is the case, and what they can do about it.

Trainees felt that the experience of treating ethnics—and the firsthand experience of the associated pitfalls—coupled with the critical discussion of their cases in the clinical conferences provided the core of this learning experience. The ethnicity course mentioned above was important for placing their experiences in the context of larger human service delivery systems.

General Weaknesses of the Program. Most of the trainees were concerned with what they saw as a lack of communication among various members of the program staff. In their opinions, poor communication resulted in occasional confusion as to the times and places of meetings, abrupt schedule changes, delays in the receipt of stipend checks, and related matters. They felt that communication among directors and field coordinators was at times confused and strained. They found it difficult from time to time to contact project directors. They were also aware that directors were often not able to contact them, because of mutually heavy schedules, and that this exacerbated the communication problems. These problems were seen by trainees as administrative and in need of correction by the directors. Trainees did, however, understand that the newness of the program was a factor and made allowances for the need to "debug" any new effort.

The second weakness related to the training process itself. Trainees felt that while opportunities were provided for them to see ethnic patients and to discuss these patients in a variety of settings, they were not clear as to how to handle the cultural aspects of the problems that were presented. Some trainees apparently wanted a specific, highly delineated model of intervention and were somewhat let down when they learned that such a model was not forthcoming. Others, understanding that one of the intentions of the program was to experiment with such models, were not clear on what "data" to collect on patients and how to utilize such data.

Related to these concerns was a theme that ran through trainee responses that could be phrased as "What exactly do I do with the ethnic patients in the counseling situation itself?" For example, they began to understand how to use the value orientations scale to interpret the patient's situation and to make a general treatment plan that was culturally appropriate. However, apart from asking certain specific questions about ethnic background, they were not sure of other clinically appropriate topics for the therapeutic dialogue, or how this cultural perspective might fit in with whatever treatment approach they were familiar with.

This proved to be a very difficult issue to resolve, given the vagueness with which the trainees described the problem. Nevertheless, it needed further consideration. Of particular importance was the development of a way to conceptually merge culturally relevant approaches with either specific (e.g., analytic, gestalt, or cognitive social learning) therapeutic methodology or an explicitly eclectic model.

This issue was dealt with in the second training year through the introduction of the seminar mentioned earlier entitled "Ethnocultural Factors in Diagnosis and Treatment." The individual presenters in this series discussed specific ethnic groups in relation to the following major parameters: (1) differential diagnosis in which cultural and psychological factors were separated out, (2) establishment of a therapeutic alliance, (3) assessment of the presenting problems in the context of the early family socialization process of the patient, (4) refinement of and monitoring the therapeutic intervention accordingly, and (5) reorientation of therapeutic goals in line with the particular acculturation conflict that the patient and/or family was undergoing.

A continuing stress reported by most trainees was that engendered by the concurrent demands of the Ethnicity Training Program and the mental health center training program. Often the effort to integrate the two segments of their training did not work well and they experienced them as competing for their time and energies. This issue was alleviated somewhat in the second training year through more concentrated work on planning the conjoint program by both the Ethnicity Program directors and by the directors of training in psychiatry, psychology, and social work for the two mental health centers. Some strain remained, however, until the end.

In both training years the trainees reported that they found the formal academic courses that were offered to be important in broadening their conceptual grasp of the psychological problems of specific ethnic groups. The individual supervision provided by Drs. Spiegel and Papajohn was also reported to be an important learning experience. The fact that Spiegel was psychoanalytically oriented and Papajohn behaviorally oriented, they felt, enhanced their understanding of the interlacing of psychological and cultural factors in the treatment process. They also reported having gained an in-depth understanding of both the Portuguese and Puerto Rican groups at the Cambridge/Somerville Center and the Chelsea branch of the Lindemann Center respectively. Some of the trainees enhanced their understanding through home visits to the families of patients they were treating.

A final weakness identified by trainees relates to the issue of interorganizational communication mentioned above. Trainees wanted the directors and the training coordinators to be more aggressive in their dealings with administrators and supervisors in placement settings. This was of particular concern at the beginning of the year, when routines and caseloads were being established. Certain trainees felt that they did not have enough control over the ethnic makeup of their caseloads and that the coordinators and directors could have taken more of an advocate role in this matter.

The main weakness related to the training process itself. They felt that in seeing ethnic patients they were not clear as to how to handle the cultural aspects of the problems that were presented. They had hoped to have learned a specific, highly delineated model of intervention and were somewhat let down when they learned that such a model was not forthcoming. While they understood how to use the value orientations scale to interpret the patient's situation and to make a general treatment plan that was culturally appropriate, they were not sure how to implement it effectively. Specifically they were not sure how to integrate this cultural perspective with whatever traditional treatment approach they were familiar with.

Although there were other individual concerns and problems mentioned by trainees, those discussed here were the ones mentioned by all or most of them.

Follow-Up. John Spiegel interviewed the trainees individually at the end of each of the two training years. Many of the views expressed to the program evaluator were shared with him also as well as some additional impressions of special relevance to planning future programs. One interesting aspect of the program, which in some ways was a major strength and at times was a weakness, was the freedom given to each trainee to carve out his or her own program. Thus, in terms of their placements, trainees had very different responsibilities and requirements and, hence, very different experiences. Most of the trainees attempted to create a learning situation that best fit their needs and backgrounds. The problem with this was that some trainees lost time at the beginning of the year as they attempted to "work the system" in order to locate themselves where they wanted to be. A typical problem for trainees involved the various rules about placements that had been created in each organization. However, once they got past the bureaucratic hassles, the trainees were to a great extent able to tailor their placements to their own needs.

For example, one trainee was specifically interested in the Portuguese and spent a great deal of time at the Egas Moniz Clinic. Another was interested in family therapy and worked closely with a family therapy training organization. Because trainees actually had a great deal of freedom within the placement aspect of the program, one cannot say that they all experienced the "same program." What they brought with them to supervision and seminars, then, and what they carried away were a variety of experiences. This gave a richness and diversity to the Ethnicity Program that would have been lost if trainees had not been given a great amount of leeway to design a program that provided the kind of education and growth opportunities they desired. *All of the trainees expressed interest in continuing to work with ethnic groups when they finished their training.*

Two years after the program was completed, John Spiegel and I contacted the trainees and gathered anecdotal reports from them, principally in the form of letters. We asked them where they were functioning and whether their training with us was indeed relevant to the work they were doing. The responses were uniformly enthusiastic. While few were working exclusively in settings where ethnic populations were in the majority, all expressed the opinion that the Ethnicity Program had been an invaluable experience in terms of their individual work with clients. Those in private practice said that their conceptualizations of the problems presented to them by their clients was enhanced significantly by an understanding of their cultural backgrounds.

After the program had been completed, John Spiegel and I continued an affiliation with the Department of Psychiatry at the Cambridge City Hospital for an additional year. This involved working as consultants on ethnicity on one of their community mental health teams. This involvement made it possible for us to assess what impact, if any, we had indeed had on one of the two systems we had worked in during the previous three years. We came away from this with two main impressions. The first was that we had actually raised the consciousness of the general staff to the point where they would contact us when they had difficulty in either the differential diagnosis of or treatment planning for an ethnic patient. Second, there was no real interest in modifying the traditional training format to include an ethnocultural component in any systematic way.

Conclusion

This overview of the Brandeis-Harvard Ethnicity Training Program represents one model among many others for introducing cross-cultural concepts and techniques to mental health personnel for the more effective and appropriate delivery of services. At the time our program was proposed (1976), we lacked preexisting training models upon which we could build our program. Since then a variety of models, as represented by this volume, have been experimentally instituted and are just now reaching an increasingly interested audience through the published literature rather than through word of mouth or preliminary presentations at professional meetings.

As far as we can determine, these models vary along different dimensions, such as (1) *intensity*—for example, one to three consciousness-raising presentations from six-week modules to yearlong efforts, such as ours; (2) *ethnic focus*—for example, one or two ethnic groups versus a broad range and diversity of ethnic populations; (3) *clinical setting*—from academic departments to freestanding service agencies; (4) *discipline*—primarily for psychiatrists, psychologists, psychiatric social workers, or some combination (such as ours) of all three; (5) *level of professional experience of trainees*—from pregraduate students through personnel with various degrees of established professional practice willing to be retrained with this new cultural emphasis; and (6) *ethnic background of trainees*—from mostly mainstream WASP or Jewish to various minorities seeking to provide service to other minorities.

All such efforts, to our knowledge, are still in the experimental stages. Their long-term effects, both on trainees and on the institutional settings in which they take place, remain to be evaluated. We who are engaged in such efforts have much to learn from each other. It is our hope that this description of our program, especially the delineation of its strengths and weaknesses, will contribute to the general pool of knowledge on which the future growth of the field will inevitably depend.

References

Kluckhohn, Florence R., and Fred L. Strodtbeck. *Variations in Value Orientations.* Evanston, IL: Row, Peterson, 1961.

Papajohn, John, and John P. Spiegel. *Transactions in Families: A Modern Approach to Resolving Cultural and Generational Conflicts*. San Fransisco: Jossey-Bass, 1975.

Clinical Applications of Value Orientations

Danilo E. Ponce

In all fairness, it must be stated at the outset that Florence R. Kluckhohn and Fred L. Strodtbeck (1961) came up with the value orientations (VO) model primarily to identify and explain *variations* in the value orientations of societies, subgroups within societies, and perhaps even the individuals in these societies. I am not at all sure that they envisioned the model being used in the service of resolving conflicts or alleviating suffering in clinical settings. I could be wrong. Assuming that I'm right, however, any methodological objections, therefore, must not be leveled at the model per se but at the clinicians (like myself) who have extrapolated from the model useful principles in clinical work.

Before I go on to describe the various ways I have used the value orientations model clinically, let me just mention a few introductory and qualifying comments. First, the obvious caveat must be made—the model is only one among many competing models that might be useful in cross-cultural work with patients/clients. (For a brief but useful introduction to some other models, see L. Robert Kohls' article, "Models for Comparing and Contrasting Cultures," in Reid 1988.) Second, since the focus in value orientations is on *organizing principles* of behavior rather than the behaviors themselves, the clinician is not saddled with the well-nigh impossible task of having to memorize the meanings of hundreds of behavioral units (e.g., what does "looking down" mean to the Filipino child when he or she is aggressively confronted by an authority figure?). Third, the use of value orientations in a clinical environment is based primarily on the premise of resolving conflicts or alleviating suffering through the twin psychological processes of "matching" or "fitting" (deShazer 1984).

A *match* is based on the assumption that it is highly desirable for the therapist to approximate the patient's whole manner of being. The therapeutic relationship is *symmetrical* or a "relationship of equals," predicated on the well-known homeopathic principle of *similia similibus curantur* ("like cures like"). Hence, efforts are expended in effecting a match in terms of gender, age, language, socioeconomic class, ethnicity, and so on—and in our particular case key and relevant value orientations modalities (e.g., matching a therapist who is Past-oriented with a patient who is Past-oriented in the Time modality). Of course, not all beneficial therapeutic relationships work in this way. As a matter of fact, in most clinical situations it is *difference that makes a difference* that oftentimes results in dramatic and lasting positive outcomes. In this instance, the relationship *and* the process are that of a *fit* rather than a match: in other words, relationships are *complementary*. A lock and key are a fit. A pair of gloves is a match. A psychoanalyst and an analysand are a fit. A support group for cancer and AIDS patients is a match. Bandler and Grinder (1975, 1979) have studied the principles of fit and match extensively and have used their insights to found an approach to psychotherapy that has come to be known as Neuro-Linguistic Programming (NLP).

I will now proceed to briefly enumerate various ways that I have used the value orientations model and the twin processes of matching and fitting in a clinical context as well as in other ancillary professional activities.

Applications of the Value Orientations Model

Individual Psychotherapy

From a value orientations perspective, a patient who is mired in *pathological mourning* because of a Past orientation in the Time modality (e.g., What will I do now without him?) might well benefit in psychotherapy by being gently nudged to shift toward a Future orientation (e.g., You know, now that you have lots of time, maybe you can do what you've always wanted to do—write that novel). This would effect a therapeutic fit. On the other hand, this could backfire because of timing. During the acute phase of the grief process, it could be that sympathy/empathy (i.e., a therapeutic match) may be more effective and appropriate (e.g., I know how you feel. I felt lost and helpless too when my mother died). Although the VO model will certainly identify an orientation, the clinician will still have to rely on clinical judgment and skills to decide whether a match or a fit is called for in a particular situation. A value orientations approach is also quite helpful in individual psychotherapy in identifying the nature of, and untangling, what has been pejoratively called "resistances to treatment," "refractory patient," "difficult client," or "therapeutic impasse." From my own clinical experience, and in years of supervising trainees and clinical staff, I have concluded that most of these so-called "treatment failures" or "therapeutic plateaus" are usually the result of unconscious mismatching or misfitting of key orientations in the patient-therapist dyad. A third possible way in which VO can be used effectively in individual psychotherapy is in matching patients with particular orientations with a particular psychotherapeutic school of thought that is congruent with the orientations of the patient. For instance, highly directive/active psychotherapists of the cognitive-behavioral school of thought (e.g., rational-emotive therapy) will have a good match with patients that have a lineal/hierarchical orientation in the relational modality. This concept of matching patients with schools of thought has been explored in more detail by Rory Remer and Pamela Remer (1982).

Marital/Conjoint Therapy

In so far as VO can reveal potentially helpful or counterproductive fits or matches between psychotherapists and their clients and patients, it just as easily reveals the same information about couples and even more so when the two are from different cross-cultural or interethnic backgrounds. The value orientations model is especially helpful in these cases because it provides the couple with a practical and easily understood frame of reference that can explain their conflicts without having to resort to blaming each other, or to having one be "right" and the other "wrong." A lot of couples are quite relieved when they discover that their conflicts are not necessarily insoluble and their only recourse divorce, when they grasp the value orientation-derived principle of "One man's meat is another man's poison."

> Therapist: Mario (a Hispanic male), I think that Jane (Mario's wife, Caucasian) seems more concerned about you

getting ahead (Mastery over Nature, Being-in-Becoming) in your office, whereas you are more concerned about getting along and not offending anybody (Harmony with, Being).

Mario: Yeah...I know. At first I kinda felt good about her egging me on during the first few years of our marriage because I tend to be passive, you know? Not making waves? So, it's good to have a cheerleader, but then...

Therapist: But then what?

Mario: But then, it was kinda like a subtle thing. I started treating my co-workers as competitors and no longer as my friends...and I started hating myself, and I began getting short-tempered with her (Jane), and sometimes I didn't even know why....

Jane: His (Mario) tendency not to speak up cost him several promotions. He didn't seem to get it that here in America, it's "looking out for number 1" (Individualistic). I was just trying to be helpful and I became the target of his anger. I'm truly hurt.

Therapist: And you couldn't see that he's the kind of person who values friendship more than getting ahead?

Jane: No..., but even if I did, I think he owes us, his family, more than his so-called friends.

Therapist: (to Mario) And you couldn't see that she's just trying to be helpful?

Mario: No.... After awhile, she was more a bitch and a nag.

Family Therapy

Clinicians who work with families intuitively know the impact of so-called generation gaps among family members. Value orientations helps the therapist define the nature of these gaps in ways that make them amenable to mediation, experimentation, and resolution.

Mr. Peters (father): I don't give a damn what she does when she turns eighteen, but so long as she is in my house, she will live by my rules (Lineal). That means I don't want her boyfriend in my house when nobody is home, and especially, not in her room!

Jennifer (daughter): But Dad, we're not doing anything wrong. Would you rather we go somewhere else? Besides,

> don't you think I'm old enough now to know what is right for me? I need to start making decisions on my own (Individualistic).
>
> Therapist: You know, Jim (Mr. Peters), it sounds to me as though we need to find a way where Jennifer can respect your wishes (Lineal), yet at the same time be able to make her own decisions (Individualistic) without feeling she is being backed into a corner. Is this possible?
>
> Mr. Peters: Well (sighing), I guess we could talk (Collateral).

Group Therapy

Value orientations profiles of group therapy members and the therapist(s) can be utilized as a map to understand and anticipate group *dynamics* and group *process.* For instance, a member whose orientation in the Human Nature modality is Evil/Immutable will consistently and predictably view other members and the therapist with suspicion. The natural tendency would be to make all attempts to disabuse that member of his orientation, with the usual result that this will only make him more steadfast in his resolve that indeed "they are out to get him." A therapist knowledgeable in the VO model, on the other hand, might attempt to effect a match rather than a fit—at least, for the time being: "Listen, Ken, I think you're perfectly correct in being cautious and suspicious—I would look before I leap, too."

The value orientations model is especially helpful in running support groups (e.g., cancer and AIDS groups) because it enables group leaders to structure the group's composition to maximize benefits *within a short period of time.* Since time is of the essence in terminally ill patients, it is imperative that patients with compatible orientations be grouped together to avoid unnecessary and costly counterproductive, mismatched therapeutic processes. Compatibility does not, however, necessarily mean matching group members all the time. In some instances, a few patients who have "given up" (Subject to) may be paired with a group that predominantly wants to "fight" (Mastery over) their illness. The latter group oftentimes provides the "spark" to "rage, rage against the dying of the light," with salutary results.

Medications

Even in what appears to be a relatively straightforward, cut-and-dried process of prescribing medications, successful compliance often depends on a host of subjective factors such as the patient's and/or the couple's value orientations. Patients with a Lineal orientation would, of course, be more receptive to "just being told" by the doctor the effects, side effects, and dosages of the medication. Not so, with somebody who has a Collateral orientation. This person will probably need to spend more time in a dialogue with the therapist about how he or she feels about medications and apprehensions about taking them. Even if there is general agreement that medications are warranted, in order to maximize compliance, the doctor will need to take into consideration how he or she presents the information. For example, one might explain the effects of Ritalin to a mother who is Being-oriented in this manner: "Your son will be able to concentrate better, and I know it will result in him getting better grades, which will considerably improve his confidence and boost his self-esteem." To a father who is Doing-oriented, the explanation might be quite different: "It will make him focus and pay attention to his work. He won't get into so much trouble and will increase his chances of success."

Ancillary Uses of Value Orientations

The method can also be used quite effectively in doing *systems analysis* of ailing systems in order to figure out whether the members of that particular clinic, center, or organization are congruent with the defined mission, values, and goals of the institution. To carry it one step further, it can also reveal not only member-system conflicts, member-member conflicts, but most significant and important, *system-target population* conflicts. Having a relatively naive staff who are mostly Caucasian middle class servicing a multicultural, lower-class population is a setup for failure. Value orientations will help identify and concretize the areas of conflict.

Another ancillary use is to enhance the effectiveness of *consultation/liaison* services. Most consultants fail or are ineffective in doing client-centered, consultee-centered, or program-centered consultation/liaison work, not so much because what they have to offer is not valuable or is irrelevant, but because it does not fit or match the prevalent orientations of the recipient of the consultation.

Supervision is another arena in which value orientations can be very useful in identifying and resolving supervisee-client conflicts. Paul, thirty-two, a social worker of Japanese ancestry, was the therapist of Joey, sixteen, Caucasian, a resident in a treatment center. Paul dreaded the sessions with Joey because the sessions usually degenerated into power struggles, where Paul could barely contain his anger toward Joey. According to Paul, Joey had a very annoying habit of saying "Yes, but..." or "I did that before and it didn't work" to all of Paul's suggestions. Paul interpreted these as part of Joey's "psychopathology," in other words, as part of his "passive-aggression." In utter frustration, he sought supervision.

In supervision, value orientations profiles of Paul and Joey were obtained and to no one's surprise showed value orientations clashes between them in several key modalities. For instance, in the Human Relations mode, Paul showed a strong preference for the Lineal (hierarchical) orientation. Hence, he viewed himself as the "authority" to whom and for whom Joey must show evidence of clinical progress. Joey, on the other hand, showed an Individualistic/Collateral orientation, therefore constantly bugging Paul: "I'm ready to be discharged. The other kids say so, and my parents agree. I think I'm ready too, so why are you saying I'm not?" Another modality in which they showed conflicting orientations was in the Time mode. Paul was Past-oriented, and Joey, Future. Paul was constantly harping on the standards and traditions of the Center "that must be upheld." Joey was talking a lot about "moving on, and getting out of here."

Once these glaring orientation clashes were pointed out to Paul in supervision, he became more sensitive to Joey's orientations and packaged his advice/counsel to fit. He also took Joey's oppositionality" less personally and more as a reflection of their value orientations differences. When Joey was discharged from the Center six months later, the staff person he thanked most was Paul. Joey's parting comment: "Paul didn't let me get away with a lot of my bullshit."

Finally, I have also personally used it as the frame of reference for *mediating* conflict and *facilitating* group process between interethnic (Native Indian patient groups/French-Canadian workers or Canadian government employees) and interreligious (Muslim and Christian workers in the Philippines) groups.

Summary/Conclusions

The value orientations model is a very useful and versatile tool that the practicing clinician can use in a variety of contexts. It enables the practitioner to meaningfully integrate culture in the bio-psycho-social-spiritual matrix. Because it can have a potentially powerful impact on one's clinical practice, it might be prudent to mention a number of caveats about the method at this time: (1) It does *not* establish normalcy or pathology. No one orientation is healthier, or "more better" (as they say in Hawaii). It does have the capability of pointing out fits or matches and hence the *appropriateness* or *adaptiveness* of certain orientations in a specific situation or context. (2) It should not be used wittingly or unwittingly as one more basis of individual or cultural stereotyping. Finally, (3) it should not be used coercively to enforce unwanted changes (Ponce 1995).

References

Bandler, Richard, and John Grinder. *Frogs into Princes.* Moab, UT: Real People Press, 1979.

———. *The Structure of Magic,* vols. 1 and 2. Palo Alto, CA: Science & Behavior Books, 1975.

deShazer, S. "Fit." *Journal of Strategic and Systemic Therapies* 3 (1984): 34–37.

Kluckhohn, Florence R., and Fred L. Strodtbeck. *Variations in Value Orientations.* Evanston, IL: Row, Peterson, 1961.

Kohls, L. Robert. "Models for Comparing and Contrasting Cultures." In *Building the Professional Dimension of Educational Exchange*, edited by Joy Reid. Yarmouth, ME: Intercultural Press, 1988.

Ponce, Danilo E. "Value Orientations: Clinical Applications in a Multicultural Residential Treatment for Children and Youth." *Journal of Residential Treatment for Children and Youth* 12 (1995): 29–42.

Reid, Joy, ed. *Building the Professional Dimension of Educational Exchange.*Yarmouth, ME: Intercultural Press, 1988.

Remer, Rory, and Pamela A. Remer. "A Study of the Discrepancies among the Value Orderings of 12 Counseling Theories: The Quantification of Value Differences." *Counseling and Values,* 1982.

Values and Conflict in Clinical Settings

Pamela J. Brink

The purpose of this article is to demonstrate how values differ depending upon an individual's profession or cultural role. To demonstrate this point, I am using the published professional codes for nursing, medicine, dentistry, and pharmacy as one set of data (Beauchamp and Walters 1994). The second set comes from my own research among the Annang of Nigeria using the Rural Value Orientations Schedule (Brink 1984). To analyze this data, I will draw upon the work of Clyde Kluckhohn and O. H. Mowrer (1944) as well as the work of Morris Freilich (1964). Using these as my referent points, I will attempt to show how cultural conflict can arise between health professionals, how values differ between health professions, and how values differ according to ascribed social roles. These differences can be documented using the Florence R. Kluckhohn and Fred L. Strodtbeck Value Orientations Survey (1961).

I would like to begin with health professional codes of conduct (Beauchamp and Walters). Using ethics terminology, the code of conduct for medicine emphasizes the ethical principle of *beneficence* (do good) and *nonmaleficence* (do no harm). The code of conduct for nursing, in contrast, emphasizes the ethical principle of *autonomy* (the individual decides). What does this mean? First, physicians are a self-directed health professional group who intervene in people's lives. They wish to do no harm and to do good, but it is they, the professionals, who decide what is good and what is harmful, putting them in a paternalistic role. They are also Individualistic according to the Kluckhohn theory of value orientations. They are consulted for their knowledge and expertise, to which the patient defers. It is the professionals who recommend what they believe to be the best course of action. For physicians, in particular, "the buck stops here." They must make decisions as individuals. They may ask for consultation, but they are trained from earliest medical school days to understand that they are responsible and only they can act. This creates an independent practitioner who believes his or her decisions are right and tries to convince the patient and the patient's family of the correctness of the diagnosis and treatment. This belief is not always true; nevertheless, this is the way physicians operate within our cultural system. I would predict that physicians would score the value of Individualism highest and Lineality second.

Nurses, on the other hand, are trained not to make decisions for patients but to work with them to enhance their healing capacities. This value of Collaterality is mandated in the professional code of conduct and is expressed as the ethical principle of autonomy. Nurses believe that patients and their families have the right to make their own decisions, that patients and their families should be given information *at their own level of understanding* and then decide for themselves what is best for them in light of their own lives and responsibilities. Nurses do not believe anyone else can or should make these decisions. The ethical code of autonomy under which nurses work places them in direct conflict with the medical code of conduct, beneficence, with the physician deciding what is good and what is harmful. In many cases, Canadian and U.S. cultures support the physician's right to decide for the patient, even when the decision is in conflict with the patient's or family's wishes.

An example of such a cultural and ethical conflict of values was demonstrated in a TV documentary in 1989. A child in a Meti family in Alberta, Canada, was under the care of a famous pediatric surgeon. The surgeon recommended a liver transplant for the two-year-old child. This family lived a great distance from the university hospital. They refused the treatment (finance was not the issue here) on the grounds of distance and disruption of family life. (Following a transplant, patients and families must attend clinics regularly, receive medications and have them monitored, and generally live close to a major medical facility in order to receive medical care.) The physician called the Royal Canadian Mounted Police (RCMP) and also had the child placed as a ward of the court so that the child could receive the transplant. To avoid the RCMP, the family moved to Saskatchewan until they could arrange to have the court reverse its decision, which it did eventually, and the family returned to Alberta, where the child died.

This example demonstrates the power of physicians to make decisions for patients under the ethical principle of beneficence and to obtain legal support for their decisions. Many nurses would respond with great discomfort to this story, believing that the family had the right to decide and that nurses should support the family in these kinds of decisions. The conflict between these two health professions, then, is mandated by their professional codes of conduct.

Nurses work with physicians in the treatment process and with the family to support the patient. They value Collaterality. They are not just supportive, however, but are also protective of their patients. Their mandate is to protect the patients from perceived harm from others—including the physician. In every state in the United States, there is a legal requirement for nurses to disobey physicians' orders if those orders are wrong. But how do nurses know which orders are wrong and harmful to the patient? Because nurses must know as much about the care and treatment of the classes of patients under their care as do the physicians. If they don't, they are not acting responsibly according to their legal guidelines. Nurses, therefore, are required by law to protect patients from physicians, which obviously causes friction when a nurse questions a physician.

Not only does this legal mandate cause friction, it also causes nurses to lose their jobs. A friend of mine was the director of nurses in a large hospital in Wisconsin in the 1980s. One of her nurses questioned a drug order by a physician and refused to give the drug. The physician, angered, protested to the chief-of-staff, who took it to the hospital board. The director of nurses supported her nurse, as the nurse was legally required to act in her own best judgment. Both the nurse and the director of nurses were fired that day.

We are faced, then, with health professional role conflict created by the codes of conduct of the professions themselves as well as the legal mandates of those codes.

A second source for potential role conflict was clearly demonstrated by Kluckhohn and Mowrer in their 1944 paper published in the *American Anthropologist* called "Culture and Personality: A Conceptual Scheme." If we look at the chart they created entitled "Components of Personality," we can see just how cultural conflict can be identified. (I have found this model extremely useful in teaching nursing students about the components of a cultural assessment.) We generally refer to cultural values as those that are held communally and have been derived from the biological, physical, environmental, and social determinants for a culture group. In other words, cultural values arise from both universal and communal determinants.

Determinants	Universal	Communal	Role	Idiosyncratic
Biological	Birth, death, hunger, thirst, elimination, etc.	"Racial" traits, nutrition level, endemic diseases, etc.	Age and sex differences, caste, etc.	Peculiarities of stature, physiognomy, glandular makeup, etc.
Physical-environmental	Gravity, temperature, time, etc.	Climate, topography, natural resources, etc.	Differential access to material goods, etc.	Unique events and "accidents" such as being hit by lightning, etc.
Social	Infant care, group life, etc.	Size, density, and distribution of population, etc.	Cliques, "marginal" men, etc.	Social "accidents" such as death of a parent, being adopted, meeting particular people, etc.
Cultural	Symbolism, taboo on incest and ingroup murder, etc.	Traditions, rules of conduct and manners, skills, knowledge, etc.	Culturally differentiated roles	Folklore about accidents and "fate," etc.

I would like to move now to the box that demonstrates the determinants of role and culture. Here we can clearly see the components that enter into culturally differentiated roles based on biological, environmental, and social roles. Not only does every culture have values that differentiate one group from another, there is also the fact that value orientations will be expressed differently depending on gender and age (biological role determinants) and on education, status, and culturally prescribed roles (social role determinants). As Kluckhohn and Mowrer point out, one's cultural perspective is modified and colored by one's social role as determined by one's biological role as further determined by one's environment. It is only logical to assume, therefore, that one's value orientations will be affected by these role requirements, just as they are in the above demonstrated professional codes of conduct. Every culture has these determinants of personality, and it is important that we look at the differences in values associated with roles and not just at the overarching value orientations associated with groups. Here's why.

At an American Anthropological Association convention, I spent an evening with Morris Freilich, when he told me about his model of the Natural Triad (1964) published in the *American Sociological Review* in 1964. Following that meeting, he sent me a reprint of his article, which I read. On the basis of our meeting and discussion, I published two papers (Brink 1972, 1980). The first appeared in the *American Journal of Nursing* in 1972 and the second was published in a book of readings. A synopsis of our conversation follows.

Freilich's Natural Triad model was based on the relationships between the mother's brother, nephew, and father in both the Trobriand and the Andamans Islands. In the first instance Malinowski had described the mother's brother as the authority figure for the nephew and the father as an informal friendly relationship. He diagrammed this as an inverted triangle with the mother's brother signified as the high-status authority (HSA), the father as high-status friend (HSF), and the son/nephew as the low-status subordinate (LSS). Freilich then went on to show how the relationships between HSA, HSF, and LSS were either negative, as demonstrated by authority, distance, formality, or nonexistence or were positive, as demonstrated by friendliness, helpfulness, and informality. Freilich further demonstrated that this Natural Triad was held together, and survived, only if one of the relationships was positive and the other two were negative.

In the instance of the Trobriands, the relationship between the son (LSS) and the mother's brother (HSA) was designated as negative because the relationship was formal, distant, and dominated by the uncle's authoritative role. They called each other by title, and their conversations were respectful and formal. On the other hand, the relationship between the son (LSS) and his father (HSF) was one of friendliness and informality. The father had no authority over his son; therefore, father and son could enjoy each other and be friends. This relationship was designated as positive. What Frielich found was that the relationship between the father and the mother's brother was formal, distant, and sometimes totally nonexistent. Frielich designated this relationship as also negative.

Frielich then showed that in the Andaman Islands the same triadic relationship occurred and the same culturally programmed behaviors were in evidence, even when it was the father who was the HSA and the uncle who was HSF to the LSS son. The relationship between the father and mother's brother was negative, the relationship between the father and the son was negative, and the relationship between the mother's brother and the son was positive in the form of a joking and friendly relationship.

Freilich then asked me if similar natural triads occurred in health care—specifically hospitals. As we talked, we found the most common Natural Triad in a hospital setting was the physician as HSA, nurses as HSF, and the patient as LSS. If the relationship between the nurse and the patient is positive, warm, friendly, and informal, and the relationship between the physician and the patient is formal and distant (and therefore negative), the relationship between the nurse and the physician *must be* negative in order for the triad to survive and work well. This relationship was unexpected yet often seen in hospital wards, where the relationships between nurses and physicians were often antagonistic and argumentative. That this is a culturally programmed role with culturally programmed values is completely unknown and unrecognized by both groups.

If, on the other hand, the relationship between the physician and the nurse is close, friendly, and informal (positive), then the relationships between nurse/patient and physician/patient *must be* negative or formal, distant, or nonexistent. When we examined the role relationships in the surgical theatre, that is exactly what we found. The patient is "out of it," being acted upon and unconscious. The physician and nurse can "banter" and "play" with each other. The model holds up.

The Natural Triad model also holds up when we look at the relationships between registered nurses, licensed vocational nurses, nursing assistants, and patients. If the relationship among the nursing staff is close, positive, and friendly, there is little room for a positive, warm, friendly relationship between staff and patients. If, on the other hand, the relationship between the registered nurses, for example, and the patients is positive, the relationship between the nursing assistants and the patients and the nursing assistants and the licensed vocational nurses must be negative or distant. This surprises everyone. It is unexpected.

How, then, can we document this using the Kluckhohn and Strodtbeck Value Orientations Survey? In my research on the Annang of southeastern Nigeria (Brink 1984), the data indicated a Human Relations value orientation difference: men were more likely to value Individualism and women, Collaterality. For the Annang, the professional nurse was more Collaterally oriented than the native healer, who was very Individualistic. There were also differences in value orientations depending on the level of education of the informant.

I believe it is this Human Relations value orientation that highlights role conflicts between health professionals. Physicians demonstrate Individualism while nurses prefer Collaterality. The possible confounding or intervening variable here is the biological role of gender. Since nursing is a female-dominated profession, it would be difficult to tease out whether collaterality was a nursing value or a feminine value.

In North America, however, the medical profession is no longer primarily a male-dominated profession. Because of this, many nurses have assumed that women physicians would be easier to work with than male physicians. This has not proven to be the case, however, and nurses have become disenchanted with their "sisters," feeling that women physicians have violated their gender role relationships. Instead, women physicians value their social role relationships over their biological role relationships. In a sense, women physicians are valuing a role that has been achieved through hard work on their part over a role that was ascribed to them at birth and over which they have no control.

Further value orientations research could examine the responses to the Human Relations value orientation by both gender and profession within the same culture. It would be an interesting analysis.

References

Beauchamp, T. L., and L. Walters. *Contemporary Issues in Bioethics*. 4th ed. Belmont, CA: Wadsworth, 1994.

Brink, Pamela J. "Value Orientations an Assessment Tool in Cultural Diversity: Theory, Method and Examples." *Nursing Research* 33, no. 4 (1984): 198–203.

———. "Natural Triad in Health Care." *American Journal of Nursing* 72, no. 5 (1972): 897–99; and "Systems Analysis of Health Care Delivery: The Case of the Natural Triad." In *Conceptual Models for Nursing Practice*. 2d ed. 341–49. Grosse Point, MI: Appleton-Century-Crofts, 1980.

Freilich, Morris. "The Natural Triad in Kinship and Complex Systems." *American Sociological Review* 29 (1964): 529–40.

Kluckhohn, Clyde, and O. H. Mowrer. "Culture and Personality: A Conceptual Scheme." *American Anthropologist* 46 (1944): 1–29. Reprinted in *Transcultural Nursing: A Book of Readings*, edited by Pamela J. Brink, 93–125. Prospect Heights, IL: Waveland Press, 1990.

Kluckhohn, Florence R., and Fred L. Strodtbeck. *Variations in Value Orientations*. Evanston, IL: Row, Peterson, 1961.

Part 3

Value Orientations and Education

Comparing and Contrasting Cultures

L. Robert Kohls

The husband and wife team of Clyde and Florence R. Kluckhohn, along with fellow anthropologist Fred L. Strodtbeck, have provided us with one of the needed tools for comparing and contrasting cultures. Looking at the phenomenon of culture analytically and philosophically, they came up with five basic questions that get at the root of the value system of any culture, no matter how different or seemingly exotic.

1. What is the character of innate human nature? (Human Nature orientation)
2. What is the relation of humans to nature? (Person-Nature orientation)
3. What is the temporal focus (time sense) of human life? (Time orientation)
4. What is the mode of human activity? (Activity orientation)
5. What is the mode of human relationships? (Human Relations orientation)

How would you describe the attitude of the majority of Americans toward each? What do Americans think human beings are like basically? What kind of relationship do they have to nature? What does time mean to them? How important is action? What kind of relationship do they have with each other?

The chart that follows is an adaptation and simplification of a model developed by Kluckhohn and Strodtbeck. It indicates the range of possible responses to the five orientations. It is intended to be read horizontally, each row relating to one of the five orientations listed above and in the left-hand column.

Orientation	Beliefs and Behaviors		
Human Nature	Basically Evil (changeable/ unchangeable)	Mixture of Good and Evil (changeable/ unchangeable)	Basically Good changeable/ unchangeable)
Person-Nature	Humans Subjugated by Nature	Humans in Harmony with Nature	Humans the Masters of Nature
Time	Past-oriented	Present-oriented	Future-oriented
Activity	Being (stress on who you are)	Being-in-Becoming (stress on self-development)	Doing (stress on action)
Human Relations	Lineal	Collateral	Individualistic

We recognize that in any culture consisting of a large number of people, the whole range of possible human values and behaviors will probably be found, if only in a few individuals. When we talk of American or French or Chinese values, we mean those that *predominate* within that group, those that are held by enough of its members to make the values an evident and prominent part of the culture as a whole. Let's take a look at each of the five orientations to determine where a typical middle-class American might be expected to fit.[1]

With respect to Human Nature, middle-class, mainstream Americans are generally optimistic, choosing to believe the best about a person until that person proves otherwise. Will Rogers, the American humorist, was being very American when he said, "I never met a man I didn't like." We would place the average American's beliefs about Human Nature in the right-hand column (Basically Good). This classification explains the interest Americans have in such activities as prison reform and social rehabilitation. Americans generally believe that in order to bring out the basic goodness in human beings, all you have to do is change the negative social conditions in which they exist.[2] Indeed, deep down, Americans in general believe humans and human society are ultimately perfectible—if only enough effort is made in that direction.

In their relationship to Nature, Americans see a clear separation between humans and nature (this would be incomprehensible to many Asians), and humans are clearly in charge. The idea that people can control their own destiny is totally alien to most of the world's cultures. Elsewhere, people tend to believe either (1) that they are driven and controlled by fate and can do very little, if anything, to influence it or (2) they are meant to live in Harmony with Nature. Americans, on the other hand, have a strong drive to subdue, dominate, and control their natural environment.

Concerning orientation toward Time, Americans are dominated by a belief in progress. We are Future-oriented. This implies a strong task, or goal, orientation. We are very conscious, too, that "time is money" and therefore not to be wasted. We have an optimistic faith in the future and what the future will bring. We tend to equate change with improvement and consider a rapid rate of change as normal.

As for Activity, Americans are so Doing-oriented that they cannot even conceive of what it would be like to be "Being-oriented." Indeed, we are hyperactive, to the degree that one sociologist has described the American as an "Electric Englishman." We believe in keeping busy and productive at all times—even on vacation. Horatio Alger's faith in the work ethic is very much with us. As a result of this action orientation, Americans have become very proficient at problem solving and decision making.

Our Human Relations orientation is toward the importance of the individual and the equality of all people. Friendly, informal, outgoing, and extroverted, Americans scorn rank and authority, even when they are the ones who possess it. American bosses are almost the only supervisors in the world who insist on their subordinates calling them by their first names. We find it extremely easy to make friends, and we think there are unlimited friends out there just waiting to be discovered. Extended family ties in America are weak due to our strong sense of individuality, especially when compared to the rest of the world. We have succeeded in reducing the family to its smallest possible unit—the nuclear family.

Look back at the Kluckhohn-Strodtbeck model (page 120). If we fill in the boxes into which the predominant American values fall, we come up with a picture of the American value system that looks like the first chart on the next page.

Now let's look at the value systems of several other societies and compare them with the American system.

We recognize that models of this kind are oversimplifications and can only give approximations of reality. Their use is in giving rough pictures of the striking contrasts that may be encountered in societies where certain values predominate, even though these so-

American Value System

			Basically Good (changeable)
			Humans the Masters of Nature
			Future-oriented
			Doing (stress on action)
			Individualistic

cieties may be in the process of marked change because of rapid modernization. Fundamental values, however, have a way of persisting in spite of change. The evolution of values is a slow process, since they are rooted in survival needs and passed on, almost fanatically, from generation to generation.

We see many of the world's traditional cultures as follows:

Traditional Cultures' Value System

Orientation	Beliefs and Behaviors		
Human Nature	Basically Evil (unchangeable)	Mixture of Good and Evil (unchangeable)	
Person-Nature	Humans Subjugated by Nature		
Time	Past-oriented		
Activity	Being (stress on who you are)		
Human Relations	Lineal		

Here's how we view Arab cultures from a generalized perspective. There would be important variations, of course, from one specific culture to another—Egyptian, Saudi, Lebanese, and so on. Notice that in one category (humans' relationship to the natural environment), Arabs seem to fall more or less equally into two of the classifications.

Arab Value System

Orientation	Beliefs and Behaviors		
Human Nature		Mixture of Good and Evil (unchangeable)	
Person-Nature	Humans Subjugated by Nature	Humans in Harmony with Nature	
Time	Past-oriented		
Activity	Being (stress on who you are)		
Human Relations	Lineal		

Here's how we see the Japanese (a very complex culture and even more "contradictory" than the Arabs'):

Japanese Value System

Orientation	Beliefs and Behaviors		
Human Nature		Mixture of Good and Evil (unchangeable)	
Person-Nature		Humans in Harmony with Nature	
Time	Past-oriented		Future-oriented
Activity		Being-in-Becoming (stress on self-development)	Doing (stress on action)
Human Relations	Lineal	Collateral	

The Kluckhohn chart only shows three variations out of an infinite variety of possibilities, and it only compares culture on five basic orientations. It does not claim, therefore, to tell you everything about every culture; yet it is impressive in the differences in values that it does reveal. In a sense, the values expressed in the right-hand column can be said to be 180 degrees away from the values in the left-hand column.

Is it any wonder that putting Americans into cultures with complex and/or radically different value orientations sometimes causes stress, disorientation, and breakdowns in communication? In a very simple format, the Kluckhohn model indicates where these problems are likely to occur.[3]

---

[1] Members of American ethnic and other minority groups would probably find their values diverging in some significant respects from those discussed here. If you are a member of a minority or have a strong ethnic identification, try to identify ways in which your values and behavior differ from those indicated here as characteristic of mainstream American culture.

[2] The Kluckhohns placed Americans in the left-hand column (basically Evil), citing the Christian belief in original sin. This may have been an accurate reading for the 1950s, though we have our doubts. But whether Americans see Human Nature as Good or Evil, it is certainly fair to say they accept it as changeable.

[3] For a study that elaborates on the Kluckhohn model and includes some interesting cross-cultural comparisons, see Edward C. Stewart and Milton J. Bennett, *American Cultural Patterns: A Cross-Cultural Perspective*, rev. ed. (Yarmouth, ME: Intercultural Press, 1991).

Values and Education in the Emerging Multicultural Society: Awareness and Fairness

Marian M. Ortuño

The emergence in the 1980s of the cultural phenomenon known as multiculturalism, has, for some, brought with it the highly laudable promise of fairness and inclusion for previously marginalized groups, while in the minds of others, it threatens divisiveness and nothing less than the disintegration of society. Indeed, human existence is "inherently and universally multicultural," even though humankind at times has rejected this notion (Wurzel 1988, 1). The United States, in particular, which prides itself on being a democratic society, has throughout its history been multicultural, multiethnic, and multiracial. This is not to say that all peoples have reaped the benefits of full participation in the American cornucopia of opportunities. Poverty, racism, discrimination, and other forms of disenfranchisement have exacerbated the problems of social inequity, and marginalized peoples have, as a result, retreated to the emotional comfort and psychological safety of their own ethnically and racially polarized enclaves.

Technological advancements of the twentieth century have rapidly transformed our world by reducing physical space, enabling us to cross formerly impenetrable information barriers. Because of these technological breakthroughs, along with overwhelming social, demographic, and economic changes, the basic assumptions underlying the social contracts that bind together societal and academic communities are in a state of transition. The role, mission, and organization of curricula in schools and universities have been called into question. In order to prepare an ever increasing ethnically and racially diverse student body for life and leadership in the twenty-first century, there is a growing need for a more inclusive curriculum. From elementary to university level, the curriculum will need to have not only an international focus but a domestic multicultural focus as well (Darder 1991, xvi). According to projected statistics from the United States Bureau of the Census, persons of Hispanic origin will comprise 13.8% of the resident population by the year 2010, and by 2050, 24.5%. The white population (not of Hispanic origin) will comprise 68% by 2010, and 52.8% by 2050; Asians, 4.8% by 2010 and 8.2% by 2050; and blacks, 12.6% by 2010 and 13% by 2050 (*Statistical Abstracts* 19). What we call a "good education," then, will need to take into account the cultural and linguistic diversity of the student body. It will also have to take into account that our society needs "to respond to changing world situations in which economic competition and political/diplomatic relations will depend on the capacity of our people to communicate and function in more multilingual and cross-cultural settings" (Saravia-Shore and Arvizu 1992, 496). The first step toward achieving a reasoned multicultural perspective would be, logically, the acquisition of the awareness that differences, sometimes resulting in insoluble conflicts, exist between groups. But differences do not have to lead to divisiveness. Learning to deal with these differences will be of vital importance in the coming century. The ability to minimize factionalism should serve as a unifying force in the struggle to promote democratic principles of social justice through understanding.

The term *multicultural* elicits a strong, emotional response from some quarters, as it has become charged with political overtones. It is thought by some to be part of a revolutionary political agenda, a vehicle of social empowerment leading to political empowerment, pitting minority against majority, liberal against conservative, and advocating ethnic separatism—"Balkanization," "ghettoization"—over democratic assimilation. In the words of Zbigniew Brzezinski,

> The emergence of potentially divisive multiculturalism—which on the one hand represents the unavoidable recognition of the reality of the American mosaic,...on the other threatens to balkanize multiethnic America by the deliberate de-emphasis of the nationally unifying and socially equalizing effects of a common language and of shared historical traditions and political values. (1993, 107)

Notions such as this invariably lead to fear, distrust, animosity, and sometimes outright confrontation between diverse groups in their attempts to give more weight and value to the achievements of one culture over those of another. The dilemma presents itself thus: Does one have to sacrifice unity in order to recognize and accommodate diversity, sacrifice the "unum" for the "pluribus," so to speak (Schlesinger 1992, 16), and in so doing, discard the ideal of "one nation, indivisible" (Malone 1997, A8)? Disputes such as this, centering around multiculturalism and the need for multicultural education, are basically philosophical, moral, and ethical in nature, so there can be no definitive solutions (Brzezinski, 108).

What I offer in this brief study are not solutions, but rather suggestions for making an accommodation between the opposing viewpoints, while at the same time acknowledging the essential goal of fairness through awareness. Some of my suggestions are of a broader nature and relate to education in general, from elementary to university levels. Other observations will specifically refer to university-level foreign language instruction and the role it plays in multicultural education.

The Value Orientations Perspective

Awareness of culture and cultural diversity is at the core of the multicultural perspective (Nieto 1995, 379). *Culture* may be defined as "...the ever changing values, traditions, social and political relationships, and worldview created and shared by a group of people bound together by a combination of factors that include a common history, geographic location, language, social class, and/or religion, and how these are transformed by those who share them. Thus, it includes not only tangibles such as foods, holidays, dress, and artistic expression, but also less tangible manifestations such as communication style, attitudes, values, and family relationships" (138). But how does one begin to approach so complicated an issue as cultural diversity without a model or organizational framework? Here, value orientations can provide educators with a *perspective*, a crucial term defined as "the relationship of aspects of a subject to each other and to a whole" (*American Heritage Dictionary,* 619). A value orientations perspective would enable students to identify their own ways of thinking and approaches to problem solving and then, as a next step, help them to realize that there are ways of approaching and solving those problems that may be just as valid, yet very different from their own. They would see that some value systems will not be compatible with others, while some will overlap. Opposing views can and do conflict, and this strikes at the very heart of education and its purposes. Critical examination of diverse viewpoints forms the very basis of intellectual inquiry, and if an individual's views are never challenged in the educational process, then that individual's beliefs and commitments are of questionable authenticity (Gonzalez 1994, 10). Calling into question one's essential beliefs and worldview is not an easy process. One way to begin to establish the dialectic of self-understanding and other-understanding is by focusing on cross-cultural differences, domestically and internationally, through the Kluckhohn value orientations model (Kempf 1995, 44). This method, I propose, can help create a sense of community and establish common ground between diverse groups by fostering understanding and respect for differences and similarities across cultural boundaries.

By using the Kluckhohn value orientations model, one has readily available a perspective, a cognitive organizer that shows how the parts relate to one another and then to the whole. With the model one can analyze and understand a cultural conflict within a framework that highlights one community's response to a particular issue against the backdrop of other possible responses. When differences do occur, they can, according to the model, be shown to have a logical justification for their existence, one rooted in a society's (1) perception of self and others, (2) worldview, (3) temporal focus, (4) forms of activity, and (5) human relations.

When one becomes familiar with the Kluckhohn model, one can, through comparison, derive the dominant or variant value orientations within one's own culture or another culture. Once having obtained this valuable tool, students and instructors are enriched with a global perspective and the ability to recognize the diversity of the methods by which different peoples attempt to solve humanity's common problems. The origins of stereotypes can be readily identified, and potential cultural conflicts in social, business, and political interactions with other ethnic groups, racial groups, or foreigners can be perceived beforehand and perhaps avoided. Sometimes interactions between representatives of diverse cultures will not be harmonious, and in such cases reference to the values model can serve to identify and manage conflict (Ortuño 1991, 450–51).

The word *enculturation* refers to the process by which individuals acquire and assimilate the values and behavior patterns of a parent society. Yet while serving to strengthen the common bonds among the members of a group, the enculturation process also gives rise to an essential ethnocentrism, or deep-rooted sense of cultural superiority. And if we are not always consciously aware of the values inherited from our parent culture, how can we begin to compare, let alone understand, those of others? Most of us do not even question the assumptions underlying our cultural beliefs and behaviors. They are so much a part of what we perceive to be "real life" that the philosophical divisions between existential premises and normative assumptions become blurred. Our cultural nearsightedness leads us to equate what "is" with what we think "ought to be." So when confronted with values different from our own—and such confrontations are inevitable in a pluralistic society—without the ability to conceptualize cultural variables, we often react judgmentally. We may retreat even deeper into our own ethnocentric shell, all the while justifying our defensiveness through a bipolar comparison with our own culture as the universal yardstick: "We are right, and they are wrong" (Ortuño, 450). By analyzing dominant and variant American cultural patterns, educators can draw students away from cultural presumptuousness and point them in the direction of self-understanding. By realizing that our dominant values are not universal, but particularistic and subject to change, we take a vital first step toward cross-cultural awareness, or "other-understanding" (Nieto, 349).

In the Kluckhohn taxonomy of values, there is no hierarchical ranking or demeaning of cultures, which does not necessarily signify that cultures are static, or that the practices and traditions of a particular culture can never be questioned. Because of its neutrality, however, the taxonomy can serve, in the area of education, as a bridge to mutual understanding, or as a vehicle for amelioration on two levels—first, on an interpersonal level, and second, on an instructional level.

Interpersonal Relations in an Educational Setting

Familiarity with the Kluckhohn taxonomy can help teachers and students value bicultural students and the resources they bring to the school setting. By not reacting to differences emotionally and by not judging diversity in worldview, self-perception, time, activity, and social relations as signs of genetic or environmental inferiority (Darder, 3), students and teachers alike can help combat racism, discrimination, ethnocentrism, and the tendency to stereotype.

Value orientations can also help bicultural students, and indeed all students, in attaining self-identification, and, in so doing, aid them in transcending the limitations of the world of their own personal experiences. The value orientations model illustrates that there is no superior culture, and in this way it can help dispel feelings of inadequacy, fear, and rejection based on perceived racial or cultural differences. Value orientations can foster a sense of self-worth and belonging by providing a format through which the marginalized may express their divergent views and make them understandable to others in a nonthreatening context. An understanding of value orientations can also promote acceptance at the university level of the so-called "nontraditional student"—a female or minority individual who embarks on a college career at a middle-age stage in life. Furthermore, the value orientations model also gives teachers a means of achieving "attitudinal openness" and of facing their own ethnocentricities (Lou 1994, 23). Given the diversity of today's classroom, an instructor would benefit greatly from the foreknowledge of which groups of students would be most likely to experience cultural incompatibility.

Third, understanding of values and the cultural underpinnings of individual versus group dynamics can help establish a dialogue and ameliorate the inevitable conflicts that arise among administrators, faculty, and different groups of parents and students.

The Kluckhohn schedule of values, in the form of an interview, can be helpful in creating a personality profile that can outline an individual's worldview and help break down barriers to achievement. This information could prove invaluable in the creation of curricula (teaching and testing) and support programs, in the understanding of the roots of conflict among students and faculty, in counseling, and in the assessment and implementation of disciplinary measures. The value orientations model could be used to evaluate a culturally based questionnaire such as the one offered by Johns (1994, 63), which asks the following: What are dominant student/teacher roles? What sort of instructional techniques would prove most fruitful—lecture, discussion group, group work, or independent study? What about gender relationships and physical closeness? What do students perceive the purpose of reading to be—to remember (memorize), to analyze, or to critique?

Finally, values can be of use in the area of academic advisement by providing insight into the cultural differences that affect learning style and, ultimately, academic success. The acquisition of cross-cultural sensitivity can enable advisers to see how life experiences may have influenced and shaped an individual's view of the self and the world.

Instructional Level of Education

A highly competitive, individualistic instructional mode favors dominant-culture children and males, and it puts others and females at a disadvantage (Nieto, 147). Value orientations highlight how some students might feel more at ease in a group-centered, collaborative-style learning environment. Nevertheless, many first-generation Asian Americans, it should be noted, who view education as hierarchical and the instructor as an unimpeachable authority figure, will not react favorably to this approach (Lou, 34).

Class participation, competition, and aggressive and original thinking are values commonly rewarded in most American classroom settings, along with an emphasis on technical knowledge, or knowledge that is "objective, separate, and devoid of the knowing subject" (Darder, 5). Some students, as the Kluckhohn model reveals, may have a cultural orientation that does not see such a strong dichotomy between human beings and the natural world. Traditional assessment and learning environments are, for the most part, biased toward the analytic style. For some students, both cognitive learning styles need to be developed—the inductive approach of graphs, formulas, and scientific abstraction and the deductive approach, which stresses a more humanized, personal approach to the presentation of material (Ramirez 1988, 205). The value orientations model can help in this regard by providing insight into the strong connection between social relations and styles of thinking and learning. Consider how valuable it would be for an instructor to realize that the dominant analytic style is more suited to a student from an individualistically oriented culture, while the more abstract relational style is closely tied to group context and relationships (Stewart and Bennett 1991, 42–43). Stewart explains,

> The social organizations, curricula, pedagogy, and discipline in the schools provide unfavorable environments for the relational conceptual style. This condition may cause difficulties for many foreign and American students [i.e., those from

> lower socioeconomic backgrounds] in higher education.... These students tend to give equal value to personal experience, empirical fact, and concepts derived from persons in authority. They fail to make the distinction between the objective and the subjective, which is required in the analytical academic world. (43)

Values can also help in the process of moving beyond the Eurocentric "canon" toward integrating nontraditional works into the curriculum by providing cohesiveness and purpose through an organizational framework.

In addition value orientations can play an important role in teacher training and professional development programs in helping current and future instructors to recognize their own biases as well as the attitudes and biases of their students. Nieto points out that "...in far too many cases teachers have professional development programs without any direct or even indirect information concerning cultural differences" (379). Teachers are generally unprepared for the diversity awaiting them in the classroom, and "teacher education programs continue to teach as if diversity did not exist, or was a pesky problem to overcome."

The value orientations approach can, in short, help steer the two opposing sides of the multicultural paradigm away from the excesses of (1) extolling the values of one culture while denying validity to others and (2) encouraging the notion of victimization and minority ethnocentrism. It has been suggested by Bowser, Jones, and Young (1995, 180) that, in the future, in the course of a university education, students should ideally "master their own as well as one or two other social cultures" while emphasizing common threads that unite cultures and their appearance across disciplines. Such an outcome would of necessity require the training of cross-cultural faculty, domestically and internationally. Foreign language educators in particular can play a vital role in the establishment of a common core of multicultural knowledge, since the foreign language class is, and has been, inherently multicultural. Perhaps in no other course are students required to confront their views of themselves and those of others in quite the same way. In this multicultural environment, they are asked not only to tolerate what may be an alien culture but also to transcend their ethnocentric limitations by accepting the target language and culture as legitimate means through which learning can take place.

Because language transmits culture and is, in turn, transmitted by cultural means, value orientations can serve as a bridge joining grammar and literary, as well as nonliterary, texts to sociocultural and historical contexts (Dimen-Schein 1977, 35). By using the Kluckhohn matrix to study the similarities and differences across cultures, the language teacher can move beyond the "folk dances, festivals, fairs, and food" approach (seen so often in elementary texts) to one that fosters a deeper understanding of the diverse beliefs, values, and practices of the target culture (Omaggio 1993, 360). Furthermore, by including the study of not only literary works but also that of aesthetic manifestations of high culture such as painting, sculpture, architecture, music, and political and historical discourse, one can transform a language class into a cross-disciplinary course. This would help students take a major step toward reaching not only oral proficiency standards but cultural proficiency standards as well (Ortuño 1994, 500).

In conclusion, the challenge of education today is to prepare students to function in a multicultural and interdependent world of international cooperation and competition—a world in which we can no longer afford to be complacently monocultural or monolingual. Value orientations provide students and educators at all levels with a comparative perspective of cultures, domestic and international, which can help prepare them for the diversity they will encounter at home as well as for firsthand cross-cultural opportunities abroad. Inevitably, with interaction comes conflicts, and value orientations can serve to identify and manage these by enabling students and educators to see that differences can be enriching resources that lead to a fuller understanding of self and others. The university plays a vital role in this process. It should strive to be truly universal in its search for truth through the history, accomplishments, strengths, and weaknesses of all humankind and in its recognition that knowledge is not absolute but belongs to all (Bowser, Jones, and Young, 185). It will be the responsibility of individual communities, schools, and universities to decide how to address the thorny issues of what constitutes the core that holds a multicultural society together and what are the most equitable ways of achieving fairness through awareness in a pluralistic society. The Kluckhohn value orientations model can provide needed direction in the search for answers to those difficult questions.

References

Bowser, Benjamin P., Terry Jones, and Gale Auletta Young, eds. *Toward the Multicultural University.* Westport, CT: Praeger, 1995.

Brzezinski, Zbigniew. *Out of Control: Global Turmoil on the Eve of the 21st Century*. New York: Macmillan, 1993.

Darder, Antonia. *Culture and Power in the Classroom: A Critical Foundation for Bicultural Education*. New York: Bergin and Garvey, 1991.

Dimen-Schein, Muriel. *The Anthropological Imagination*. New York: McGraw-Hill, 1977.

Gonzalez, Juan C. "Once You Accept, Then You Can Teach." In *Teaching from a Multicultural Perspective*, 1-16. Thousand Oaks, CA: Sage, 1994.

Johns, Ann M. "Languages and Cultures in the Classroom." In *Teaching from a Multicultural Perspective*, 60–76. Thousand Oaks, CA: Sage, 1994.

Kempf, Franz R. "The Dialectic of Education: Foreign Language, Culture, and Literature." *ADFL Bulletin* 27 (1995): 38–46.

Kluckhohn, Florence R., and Fred L. Strodtbeck. *Variations in Value Orientations*. Evanston, IL: Row, Peterson, 1961.

Kohls, L. Robert. *Survival Kit for Overseas Living*. 3d ed. Yarmouth, ME: Intercultural Press, 1996.

Lou, Ray. "Teaching All Students Equally." In *Teaching from a Multicultural Perspective*, 28–45. Thousand Oaks, CA: Sage, 1994.

Malone, Julia. "'Indivisible': A Vanishing Word in U.S." *Waco Tribune Herald,* 15 January 1997, sec. A, 8.

Nieto, Sonia. *The Sociopolitical Context of Multicultural Education*, 2d ed. New York: Longman, 1995.

Omaggio Hadley, Alice. *Teaching Language in Context*. Boston: Heinle & Heinle, 1993.

Ortuño, Marian M. "Teaching Language Skills and Cultural Awareness with Spanish Painting." *Hispania* 77 (1994): 500–511.

———. "Cross-Cultural Awareness in the Foreign Language Class: The Kluckhohn Model." *Modern Language Journal* 75, no. 4 (1991): 449–59.

Ramirez, Manuel. "Cognitive Styles and Cultural Democracy in Action." In *Toward Multiculturalism: A Reader in Multicultural Education*, edited by Jaime S. Wurzel, 198–206. Yarmouth, ME: Intercultural Press, 1988.

Saravia-Shore, Marietta, and Steven F. Arvizu. *Cross-Cultural Literacy: Ethnographies of Communication in Multiethnic Classrooms*. New York: Garland Publishing, 1992.

Schlesinger, Arthur. *The Disuniting of America*. New York: Norton, 1992.

Stewart, Edward C., and Milton J. Bennett. *American Cultural Patterns: A Cross-Cultural Perspective*. Rev. ed. Yarmouth, ME: Intercultural Press, 1991.

U.S. Bureau of the Census. "Resident Populations, by Hispanic Origin Status, 1980 to 1997, and Projections, 1998 to 2050." In *Statistical Abstracts of the United States*. Washington: Government Printing Office, 1998, no. 19, 19.

Wurzel, Jaime S., ed. *Toward Multiculturalism: A Reader in Multicultural Education*. Yarmouth, ME: Intercultural Press, 1988.

Developing Student Awareness of Value Orientations: Building a Foundation for Multicultural Education

Ann D. Chapman

> *I don't know anyone who is different from me and I don't need to know them.*
> *I believe what my family has taught me to believe—my friends believe the same, so it must be the truth.*
> *The way I do things is the right way. Everybody I know does them this way.*

Ethnocentric statements and thoughts such as these are common among students as they enter my undergraduate education and graduate counseling classes. At professional meetings colleagues from universities throughout the country relate that they hear similar statements from their students (Kiselica and Locke 1996). Many college and university students are monocultural, have not left home psychologically, and have a worldview that is aware of and sensitive only to the culture in which they grew up. These students present a special challenge in the multicultural classroom.

National standards in both education and counselor education require that academic programs help students develop an understanding for and appreciation of multiculturalism (American Counseling Association 1995; National Council for the Accreditation of Teacher Education 1995). Therefore, professors in education and counselor education must learn how to better understand and overcome the resistance some students have toward the exploration of new worldviews and how to help students develop an appreciation of different cultures.

This article will describe one effective method, value orientations analysis (VOA), for helping monocultural students recognize the importance of understanding diverse worldviews. In order to appreciate why VOA is so effective with monocultural students in the multicultural classroom, it is helpful to be aware of the effects of identity status on students' reactions to multicultural content and the essential dimensions of multicultural education.

Student Identity Status and Multicultural Content

The author has found Marcia's (1966, 1976, 1989) work regarding identity statuses to be helpful in understanding and predicting student enthusiasm, interest, hesitancy, fear, and indifference regarding multicultural content. This ability to understand and predict has enhanced curriculum development.

According to Marcia, during the resolution of the late adolescence/young adulthood identity crisis defined by Erikson (1959, 1963), at any one point in time individuals are in one of four identity statuses. These statuses (*not* developmental stages) differ in two ways, depending on (1) whether or not the individual has been actively involved in developing a personal identity and (2) whether or not the individual has committed to values, beliefs, and a lifestyle or career.

The Four Identity Statuses

Two of the identity statuses indicate active involvement in the development of personal identity. In the *identity achievement* status, an individual has been actively involved in developing a personal identity and, as a result of this involvement, has committed to certain values, beliefs, and a lifestyle or career. In the *identity moratorium* status, an individual is currently involved in actively developing a personal identity but has not yet committed to a particular worldview.

The remaining two identity statuses indicate that active involvement in the development of a personal identity never occurred or ceased before a secure identity developed. In the *identity foreclosure* status, an individual has never been actively involved in developing a personal identity but has committed to certain values and a worldview by accepting the beliefs and goals of those (usually their parents) around them. In the *identity diffusion* status, an individual has not committed to a particular worldview or set of values and is not currently motivated to actively search for a personal identity (see Table 1).

Table 1: Identity Matrix

	Actively Involved	Not Actively Involved
Committed	identity achievement	identity foreclosure
Not committed	identity moratorium	identity diffusion

Identity Status and Student Reactions

Students who are most enthusiastic in their classroom exploration, examination, and comparison of worldviews and value systems fall into one of Marcia's two active involvement statuses described above. Students who are most similar to the identity achievement status are usually the older (over thirty years of age) graduate students and the more mature, nontraditional undergraduate students. They indicate through class or private discussions that they have considered their personal beliefs and attitudes and are quite knowledgeable about and secure in their personal worldview and values. This self-awareness and security appear to enable these students to look beyond themselves and to appreciate and respect differing value systems. They do not fear that an understanding of other values and worldviews will result in the loss of their own. Perhaps because they have questioned, explored, and conceivably altered their views once before, the prospect of the personal change that could result from further questioning and exploring is not fear-inducing for these students.*

Another group of students who enthusiastically embrace multicultural education consists of those who are in the process of forming a personal identity. These students fall mostly into Marcia's identity moratorium status and tend to be traditional-age undergraduate and graduate students. While completing the normal developmental task of identity achievement (Erikson 1959, 1963), these students express their eagerness to learn about and compare the

* It should be noted that the author has also had a few students who would be classified as identity achievers whose self-awareness has led to rigidity and a total lack of interest in knowing about other worldviews and cultures. These students will complete all assignments with little complaint. However, they express disagreement with and dislike for differing values and will not allow the new knowledge or experiences to impinge on their current worldviews.

worldviews and value systems into which they were acculturated with those from other cultures and diverse groups. They fall along a continuum from those who want to confirm beliefs with which they are already fairly comfortable to those who currently do not feel connected to any belief system and are searching for a worldview with which they are compatible. Regardless of where they are on this continuum, these students want to absorb as much multicultural information as possible.

Students who developed their personal identity without active personal involvement provide a great challenge in the multicultural classroom. Those students are similar to those defined in Marcia's identity foreclosure status and are found largely among graduate students. They have simply accepted (without question) the values, attitudes, and beliefs of their family, friends, and immediate environment. They have not chosen to avoid exploration and questioning; the idea of doing so has simply never occurred to them and the need to do so has never presented itself. Most of these students have grown up, gotten married, and currently live in one region. They enjoy the comfort, peace, and connectedness they feel among those who are like them.

For these students the multicultural class is their first opportunity, or challenge, to experience the normal developmental process of active identity examination. The idea of questioning or challenging their personal worldviews and value systems, especially when presented as a requirement in a class, seems a bit ridiculous to these students, but most will cooperate—initially. As it becomes clear that peers whom they believed were just like them actually have worldviews and value systems that differ from their own, these students react with a combination of skepticism and pride. There is doubt about a process that brings into question the similarity they had assumed between themselves and their friends. However, pride and deeper interpersonal understanding emerge as the class members discuss similarities and justify differences in their basic values and personal interpretations of heritage. Nevertheless, when worldviews and value systems that differ dramatically from theirs are presented and discussed in a manner that indicates respect for diverse worldviews, it is not uncommon for these students to express varying degrees of antipathy for the whole process. Upon inquiry, many will disclose fear that this exploration of differing worldviews may cause them to question beliefs that they cannot change without disrupting their lives and, therefore, they balk at such examination. The professor's acceptance of the emotional struggle of these students is essential and will often enable them to risk the exploration.

The second group of students who provide a particular challenge in the multicultural classroom are similar to those in Marcia's identity diffusion status. Although these students may have in the past attempted unsuccessfully to define their values, they currently find the whole area of worldviews and values to be irrelevant and uninteresting or, perhaps, threatening. They are not antagonistic and usually complete requirements in a perfunctory manner. However, they absent themselves from class psychologically and physically whenever possible. These students do not reveal enough about themselves for the professor to even hypothesize a cause beyond disengagement for their lack of interest. Very few students fall into this group, either among graduate or undergraduate students, and many who appear to be in this category at the beginning of the semester later fit better in the identity foreclosure status.

Undergraduate and Graduate Identity Status Distribution

As mentioned earlier, student identity statuses are determined informally by the professor, based on student comments in class or in private discussions regarding current or previous value exploration and commitment. The distribution of the four statuses differs in graduate and undergraduate classes, as also observed in the foregoing pages. In the author's regional, open-admission, tuition-driven institution in a state where graduate work is required for teachers, the identity status of students in her typical graduate multicultural counseling classes are distributed as follows:

Foreclosure	50-55%
Achievement	25-40%
Moratorium	10-20%
Diffusion	0-5%

Her typical undergraduate classes, however, are distributed differently:

Moratorium	45-55%
Foreclosure	20-35%
Achievement	10-20%
Diffusion	5-20%

Essential Multicultural Learning Domains

Vacc, DeVaney, and Whittmer (1995) suggest that to be most effective, multicultural counseling classes must include affective, cognitive, and experiential content. This same paradigm is appropriate for all multicultural education. The cognitive is essential as a knowledge base. We cannot respect or appreciate that which we do not know. However, particularly in the area of multiculturalism, long-standing attitudes, emotions, and feelings of both the dominant and minority cultures must also be examined. One problem with political correctness can be a focus on verbal or cognitive valuing without an accompanying affective appreciation. Experiential learning is also essential. In the area of multiculturalism, it is quite possible (in fact, common) for an individual to have intellectual knowledge about and abstract caring for a different cultural group but still find direct interaction with a member of that cultural group to be uncomfortable or even frightening. Only direct experiential learning can alleviate that discomfort. Further, the author has found that experiential activities increase positive affective learning and instill a desire for knowledge about a group.

Thus, the multicultural educator must consider how to facilitate learning in the cognitive, affective, and experiential domains for every identity status represented in the class (see Table 2). To be most effective, a multicultural class must have a teaching/learning component that fulfills the learning need in each of the three learning domains.

Table 2
Grid for Student Identity Statuses and Essential Multicultural Learning Domains

Identity Status	Multicultural Learning Domain		
	Cognitive	Affective	Experiential
Achievement			
Moratorium			
Foreclosure			
Diffusion			

Effective Approaches in Multicultural Education

To accomplish what is needed, the instructor or professor can use several approaches. Many of the methods mentioned below enhance learning in more than one essential domain. However, the methods are listed only in the domain they most directly influence.

Approaches for Specific Domains

Methods used successfully by the author to enhance *cognitive* learning include (1) assigned reading, (2) traditional lecture, (3) diverse guest speakers, (4) films, and (5) student reports (which must include affective and experiential as well as informational components) regarding minority populations.

In regard to *affective* learning, important elements of the class include the expression, exploration, discussion, and analysis of both personal and minority attitudes, behaviors, and value orientations patterns (Kluckhohn and Strodtbeck 1961). Class members try out nonverbal communication styles of minority cultures in order to compare the resulting affective component with that of their usual nonverbal style. The students, in groups, also build statues that reflect selected positive and negative aspects of their personal cultural backgrounds. These statues often provide new insights into the attitudes of both the statue builders and the observers.

Finally, for *experiential* learning, students participate in a wide variety of out-of-the-classroom activities such as (1) visiting and socializing with people of minority-group background, (2) eating ethnic foods, and (3) attending minority activities and celebrations. These experiential activities are both formal (arranged by the professor) and informal (arranged by the student).

A Method for All Domains—Value Orientations Analysis

Each of the above methods makes a unique and valuable contribution toward meeting the cognitive, affective, and experiential learning needs of the variety of students found in a typical multicultural class. However, there is one method that, more than any other classroom activity listed, can be adapted to promote cognitive, affective, and experiential learning among students in all identity statuses: value orientations analysis (Chapman 1993). The VOA process consists of the development of six phases of awareness: exterior self-awareness, integrated self-awareness, difference awareness, micro- and mesosystem awareness, cultural awareness, and experiential awareness. The author has found that the study of value orientations is most effective when it begins with application to the self, then moves through application to others, institutions, and social and educational programs and, finally, is applied to cultures and direct experience with members of minority populations.

Exterior Self-Awareness. The first awareness phase, exterior self-awareness, begins with students completing an instrument that will help them develop an awareness of their personal value orientations ordering. Two such instruments are the pencil-and-paper Value Orientations Questionnaire (Green and Haymes 1973) and the computerized Value Orientations Survey (Florence R. Kluckhohn Center for the Study of Values 1995).† After the instrument is completed, information about value orientations theory and its applications is presented. Students are then given the results of their value orientations assessment. This content is purely cognitive and informational. Students can disagree with the orderings resulting from the instrument and replace them with others. Reasons for the replacements are accepted but not required at this time. Since the content is objective, self-descriptive, and open to question, interested students find this exercise motivating, while cautious students find it nonthreatening.

Integrated Self-Awareness. Integrated self-awareness is a natural expansion of students' initial examination of the validity of their instrument-determined value orientations ordering. During this phase students are asked to write a brief paper giving examples of their behaviors, beliefs, feelings, or attitudes that validate the correctness of their value orientations ordering. This exercise involves both cognitive (thoughts and beliefs) and affective (feelings and attitudes) dimensions. The students begin to see how value orientations ordering is an integral part of their lives. They begin to accept the validity of value orientations intellectually and personally. Also, although the content in this awareness phase is subjective as well as objective, affective as well as cognitive, it is still purely descriptive. Only rarely has the author had students who were less than enthusiastically involved in the process at this point.

† The Green and Haymes instrument can be obtained from the author of this article (1840 Traveller Road, Lexington, KY 40504). The computerized Value Orientations Survey can be obtained from the Florence R. Kluckhohn Center for the Study of Values (119 N. Commercial, Room 820, Bellingham, WA 98225).

Difference Awareness. The third awareness phase, difference awareness, results in an awareness among students that the individuals in their class differ in their value orientations ordering. Class value orientations orderings are listed on the board or in a computer printout. The reasons for the orderings and their impact on students' lives are discussed. Student reaction to the differences is varied. At one end of the continuum are those who are not surprised and find the divergence interesting and motivating. At the other end of the continuum are students, often the ones in identity foreclosure status, who are shocked to discover that they differ from the friends they have made in class and, sometimes, have known for years.

In this classroom situation with friendly acquaintances and longtime friends, students *want* to bridge differences rather than create gaps. For example, the student who places least emphasis on Lineal and most on Individual in Kluckhohn's Human Relations dimension has quite a different approach to life from the student who places most emphasis on Lineal and least on Individual. When students discover this difference, as two good friends did one semester, they can argue over who is correct, agree to differ, or attempt to understand and bridge the difference. Because of the value orientations assumption that all people value the same orientations with varying degrees of emphasis, value orientations theory facilitates bridging between differing value systems. "I value what you value, but with a different emphasis" becomes a basis for conversation rather than argument. It is very important to stress that the differences are not absolute but a matter of emphasis. Students learn they can understand and respect differences while maintaining their own value systems. Thus, during the difference awareness phase students learn "bridging" skills, or how to connect with and respect, cognitively and emotionally, individuals with different value orderings. The two friends mentioned above used their new difference awareness to explain behaviors they had previously found irritating, and both indicated a deepened understanding of and respect for the other. The learning during this awareness phase is more affective and experiential (as students encounter each other) than cognitive. The difference awareness phase is difficult for foreclosure status students. However, most participate fully and try to understand the value orderings of their peers. On the other hand, students who are in identity diffusion status tend to be only passively involved in the process during the difference awareness phase.

It is not unusual for them to indicate that, although they will comply in a perfunctory manner, they are not interested in comparing, contrasting, and understanding values.

Micro- and Mesosystem Awareness. Micro- and mesosystem awareness begins to move students beyond self, friends, and the classroom into the world. The terms *microsystem* and *mesosystem* are based on Bronfenbrenner's (1979, 1988) work and include those aspects of an individual's environment that in some way impinge directly on him or her. In this phase, students use a process developed by the author (Chapman 1981) to analyze the value orientations ordering of a public figure, institution, or program that affects them personally and to compare that ordering with their own. They explore potential areas of conflict and consider ways to decrease the probability of its arising. Most of the students come to a better understanding of conflict situations in their own lives and often find new ways to deal with work-related problems they are experiencing. Micro- and mesosystem awareness is less personally involving and less threatening than difference awareness to students who are in an identity foreclosure or identity diffusion status. The learning is largely cognitive and objective, though it has some affective components.

Cultural Awareness. Cultural awareness involves the introduction of value orientations ordering as a descriptor of culture and a representation of cultural and subcultural similarities and differences. This awareness involves affective and cognitive exploration, and it can be difficult for students with little experience in questioning or defending their personal value systems. Caucasian students who have thought of themselves as nothing but Americans and who believe that everyone believes just as they do can be quite shocked to discover that their value systems differ in many ways from what research (Kluckhohn and Strodtbeck 1961; Wagner and Hald 1986; Carter 1991) has found to be the dominant American value system. This discovery can be especially difficult when students find that their value orientations orderings are most similar to those of a minority group. At this point some foreclosure status students will retreat into passive resistance for a period of time that varies from a part of one class period to the remainder of the semester. However, with encouragement and support from the instructor and others in the class, most of these students either immediately or within a short period of time use the bridging skills they have developed in previous awareness phases to develop a better understanding of their relationship to the dominant culture and to minority cultures. They begin to see that as counselors or teachers they must consider and respect cultural differences and similarities.

Experiential Awareness. The sixth and final awareness phase, experiential awareness, requires that students interact directly with a member of an ethnic or racial group other than their own.† These interactions often include meals, observations, social activities, and a conversation in which value orientations are discussed. The knowledge and understanding obtained and the bridging skills developed in the previous phases have prepared students to engage in a respectful conversation regarding values, attitudes, beliefs, and behaviors with individuals from differing subcultures. Students may design the discussion as they wish; however, most begin the conversation by explaining value orientations theory and by describing their value orderings and the attitudes, beliefs, and behaviors associated with them. They then help the individual with whom they are interacting to describe his or her value ordering. This leads naturally to a discussion of similarities and differences in their attitudes, beliefs, and behaviors. The main difficulty students report concerning this exercise is ending the conversations, which they find to be personally involving and very interesting. This awareness phase is focused on experiential learning, but there are clear affective and cognitive components as well. Some students who are in identity foreclosure or identity diffusion status find the direct interaction regarding values, attitudes, beliefs, and behaviors too difficult to take on individually and participate by accompanying another student and observing the exchange.

The author has found the use of the awareness phases framework to be most effective when implemented in the order described. However, there is nothing sacred about the order, and classes consisting of differing combinations of identity statuses may even skip phases. For example, a recent class of the author's seemed to intuitively grasp the micro- and mesosystem awareness phase and went almost directly from integrated self-awareness to cultural aware-

† Although students may initially feel awkward at the prospect of asking someone to spend time with them and to share about their cultural subgroup, almost always they find that the individual is very pleased by their interest. The key is that the student be genuinely interested in the individual and his or her culture.

ness. The progression proposed in this article is only a suggested framework for faculty who would like to introduce value orientations into their multicultural classes. The beauty of the technique, like the beauty of the theory, is its flexibility and variability.

Conclusion

Multicultural education is not an option in undergraduate teacher education and graduate counselor training. It is an imperative. Teaching and counseling require sensitivity to and appreciation of differing cultural backgrounds. Faculty in these areas must find ways to understand and overcome resistance in their students. The identity status of students can help predict which of them may resist multicultural content, especially in the affective and experiential domains. Classroom value orientations analysis is an effective approach with most students. All three important learning domains—cognitive, affective, and experiential—are involved. Points of resistance can be predicted, prepared for, and ameliorated. Finally, the method is flexible and can be adapted to the needs of the individual classroom.

References

American Counseling Association. "Code of Ethics and Standards of Practice." *Kentucky Counseling Association Journal* 14 (1995): 33–40.

Bronfenbrenner, U. "Interacting Systems in Human Development." In *Persons in Context: Developmental Processes,* edited by N. Bolger, A. Caspi, G. Downey, and M. Moorehouse, 25–49. New York: Cambridge University Press, 1988.

———. *The Ecology of Human Development*. Cambridge: Harvard University Press, 1979.

Carter, Robert T. "Cultural Values: A Review of Empirical Research and Implications for Counseling." *Journal of Counseling and Development* 70, no. 1 (1991): 164–73.

Chapman, Ann D. "Educational Applications of Kluckhohn's Value Orientations Theory: Focus on Two Graduate Education Classes." Paper presented at the Kluckhohn Values Symposium, Seattle, WA, October 1993.

———. "Value Orientation Analysis: The Adaptation of an Anthropological Model for Counseling Research." *Personnel and Guidance Journal* 59 (1981): 637–43.

Erikson, Erik. *Childhood and Society,* 2d ed. New York: W. W. Norton, 1963.

———. *Identity and the Life Cycle.* New York: International Universities Press, 1959.

Florence R. Kluckhohn Center for the Study of Values. "User's Manual for the Value Orientations Method." Bellingham, WA, 1995.

Green, L., and M. Haymes. "Value Orientations and Psychosocial Adjustment at Various Levels of Marijuana Use." *Journal of Youth and Adolescence* 2, no. 3 (1973): 213–31.

Kiselica, M. S., and Don Locke. "Can We Confront Racism without Undermining Appreciation for Cultural Diversity?" Discussion session at the Third National Association for Counselor Education and Supervision Conference, Portland, OR, October 1996.

Kluckhohn, Florence R., and Fred L. Strodtbeck. *Variations in Value Orientations*. Evanston, IL: Row, Peterson, 1961.

Marcia, J. E. "Identity and Intervention." *Journal of Adolescence* 12 (1989): 401–10.

———. "Identity Six Years Afterwards: A Follow-Up Study." *Journal of Youth and Adolescence* 5 (1976): 145–60.

———. "Development and Validation of Ego Identity Status." *Journal of Personality and Social Psychology* 3 (1966): 551–58.

National Council for the Accreditation of Teacher Education. *Standards, Procedures and Policies for the Accreditation of Professional Education Units.* Washington, DC: National Council for the Accreditation of Teacher Education, 1995.

Vacc, N., S. DeVaney, and J. Whittmer. *Experiencing and Counseling Multicultural and Diverse Populations*. Muncie, IN: Accelerated Press, 1995.

Wagner, Eric A., and Lawrence G. Hald. "Sport as a Reflector of Change: Football, Wilderness Sport and Dominant American Values." *Arena Review* 10, no. 1 (1986): 43–54.

Value Orientations and Foreign Language Study

Marian M. Ortuño

Before the Second World War, most foreign language instruction in the United States centered around the development of literary skills—reading and writing. From the beginning of the twentieth century, the techniques used in teaching modern foreign languages were not unlike those employed by teachers of classical languages. Students would be given grammatical rules to memorize and then be required to read and translate materials of increasing difficulty.

During World War II, it became very apparent that those individuals trained in the so-called "classical manner" were not capable of interrogating prisoners, understanding foreign radio broadcasts, or communicating with the Allies (Lisken-Gasparro 1987, 2). The changes that the U.S. Foreign Service Institute then implemented in order to address the pressing national need for developing *practical* skills in foreign language penetrated academia and provided the dynamic behind what has come to be known as the *oral proficiency movement*. This new approach emphasized the development of oral skills and practical communication, especially listening and speaking. To this day, emphasis on practical applicability has been the driving force behind virtually all foreign language instruction in this country. Nevertheless, in considering the four skills of listening, speaking, reading, and writing, one realizes that a crucial component is missing. For students to be able to function adequately in a host country, good language skills are not enough. Miscommunication can result because of a basic ignorance of cultural differences.

More recently, teachers and writers of textbooks have come to realize that culture cannot be separated from language. But what exactly constitutes "culture," and how does one incorporate it into the curriculum? Most authors of texts, as language professionals with some experience abroad, have at least a subjective "sense" of what constitutes culture, and their attempts to incorporate it into the curriculum range from the naive to the sophisticated—from instructions on how to make a Spanish "tortilla" (a potato-egg omelet) or more cryptic advice in the form of "dos" and "don'ts" to an understanding of underlying Spanish and Latin American assumptions and values.

For instance, one textbook author recommends, when you are in Latin America, "don't be open, frank and direct about feelings, like most North Americans," because Latin Americans consider such verbal expressions too blunt and rude. Instead, the author advises, be tactful and diplomatic, because "... in Latin America, it is better to tell people what they want to hear rather than to disturb them with the unpleasant truth" (Hendrickson 1986, 394). To the unprepared, this information comes across, at best, as a peculiarity of behavior. At worst, it could lead to misinterpretation and the reinforcement of stereotypes. The inquisitive student cannot help but ask why.

The introduction to another recently published textbook explains, "No attempt has been made to present a complete cultural view, but rather to convey 'impressions' of life in Spain, Latin America, and the United States as seen through the eyes of Hispanic writers, artists and commercial advertisers" (Marks and Blake 1989, preface). The weakness of this approach is that one cannot convey cultural awareness and understanding through "impressions." One needs a metric, an organizing principle, to accomplish this.

I have found that the Kluckhohn taxonomy of value orientations provides the type of systematic schedule needed for analyzing a particular culture, for answering the question "Why?" So when differences in behavior patterns do emerge, they can be understood and analyzed within a framework that, at a glance, highlights one community's response to a particular issue against the backdrop of other possible responses.

Perhaps in no other university course do cultural differences collide so dramatically and with such lasting impact as in a foreign language class. A challenge immediately presents itself to the instructor from the very first day of class because quite often the courses are required, and that means that one's audience might be somewhat less than receptive to new sounds, ideas, and ways of looking at life. Some linguistics experts have even gone so far as to say that no matter how motivated the prospective learner may be, the process involved in learning a foreign language and culture is so unique that it threatens the individual's sense of self in a way that no other discipline seems to do. Since language and culture are major factors in the development of an individual's social identification, coming face-to-face with a new system clearly involves a reevaluation of one's old system. Reliance on the Kluckhohn model puts the instructor in an ideal position to guide students through this reevaluation process—to shake the foundations of their cultural prejudices and to make them more receptive to the language and culture of another people.

The Kluckhohn model I use is the original, along with an adaptation done by L. Robert Kohls, who, in his *Survival Kit for Overseas Living* (1996), has simplified the categories and has explained each one in terms the average person can understand (85). Most of the time students can readily see that U.S. values come straight down the right-hand side of the chart. By asking leading questions, I can get them to identify what may be termed Hispanic values. By asking leading questions, I can get them to identify what may be termed "pan-Hispanic" values. I refer here to core values shared by the Spanish-speaking cultures in the Americas and the mother country, Spain. I do not wish to minimize cross-cultural or intercultural distinctiveness, nor do I want to imply that culture is linguistically determined. Nevertheless, the peoples of Spain and Spanish America will, on a very basic level, tend to identify more with certain core, pan-Hispanic values than with the dominant values of the more culturally distant United States. The students can now determine this for themselves by looking at Kohls' modification of the Kluckhohn model. I ask, "What does our culture have in common with the cultures of the Spanish-speaking world?" The chart reveals striking evidence—"We seem to have nothing in common!" When Florence R. Kluckhohn came to that same conclusion back in 1959, she went on to elaborate, "The value system of the Spanish Americans [i.e., those living in the southwestern United States], a system which has been, and still is, in most respects, a mirror image of the dominant American culture, has been a key factor in the extremely low rate of assimilation of Spanish-Americans into the dominant American culture" (1961, 355).

To give students at all levels, elementary to advanced, some practice in using the Kluckhohn model, I invite them to solve cultural miniproblems. We begin with an explanation of the folk wisdom in Spanish proverbs, a technique suggested by Kohls (28–30). For instance, "*La plenitud no está en lograr lo que anhelas sino en valorar lo que tienes*" ("Fulfillment is not in achieving what you desire, rather in valuing what you already have"). I ask my students, "How would you change this proverb to match American cultural values?" Of course, you reverse it—the mirror image Florence Kluckhohn referred to—and you read, "Fulfillment is in achieving what you desire rather than in being contented with what you have."

At the intermediate level, where we can discuss culture in Spanish, we practice using the Kluckhohn model by analyzing more elaborate versions of the miniproblem. These descriptions of situations involving individuals who have varying degrees of language skills but little or no cultural literacy are based on actual personal experiences. They dramatically point out that linguistic skills alone are often not enough to enable a person to function adequately in a foreign environment. In small groups, students discuss and analyze the roots of a particular conflict and then offer suggestions as to how the resulting negative psychological reaction could have been avoided. Here are some examples.

Situation One

An American man in a Madrid subway, who, being very democratically minded, gives up his seat to a rather scruffy-looking gypsy mother and her baby. Suddenly he notices that he's getting dirty looks from disapproving *madrileños*. As reprehensible as this attitude may be from a moral standpoint, the reactions of the Spaniards can be explained in terms of the Human Nature and Human Relations orientations. Some people are simply undesirable—that is, inherently not good because of what they are—gypsies, for instance. They are not part of "my social group" of decent individuals, the average Spaniard reasons. Their system of values is at odds with the dominant system, and to the Spaniard, they conform to the stereotype. They lie, cheat, steal, and are a blight on society. Yet, in an interesting variant of the dominant Activity orientation—Being—through their own individual efforts (Doing), gypsies become perfectly acceptable socially should they achieve fame as performers—bullfighters and flamenco singers and dancers. This, incidentally, provides a parallel to a similar situation with minorities in U.S. culture, where success in the fields of sports and entertainment leads to social acceptability.

Situation Two

An American tourist in Madrid who speaks some Spanish enters a small fruit and vegetable market. All of the produce is displayed in open boxes, and since the woman needs only four peaches, she begins to examine the fruit and chooses the ones she wants, very much like she would do in the United States. All of a sudden the proprietor appears and begins to reprimand her in a very unpleasant tone of voice. The woman puts back the fruit and leaves, feeling confused and upset.

Situation Three

An American professor manages to rent an apartment in Madrid for himself and his family for a stay of two months. When he complains to a Spanish friend that the rent is two thousand dollars a month, instead of the anticipated sympathetic response, the friend replies, "Why complain? You ought to be proud that you are a professional man capable of paying that much for an apartment."

Situation Four

A young American couple, who speak Spanish well, check into a hotel in Lérida, Spain. The desk clerk tells them there are plenty of rooms available. Minutes later, a British woman, traveling alone and dressed very casually, also enters the hotel. She has been driving all night and looks it. When she asks for a room, the desk clerk tells her the hotel is full. When the American couple tries to intercede on her behalf, the desk clerk says, "If you want her in your room, we'll give you an extra bed."

As one can see, conflicts in almost all five of the basic orientations come into play in these four situations. In Situation One, apart from the Human Nature conflict, a secondary conflict arises involving different perceptions of Human Relations. Before hastily condemning the Spaniards for what appears to be overt prejudice, students are encouraged to examine more closely the sincerity and depth of social acceptance displayed by Americans in their dealings with those of "other groups." Quite often the American cultural value of equality is severely restricted (Stewart and Bennett 1991, 93). Similarly, in Situation Four the values of an American couple steeped in the belief of equal treatment for all (at least superficially) collide with those of a Spaniard who acknowledges social hierarchies. He displays a greater sensitivity to "analog" perception, that is, perception based on observed physical data such as nonverbal behavior (29). For the innkeeper, as discriminatory as it may seem from the American standpoint, outward appearances mark the English tourist as a person of dubious moral character and definitely not the sort of clientele he would welcome in a respectable establishment.

Again we see a conflict in the area of Human Relations. Americans have a segmented view of the individual which enables them to overlook what might be considered objectionable aspects of a person's character or lifestyle and to focus on that person's essential "humanness" (90). The Spaniard, for whom the group takes precedence over the individual, views others in their totality as either acceptable or not. A foreign woman traveling alone and inappropriately attired is clearly unacceptable. The innkeeper has no qualms about equality and fair play. His concerns center on group pressure as he ponders, "What will the 'respectable' people in the hotel say if I give a room to someone who looks like a woman of ill repute?"

In Situation Two conflicts in the Time, Activity, and Human Relations dimensions subtly combine to produce negative emotional reactions in both parties. The American tourist is clearly impatient and concerned only with accomplishing her task in the most expeditious manner possible. In her self-perception as an individual, she sees no need to waste time in greeting the proprietor and waiting to be served. Had the woman been a little more culturally sensitive and less inclined toward literally "taking matters into her own hands" (Doing, on the Kluckhohn scale), she could have quickly learned the appropriate mode of social interaction required in this situation by observing other customers. Students are often surprised to discover that the independence, self-reliance, and action-oriented problem solving displayed in this situation and so highly valued in American culture, are seen as aggressively rude and inappropriate in other cultures.

Time, Person-Nature Relationship, Activity, and Human Relations overlap to form the root of the conflict in Situation Three. The American's frugality is seen as distasteful by the Present-oriented Spaniard. He believes in enjoying the fruits of one's labors now. After all, who knows what the future will bring? This fatalistic attitude (Subjugation to unknown forces of Nature) is countered by the American's view toward the future and what he feels he can do to take control of his destiny (Mastery over Nature). One way is to sacrifice a little of the present through frugality and personal deprivation to ensure a more secure future. Form of Activity comes into play in the attitude of the Spaniard for whom "Being" is far more important than "Doing." If part of your social identity (Human Relations) derives from group membership, what better way to show others that you belong to a more prestigious social and professional class than through conspicuous consumption? So while frugality and saving money for the future through self-deprivation now may seem like prudent and highly laudable actions to most Americans, some Spaniards might, under certain circumstances, view these as foolish and incomprehensible.

The practice gained in discussing the issues that surround these and other cultural "minipuzzles" helps sensitize students to cross-cultural differences. With the aid of the value orientations model, they begin to straddle two cultures and learn how to avoid areas of potential conflict when dealing with foreigners in a foreign environment.

A cultural explanation can also help students immensely in comprehending grammar that has no parallel in English. An example is the so-called reflexive for unplanned occurrences, which can be explained by looking at the Human Relations category of the Kluckhohn model. In this construction, the individual refuses to accept personal responsibility for an action and instead blames the unfortunate result (usually forgetting, dropping, breaking) on an inanimate object. For instance, the sentence, "*Se me cayó el libro*" is translated into correct English as "I dropped the book." What the sentence literally means is, "The book fell from me." In other words, I had nothing to do with it; it was the book's fault. It often comes as a surprise to students that peoples of other cultures may not be so eager to implicate themselves personally in a failed enterprise—even on a largely unconscious grammatical level.

At the advanced level of foreign language study, literature figures more prominently in traditional course offerings. In our rapidly changing, technology-centered world, students today are not as oriented toward the written word as in years past. The study of literature for literature's sake does not justify, in many modern students' minds, the often considerable investment of time and energy they must make in the struggle to comprehend a foreign text.

With the help of the Kluckhohn model I can show these students that literature (part of what I call High Culture or "Culture" with a capital *C*) is a vital key in revealing the behaviors and attitudes of a people, that is, low culture or culture with a small *c*. A common misconception is that culture includes only big *C* categories—literature, art, music, and so forth. But as I try to point out, these artistic expressions contain within them a society's small *c* culture—that is, evidence of an integrated system of learned patterns of behavior.

At the intermediate or advanced levels of instruction, the themes that appear most frequently in anthology texts are male/female stereotypes, the Hispanic family, religion, political differences, and perhaps the most ubiquitous one of all—the Hispanic view of death. To introduce the latter topic we turn to the Kluckhohn model and see that attitudes toward death, a force of nature, fall into the category of perception of the world, Person-Nature orientations. The dominant American pattern appears on the right-hand side—"Mastery over Nature." We see a very definite separation between ourselves and nature, and we are driven to subdue and dominate most natural forces, death being no exception. Most other cultures, including the Hispanic, fall into the left-hand side—"Subjugation to Nature"—and feel that fate controls one's destiny and there is little one can do to change it.

Since my purpose in the classroom is not only to impart information but to encourage the students to speak Spanish, I often use a visual device such as a culturally relevant picture or slide to serve as the focal point of the discussion. In this instance, I show Juan de Valdes Leal's paintings *Triumph of Death* and its companion piece, *Finis Gloriae Mundi*, or *The End of the Worldly Glory.* Valdes Leal was born in Córdoba, Spain, in 1630 and was a disciple of the famous religious painter Francisco de Zurbarán, a master of the tenebrist technique. I introduce the slides by explaining that many times the way in which a culture sees death reveals much about its philosophy of life. We describe and interpret the symbols in these *memento mori* (reminder of death) paintings, including the Latin inscription in the first one, *In ictu oculi,* or "In the twinkling of an eye." As Brown describes the two paintings,

> **Death is a skeleton carrying a coffin, a shroud, and a scythe, who disdainfully extinguishes the candle of life. The eyeless sockets seem to glower with satisfaction as the light goes out**

> on the symbols of greatness and power. In the twinkling of an eye, the sum of life's achievements is obscured by dark death. The second painting, ***Finis Gloriae Mundi (The End of the Worldly Glory)***, elaborates the theme of death by a chilling representation of sepulchral existence, where fragile human substance is...merely decomposing matter. Worldly glory ends in rot and decay. (1978, 128)

We next turn our attention to an example of Medieval poetry by Jorge Manrique (1440–1479), who wrote these verses as part of a much longer work in honor of his deceased father:

> Our lives are the rivers
> that flow into the sea
> which is death;
> there go those of noble estate
> their privileges ended
> and consumed;
> there go the largest rivers,
> there the others of medium size
> and the smallest;
> and upon arrival they are equal
> those who live by the work of their hands
> and the rich. (Darst 1988, 30, author's translation)

The thematic connection with the paintings is clear—even though the time span between the works is nearly two hundred years. By showing the slides and reading the poem, I illustrate that first, cultural attitudes have deep historical roots and second, that these attitudes change very, very slowly.

As far as Time sense is concerned, we in the United States look to technology and medical science to prolong life. We search for immortality in any number of ways. We quit smoking, we exercise, we engage in artistic creativity, and we donate our organs for transplantation. "Vehicles for transcendence" include not only our children but also a belief in "resurrection, reincarnation, metempsychosis" and efforts that result in "the preservation of some natural habitat or species of life" (Kearl 1989, 216–18). In our culture today we feel we have some personal control over death, and we cannot accept it with passive resignation. We want mastery over natural forces, and we want to spare others the burden of care. A life of poor quality is not worth living (194–95). We seek pleasure and avoid pain with our modern focus shifted from the concern for the health of the soul to a preoccupation with the health of the body.

This way of thinking stands in sharp contrast with the views expressed in Spanish writer Azorín's *Vida de un labrantín (Life of a Peasant Farmer)* (Martinez Ruiz [Azorin] 1987). Although set in early twentieth-century rural Spain, it nevertheless exemplifies certain attitudes and modes of behavior that after four centuries, still form part of the Spanish cultural mentality. The fatalism, the lack of motivation, the inability to see beyond the present moment, and the total resignation to the forces of nature become more comprehensible in terms of Human Relations, Time, and Activity:

> Sometimes there is a bad harvest, a mule dies, a member of the family becomes ill or there is no money to pay the taxes. The poor farmer does not break into sobs and curse; he says: "So! What can we do? God will show the way. God will take care of our needs." The poor man has no idea of the future. The future is the nightmare and torment of many people. The poor man does not worry about tomorrow. "Each day brings its woes, says the Gospel. Don't we have enough, with today's problems? If we worry about tomorrow, won't we have two problems, instead of one?" With the passing of time either the poor man or his wife will die. If his wife dies first, he will remain alone; his noble sense of resignation, his noble serenity will never leave him. A sigh will cross his lips every afternoon and he will exclaim, "So! What can we do? God's will be done." (49–50)

As I mentioned earlier, values are slow to change, and we see, not surprisingly, that the traditional Spanish attitude toward death persists well into the twentieth century. To illustrate this point, we read an article from the *Wall Street Journal,* 1984, titled: "Spaniards' Distaste for Life Insurance Leaves Industry There Languishing" (cited in Kearl, 40–41). Given our cross-cultural preparation, the fact that only nine out of every hundred Spaniards have life insurance comes as no surprise.

The article goes on to enumerate what life insurance salesmen must contend with in Spain.

> The mother of a drowned fisherman flatly refuses to accept his death benefit from an insurance company. A village priest rails against the trade, asking, "Who but God can insure life?"

> and the Socialist General Union of Workers denounces Spain's state-controlled telephone company for providing "scandalous" life insurance and pension coverage for top executives. "The average Spaniard lives from day to day," complains an insurance executive. "It's difficult for him to program twenty to thirty years ahead. He believes in fate." (41)

In conclusion, reliance on the Kluckhohn model to teach the cultural component in language and literature classes greatly enhances instructional effectiveness. It allows students to see areas of potential compatibility and incompatibility between cultures, and it provides them with a depth of understanding they would not have otherwise. In the words of one student:

> I thought that the Kluckhohn model was extremely important and very interesting. Because one culture often looks at another as strange, or irrational, I believe that being able to see, on paper, other cultures' beliefs and customs is very beneficial and even necessary for the United States. I really enjoy looking through the eyes of people in other cultures and being better able to understand how they view the world. The Kluckhohn model, in my opinion, is a necessary teaching aid, not only for students, but for people in all fields.

References

Brown, Jonathan. *Images and Ideas in Seventeenth-Century Painting.* Princeton, NJ: Princeton University Press, 1978.

Darst, David H., ed. *Sendas literarias: España.* New York: Random House, 1988.

Hendrickson, James M. *Poco a poco: Spanish for Proficiency.* Boston: Heinle & Heinle, 1986.

Kearl, Michael C. *Endings: A Sociology of Death and Dying.* New York: Oxford University Press, 1989.

Kluckhohn, Florence R., and Fred L. Strodtbeck. *Variations in Value Orientations.* Evanston, IL: Row, Peterson, 1961.

Kohls, L. Robert. *Survival Kit for Overseas Living.* 3d ed. Yarmouth, ME: Intercultural Press, 1996.

Lisken-Gasparro, Judith E. *Testing and Teaching for Oral Proficiency.* Boston: Heinle & Heinle, 1987.

Marks, Martha Alford, and Robert J. Blake. *Al corriente: Curso intermedio de español*. New York: Random House, 1989.

Martinez Ruiz, Jose [Azorín]. "Vida de un labrantín." In *Pasajes: Literatura*, 2d ed., edited by Mary Lee Bretz, Trisha Dvorak, and Carl Kirschner. New York: Random House, 1987: 47–50.

Stewart, Edward C., and Milton J. Bennett. *American Cultural Patterns: A Cross-Cultural Perspective*. Rev. ed. Yarmouth, ME: Intercultural Press, 1991.

Part 4

Value Orientations and Conflict Resolution

A Sharing of Subjectivities: The Values Project Northwest

Kurt W. Russo

As the principal investigator for the Values Project Northwest, I had the distinct honor of working with Dr. Florence R. Kluckhohn for a number of years prior to her death in 1987. I first learned of Dr. Kluckhohn from Dr. Fremont Lyden, who at that time was teaching in the Graduate School of Public Affairs at the University of Washington. I came to him at the behest of the Lummi Indians to find a research method that would allow for the measurement and comparison of differing cultural value systems. He did not hesitate to recommend the value orientations method, suggesting that I contact Dr. Kluckhohn at her home just north of Seattle.

Over a period of four years I worked with Dr. Kluckhohn and other members of the Values Project Northwest staff, applying her method in the Lummi Indian Nation and a number of public- and private-sector groups and agencies. Our aim was, first, to test the usefulness of the value orientations method in identifying variations in values between the Lummi Nation and the organizations whose decisions have an impact on the Nation. In addition, we worked with her to begin formulating a program that would apply the results of the values research to the design of cross-cultural workshops.

I would like here to share with you some of the results of the research and training project, now being administered by the Florence R. Kluckhohn Center for the Study of Values, and would like to dedicate this article to Dr. Kluckhohn and to Dr. George E. Taylor, who have served as an inspiration for all of us at the Center over the years.

The Research Phase

In 1982 the Values Project Northwest, under the tutelage of Dr. Kluckhohn, began with interviews of members of the Lummi Nation. Over a period of twelve months we completed 110 value orientations interviews (out of a total population of 2,600), utilizing the original survey (see Appendix A for the complete survey) set forth in the book *Variations in Value Orientations* (Kluckhohn and Strodtbeck 1961). Project staff and Lummi tribal trainees interviewed three generations in each of the twelve primary families in the Lummi Nation. Included in this sample population was a subgroup of Lummi gillnet fishers, selected at random from the fisheries enrollment register. I should add that we modified the survey slightly, asking each respondent to make not only the usual field of choices but also to select what he or she felt "most other Lummi Indians" would say was best in each of the survey situations.

Our original purpose was to field-test the value orientations method in a cross-cultural context and evaluate its ability to measure variations in orientations between groups who either worked with the Nation in joint ventures or were in conflict with them over the management of natural resources. We were also interested in the area of perceptual diversity and in determining how well the instrument would serve the purpose of identifying cross-cultural as well as intragroup stereotypes. Our next step was to complete value orientations interviews in a number of groups. Over a period of two years (1983–1985) we obtained permission to conduct value orientations interviews in a timber company (Weyerhaeuser Company), a public resource agency (the U.S. Forest Service: Mt. Baker-Snoqualmie National Forest), a private utility (Puget Sound Power and Light Company), a public utility (Seattle City Light); and a prominent financial institution (Rainier National Bank).

Each of these groups had experience working with the tribal community in general and the Lummi Nation in particular. Once again, we modified the original schedule for the five groups only to the extent of asking the respondents to answer, in each of the survey situations, what they felt "most others" in their group would feel is best and what they felt "most Lummi" would choose in each of the survey situations.

The analysis of the results was published in 1985 in the document, *The Values Project Northwest: Xwlemi* (Russo, et al.), with funding assistance from the Office of Trust Responsibilities (Department of the Interior). While time does not permit a comprehensive review of the results, I can elucidate some of the more important and interesting ones.

Looking first at the Time dimension, we found some important variations between the tribe and the other participating groups. In terms of the overall orientations, the Lummi pattern was *Present = Past > Future*, while each of the other groups had the profile of *Present > Future > Past*. Moreover, we found that most individuals in each of the four groups generally undervalued the importance of the Past orientation to the Lummi Indians.

In the Human Relations dimension, all of the groups, including most of the Lummi, had the same pattern: *Collaterality > Individualism > Lineality*. Among the subsample of Lummi fishers, however, the pattern was *Collaterality = Individualism > Lineality*. It is interesting that the Lummi fishers were significantly more Individualistic than any of the other groups or subgroups sampled. We also found that there was a marked tendency among the groups to underestimate the importance of both Collaterality and Individualism in the tribe and to overvalue the significance of the Lineal orientation.

In the Person-Nature dimension we found identical overall patterns in each of the nontribal groups, that is, *Mastery over > Harmony with > Subject to*. It is noteworthy that less than 10 percent of the respondents in the nontribal groups selected the Subject to orientation as either a first- or second-order preference. In the Lummi community, on the other hand, we found the pattern to be *Mastery over > Subject to > Harmony with*. The hidden variation in this dimension for the tribe was the meaning of "large-scale" forces (MN2 and MN4 in the original schedule), where *Subject to* Nature figured prominently in the pattern. Among the Lummi gillnet fishers we found the *Subject to* orientation even stronger, with an overall pattern of *Mastery over = Subject to > Harmony with*. Note that the "Harmony with" orientation was least preferred by the tribal members. This is especially important, for most of those interviewed outside the tribe thought the Lummi members would prefer "Harmony with" over the other two orientations.

Lastly, in the Activity dimension the research revealed that the Lummi were the most Doing-oriented of the groups. The tribe was the only group that identified with this orientation (both ideally and actually) in each of the Activity situations. Also worthy of note is that an average of 62 percent of the respondents in the nontribal groups believed the Lummi Indians would reject Doing in favor of the Being orientation in each of the Activity dimensions.

Once again, time does not permit me to delve into the implications of the data; our analysis is set forth in the aforementioned publication. What I can say is that the results were sufficiently informative and important to proceed with the training phase of the project.

Training Program

In 1987 the Values Project Northwest, under the auspices of the Kluckhohn Center, initiated the training phase of the program. The program consisted of the involvement of two new groups (the Washington State Department of Natural Resources (DNR) and Tacoma Public Utilities) as well as the Lummi Nation. In both instances, the groups found themselves at odds with the Lummi Nation over the management of cultural and religious sites, areas, and resources used for cultural and religious purposes. This highly contentious issue is focused on the use of specific sites for such Lummi traditional religious practices as spirit questing, ceremonial use of streams and rivers, and the use of forestlands for depositing ceremonial regalia. As important as the specific practices, however, were Lummi beliefs about nature and the environment that were at odds with those of the DNR and Tacoma Public Utilities and, indeed, with the core American belief system.

The format for the program was the same in both cases. Project staff first completed value orientations interviews in the two new groups, using the original schedule and the modifications mentioned earlier. Interviewees were selected on the basis of the extent to which their decisions influenced the use of resources that had a cultural value to the tribe. We next completed open-ended ("issue-oriented") interviews, in which we asked the respondents to speak freely about what they felt to be the most important and problematic issues in relation to the Lummi Nation. Similar open-ended interviews were also completed in the Lummi community.

After compiling and analyzing the data, the project staff designed, coordinated, and facilitated a series of workshops. In the case of the project with the DNR as well as the subsequent project with Tacoma Public Utilities, fifteen participants were drawn from the field of interviewees to take part in the workshop sessions. Fifteen tribal participants, drawn from various parts of the community, were also asked to take part.

In both projects we began with what we termed an in-house session. In the case of the DNR project, for example, we held a separate session first with the Nation, then with the agency. These two sessions were devoted to discussing the results of the interviews in their group. The participants worked through the information and discussed it in a number of formats, examining their own value environment. They were also presented with some of the results from the Value Orientations Survey given in the other group that might shed some light on significant similarities or differences between them.

This was followed by a joint session in which the two groups were brought together. The material for discussion was largely drawn from the open-ended interviews, but the format was designed with orientations in mind. During the half-day session, the two groups met in a variety of formats, including one-on-one as well as small- and large-group discussions, ending with a Talking Circle, a Native American tradition that provides everyone the opportunity to speak openly about any subject that is, at the moment, of greatest importance to them. The central activity for the one-on-one and small-group sessions was a critical incident exercise developed by project staff to elicit discussion variations in basic values that were identified in the course of the value orientations interviews. The incident developed for the session is presented below.

Critical Incident Exercise

> **The agency and representatives from the Lummi Nation are meeting to discuss clear-cutting in an area on state forestlands used by the Lummi community for traditional spiritual practices. Representatives from the agency have met with the community before on other issues but are largely unaware of the nature of cultural uses of state forestlands.The Lummi participants are respected for their knowledge of traditional cultural practices, but they seldom meet with outsiders. After presenting their plan for cutting the area, the agency representatives ask for comments from the Lummi community members. Instead of responding to the plan, the Lummi participants talk about the treaty and how it has been continually violated over the years by non-Indians, about how their parents were forced into boarding schools, about the loss of their language and the systematic stripping away of their culture and the taking of their lands, and other seemingly**

> **unrelated topics. To the great frustration of the agency representatives, the meeting ended without any further discussion of the plan.**
>
> **How would you characterize the expectations of the agency representatives?**
>
> **What do you think accounts for the behavior of the Lummi participants?**

The incident succeeded in promoting a candid discussion between the participants on the specific issue at hand (cutting in cultural-use sites) and directing them to the hidden dimension of the conflict: variations in orientations on the meaning and relevance, today, of the past. The nature of the incident sparked a frank and open dialogue on difficulties the participants had actually encountered in a variety of cross-cultural settings. Moreover, the agency participants heard from Lummi participants some of the reasons why the hearts and minds of their members were often guided by the past when talking about present-day issues. By delving beneath the issue at hand to the underlying variations in orientations, the participants were provided the opportunity to speak openly, often in the most personal terms, about differences that affect communication, cooperation, and cross-cultural understanding.

Following the joint session, we held a second round of in-house sessions. On this occasion, however, we delved more deeply into the orientations of the other group and how well, or how poorly, these orientations were predicted by the respondents. After presenting the data, the participants discussed the meaning and importance of the data for past or present conflicts and what the data meant for communication in the future.

A final joint session was then held. It has been our experience that this second session is in most workshops both more productive and more meaningful to the individuals involved. In the instance of the DNR and the Tacoma Public Utilities projects, a degree of bonding between the participants was clearly evident and there was a willingness—even an eagerness—to communicate at deeper levels.

The workshop sessions are generally followed by a series of meetings that we call the "Group of 10." Five participants from each group meet on three occasions in sessions facilitated by project staff. During these sessions the participants attempt to institutionalize the areas of understanding gained during the course of the workshops. In the case of the DNR these meetings resulted in an accord which laid the foundation for more meaningful consultation on cultural resource management. In the Tacoma Public Utilities project, the Group of 10 worked out a management plan for the construction of a hydroelectric plant in the vicinity of a culturally significant stream. In both cases, these agreements were, in the view of the participants, made possible by what they learned during the course of the workshops.

The Implications

Let's explore some of the implications of the Values Project Northwest research. To do so I would like to concentrate on the orientations and perceptions of the DNR vis-à-vis the Lummi Nation. Let us first look at the orientations for these two groups for all four of the value spheres.

	DNR Actual	Perceives Tribe	Lummi Actual
Time	PR > FU > PA	Present	PR = PA > FU
Relational	CO > IN > LI	Lineal	CO > IN> LI
Activity	DO > BE	Being	DO > BE
Person/Nature	OV > WI >SU	Harmony with	OV >SU >WI

We can see here both similarities and differences, but, on the whole, two distinctly divergent orientation systems. It is not enough to say, for example, that the Nation has a stronger Past orientation, and leave it at that. We should also consider that the content of the past (e.g., beliefs, concepts of the world, teachings of right and wrong behavior) is also markedly different between these two "core" cultures. To understand the importance of the variation between the two groups, it is important also to know how the content of their orientations differ—or collide. Let's examine this in four specific situations.

Situation 1: Private Knowledge versus Public Information

The tribe is attempting to protect from logging an area that is used today, as it has been in the past, for purposes of a religious ceremony. The DNR seeks more information about the site, but the tribe is unwilling to provide it. The agency, with its *Present > Future* orientation, believes that people should be willing to accommodate change (even in religious matters) and that the tribe (which they perceive as Present-oriented) is being deceptive or disingenuous, hiding behind the rubric of "culture." The tribe, for its part, is oriented to the Past = Present, where people endeavor to move the past forward and where what was once believed is still believed to be true today. Their teachings forbid them to talk about the subject of religious ceremonies with anyone outside the immediate family, and they interpret the behavior of the agency as yet more evidence of racism and an anti-Indian attitude.

Looking at the Human Relations dimension, we see common ground, but again we must bear in mind the context of culture. What the two groups share is the desire to belong to, and identify with, a group. What differs is the nature of the group to which they belong. The tribe, unlike the agency, is a community of interrelated families in daily contact with each other, where consensus is an operative principle. In the agency, on the other hand, organizational hierarchy limits the actualization of the Collateral orientation.

Situation 2: Indian Time

The agency and the tribe must make a decision on a matter of mutual interest. The DNR establishes its position and communicates it to the tribal leadership, assuming the matter will be resolved by someone—or perhaps a handful of people—who are "in charge" of the community. Weeks pass and nothing is heard from the tribe. The agency, perceiving the tribe to be an age-based hierarchy (Lineal), interprets the silence to mean that either the tribe is lazy and inefficient or that they are merely stalling for (Indian) time. The tribe, meanwhile, has determined that this is a matter that involves the entire community and lets it be known that it is searching for a formal or informal consensus before going forward with the agreement. Families must meet and talk, then come together and bear witness to the decision of the tribal government. The impatience of the agency is understood to be another sign that white people always rush to judgment and want to push the tribe to do the same.

The Activity dimension would also appear to provide a good deal of common ground. After all, both groups value activities that result in practical, tangible rewards valued by others around them. They are both product—not process—oriented. We should keep in mind, however, that the DNR, like every other group interviewed, perceives the tribe as Being-oriented. This misunderstanding can, and does, interfere with communication between them.

Situation 3: The Memorandum of Understanding

The DNR wishes to frame a memorandum of understanding with the tribe. In doing so, it frames the memorandum largely in abstract terms, laying out processes in which the two parties can engage that will result in benefits in the future. Perceiving the tribe as Being-oriented, it assumes that this relaxed approach will appeal to the tribe and result in long-range cooperation. The tribe, upon reviewing the memorandum, is upset with the lack of substance and product and rejects it as a frivolous waste of time and of limited resources.

We come now to the Person-Nature dimension, where there are both similarities and differences. While both groups value most highly the Mastery orientation, with its implicit emphasis on control, they differ dramatically in their second-order preference. The agency orientation could be described as one in which "Just because you don't win doesn't mean you lose." The pattern for the tribe, however, would read differently, that is, "What you don't control, controls you." Added to this dilemma in communication is the degree to which the agency underestimates the importance of both the Mastery over and Subject to orientations in the Nation.

Situation 4: The Middle Ground

The agency and the tribe have come together to negotiate a settlement over some disputed lands. The agency comes in with its "bad cop/good cop" attitude, leading with its hardest-hitting negotiator, who spells out the conditions in no uncertain terms. Of course, the agency has a fallback position and is willing to compromise, and it expects the tribe will do much the same. The tribe, however, upon hearing the conditions, immediately feel their control threatened and engage in long and bitter discussions with the agency negotiators. Unlike the agency, they do not readily perceive the middle ground but, rather, feel that if they don't master the situation, they will lose control over hard-fought ground.

Reflections on the Values Project

As we moved through each stage of the Values Project, we encountered challenges and seemingly insuperable obstacles in both the research and training phases of the project, some of which I would like to reflect on next. Dr. Danilo E. Ponce remarks in his article on individuals' resistance to being treated as research subjects (in this volume). This is a familiar issue. In the Values Project the Lummi tribal members were perhaps least resistant of all the groups interviewed with the Value Orientations Survey instrument. This was due, in part, to the fact that I was working with the Lummi Nation and the program was endorsed and, in fact, sponsored by it. The use of tribal interviewers also encouraged participation and engendered trust among the tribal respondents.

The situation was much different, however, in the other groups. In each case we encountered an initial skepticism on the value of the method and suspicion of our motives for conducting the research. During preliminary consultations with representatives from the various groups, individuals expressed their doubts as to the veracity of the method and its ability to "get at" the subject of values. One representative from Puget Power went so far as to say that the "exercise" was pointless, for "Everyone knows we're all the same, here." This was invariably followed by a volley of questions about why we were conducting the interviews, who it was really for, and what the risks were (e.g., the fear of ambush) to the organization. Even after these doubts and fears were put to rest, some of the respondents resisted being interviewed with the Value Orientations Survey instrument. However, once the interviews were completed, the vast majority of the participants felt the experience was worthwhile and, in some cases, an illuminating one.

The workshops presented us with a new set of challenges. Tribal workshop participants were, at first, resentful of having their values described to them by a non-Indian via a survey. Their resentment gave way, however, when we made clear that orientations were merely general trends and tendencies that characterize the community. Their interest and level of involvement also greatly increased as we involved them in interpreting the data. Did the patterns make sense in terms of their experience in the community? What did they see to be the meaning of the variations within the tribe and between it and the other groups? How could the information be used to improve the workplace or relations between different groupings in the community? Their involvement as participant-observers greatly enhanced the value of the information, its meaning to the participants, and its usefulness to the community.

Interestingly, we faced even stiffer resistance from the other groups that took part in the Values Project workshops. While very interested in the data about the tribe, they often felt that reflecting on their own orientations was a dubious exercise, at best. Some complained that the 'forced choice' format of the survey was too restrictive. Others felt that the patterns did not speak, in any way, to their self-perception. Others questioned the overall validity of the instrument. Some of these problems could be attributed to weaknesses of the instrument or to the difficulty of conveying the information in a language accessible to the individual participant. In our view, however, a good deal of this resistance stemmed from a defensive reaction on the part of people who believed that in the value orientations approach their most personal values were being "picture-profiled." This resistance gradually lost steam, however, and by the end of the final joint workshop, when they had come to recognize the substantiveness and value of the exercise, even the most recalcitrant participant felt more comfortable with both the instrument and the data.

A more difficult obstacle was the issue of trust. We should keep in mind that the overall goal of the Values Project is to improve value-based understanding between groups in conflict. Based on debriefing interviews and the behavior of the participants in the final joint session as well as the Group of 10 series, the project largely succeeded in this goal. However, while the individuals may have had a better understanding of each other, they still worked within the confines of organizations with conflicting interests. This issue of confinement was often raised by participants who would, on the one hand, applaud the new levels of understanding, yet decry the fact that they were ultimately limited by the organization's mission and mandate over which they had little or no control. The question then arose: Trust who to do what? Trust the person to try to act on a better understanding of the values and perspectives of the cultural "other"? Or believe that individuals will do what they are told, regardless of what they have come to understand about each other?

While we do not have ready-made answers to these questions, it is important to remember that this project is not, in the strictest sense, a research project. It is research, yes, and it is carefully structured and monitored. But it is taking place in the real world of groups with profound, long-standing conflicts of interests. With the possible exception of our most recent project with the Lummi Nation and the Washington State Department of Ecology, we have never been asked to be mediators. Rather, we have been asked to serve as facilitators in the field of values. It was, and is, our hope that following upon this facilitation process, some of the participants, each in his or her own way, will gradually influence how the two groups resolve their conflicting interests.

Finally, I would like to call to your attention the comments of one of the land managers for the Department of Natural Resources. This individual was among the most resistant of all the participants in the early phases of the project with the agency. These remarks were made at the last joint session between the agency and the Lummi Nation.

> My experience in the workshops has left me uncomfortable and unsettled. You see, there is, in ignorance, a fine foundation for certainty, and ignorance is a solid foundation for moral rectitude. Ignorance makes a fine foundation for suspicion. I've known all of those with respect to the Lummi cultural issues as they affect our state timber sale program. But I've seen enough in these sessions to recognize your sincerity. I realize you are not coming from what I had originally perceived as bad faith. Those are behind me; the certainty and the moral rectitude are shaken; the suspicion is largely dispelled and...I don't know...in my own mind...where I'm headed from here. That leaves me unsettled and uncomfortable. (Zubalik and Russo 1988)

Conclusion

Our challenge is, and continues to be, how to inform groups in conflict as to why, and to what extent, variations in basic values and perceptions distort the communication process. We have, to that end, enjoyed a modicum of success, although we are continually reviewing and revising our research and training approach. Beyond that challenge, the overarching goal is to allow each side to share in the subjective experience of the other. This sharing implies more than merely standing in the shoes of the other, for at the end of the day what matters most is what you see, not where you stand. Whether we are working in the Pacific Northwest, in Mexico, Brazil, or the Republic of South Africa, we believe it is imperative to communicate understanding—that is, to allow a group or individual to experience, if only for a moment, the internal world of the "other."

References

Kluckhohn, Florence R., and Fred L. Strodtbeck. *Variations in Value Orientations.* Evanston, IL: Row, Peterson, 1961.

Russo, Kurt W., Phil Bereano, Robin Berez, Joseph Dupris, Tom Ensign, Michael Hills, Lyman Legters, Fremont Lyden, Leslie Rabkin, James Watson, and Steven Zubalik. *Values Project Northwest: Xwlemi.* Washington, DC: United States Department of the Interior, 1985.

Zubalik, Steven, and Kurt W. Russo. *The Values Project Northwest: Lummi Tribe and the Washington State Department of Natural Resources.* Kluckhohn Press, 1988.

Value Orientations as a Tool for Cross-Cultural Understanding

Bill Wallace

I am the northwest regional manager for the Department of Natural Resources (DNR) of Washington State and have been with the DNR twenty-two years. Eleven of those I have spent in the northwest region, where I have had an opportunity to work with a number of different Indian tribes. I was involved with the Kluckhohn Center Values Project Northwest about eight years ago with others from the department and members of the Lummi tribe. I didn't realize at the time how valuable that experience was, but since then, I've reflected back on it often and realize now that it was a turning point for me in learning about tribal values and improving my working relationship with the tribes.

The DNR has several major missions. One is as a land manager. We manage about five million acres of state land. Roughly two million acres of that are aquatic lands (bedlands, tidelands, and shorelands), two million are forest, and one million acres are agricultural. We manage much of the forest and agricultural lands for specific trust beneficiaries such as universities and schools. Some we run as businesses. In 1997 we generated over 260 million dollars for those beneficiaries. We also fight fires on state and private forestlands and administer the Forest Practices Act, which regulates forest practices on state and private land.

While serving in these different roles, I have worked with eight federally recognized tribes, out of twenty-six in the state. The eight tribes in the northwest region are the Lummi, Nooksack, Swinomish, Upper Skagit, Sauk-Suiattle (the new federally recognized tribe), the Samish, and further to the south, the Tulalip and the Stillaguamish.

The legal framework within which our agency and the state government work with the tribes is embodied in the 1989 Centennial Accord, a treaty negotiated by Governor Mike Lowry with the federally recognized tribes in Washington State.

The 1987 Timber, Fish and Wildlife Accord (TFW Accord) also shapes our working relationship with the tribes. During the 1980s there was considerable friction and litigation among the private forest landowners, tribes, and environmental groups over forest practices. Finally, the groups came together and created a "handshake agreement," promising to work together, both at the policy level and in the field, to manage the resources.

About eleven years ago, when I began working with the tribes, I was an assistant regional manager. I found it frustrating to do business with the tribes, but I couldn't figure out why. There seemed to be a number of issues involved. One of them had to do with communication. My supervisor and I had access to local legislators, leaders of environmental groups, and heads of local government, but we had difficulty accessing the leaders of the tribes. Often we worked with the tribe's staff members, but sometimes the staff members were not Indians. How, we wondered, do we gain access to tribal leaders in order to do business with them? It took me a couple of years to figure this out.

Another point of frustration resulted from different concepts of time. I felt that the tribes didn't respect the statutory time lines that I had to abide by under legislation covering forest practices. For example, we only have so much time to approve forest practice permits. Meetings must occur at specified times and with the right people there to make decisions, but there seemed to be a struggle in terms of meeting one another's time lines.

Another significant issue arose over tribal "cultural sites." While there are laws that protect archaeological sites, both Native American and non-Native American, when it comes to Native American cultural sites, there is very little in our laws that protects them, and there is very little we as an agency can do. So, first there was an issue of our being unable to either understand or respect the significance of the cultural sites. Second, the laws didn't help us much to work with the tribes in a meaningful way. That situation produced frustration for both the tribes and for us.

Fortunately, over time I learned some lessons that have decreased my frustration and helped me work more easily with the tribes. I started to understand, for instance, what "sovereign nation" means and what a "government-to-government" working relationship is. One day I was sitting in my office thinking "Why can't I gain access to a tribal chairman or to a tribal committee or the tribal council to talk about things?" when an "aha!" hit me. Because the Centennial Accord was a government-to-government relationship signed by the governor and the tribal chairman, it was an agreement between heads of state at their particular governmental levels. So my wanting to meet with the tribal chairman was like my running down to Olympia to knock on the governor's door and saying, "I'd like to talk to you about some business." That realization seems simple enough, but nobody had explained that concept to me.

Next, the Kluckhohn Center helped me understand that tribes have different values, cultures, needs, and priorities from the white mainstream *and* from each other. That was a kind of news flash to us: "Tribes are different!" Now we know we can't put them into the same box. To understand all the tribes, you have to get to know each tribe individually.

Understanding how tribal governments operate and who has authority to make decisions is also very important. It has been my experience that the tribes don't delegate authority in the same way my state agency does. The state government goes through a well-defined process of policy setting, from the legislature to boards of management to executive managers. The process is put in writing, and I am given a formal delegation of authority outlining what I can do to carry policies out within my region. If I or my staff goes to a meeting, we have some limited authority to make decisions. This does not seem to be the case with tribal representatives, who appear to have less decision-making power. Decisions are made in tribal committees and councils, so people at the meetings can represent the tribe and gather and take back information to the tribal leadership, but they cannot make decisions on the spot that would bring the meeting to a conclusion. How tribal governments function is something we began to understand, respect, and work with in our interactions with the tribes.

I also began to understand "Indian time." As I said earlier, I felt that the tribes had difficulty working within our time lines and with our need to do certain business within strict time limits. I found out through the Kluckhohn Values Project counselor that Indian time means "when the time is right." As a result, we recognized that there was a cultural conflict between the seeming arbitrariness of our operational deadlines and the tribes' need to reflect, bring information together, and come to a decision when the time is right.

Another lesson I learned was that the DNR and the tribes both have a common interest in finding ways to use resources that will best preserve our ecosystems. I think we have a lot to learn from the tribes. They have been, historically, very good stewards of the resources.

My last lesson came from the Kluckhohn Center workshop. It was recognizing the difference between the tribes' approach—saying "I feel" and coming from the heart—and my and the DNR's approach, saying "I think" and coming from the head. Normally I "think" about matters of resource management. I think in terms of economics or science. I think also in sociopolitical terms. I keep the decision process in the "I think" mode.

When I participated in the Kluckhohn Center workshop and sat down with tribal members, I heard them pour out their values. The "I feel" started coming out. I wasn't sharing what my religion meant to me, what my deep core values were, but they were. They shared some of their very innermost feelings, some of which they hadn't shared with their spouses, who were also sitting in those workshops. Tears were in everyone's eyes, including ours. That really struck me. Their comments were coming from the heart. And I said, "...I don't normally approach business this way."

It was essential for me to understand these cultural and spiritual values so I could put them into context in our business interactions. I don't pretend to fully understand the tribal cultures, but I have enormous respect for them, which I can take back to my staff and bring into play when issues of a cultural and spiritual nature come up with the tribes. When we do business, I can say to my team, "OK, let's reflect on this and try to think what this might mean to them," and then bring that understanding of their cultural values to our daily business.

In summary, over the past eleven years, I have developed what I call "Keys to Improved Working Relationship between DNR and the Tribes."

- *Get to know each tribe; each is different.* It is crucial to know their leaders, their priorities, things that are important to them, who their decision makers are, and the people who have access to them and might be able to influence them, so that we can communicate better.

- *Maintain communication with the tribes.* Be responsive to issues that concern them.
- *Be flexible and resourceful.* In most organizational structures there is some flexibility. If you focus on better understanding tribal needs, you can use that flexibility to respond in ways that meet both your official needs and the needs of the tribes.
- *Be respectful, understanding, professional, and patient.* We talk to DNR staff, explaining that they need to develop a good working relationship with the tribes and, ultimately, feelings of mutual trust. We believe that the DNR and the tribes need to approach resource management issues as partners, not adversaries. We both have a lot to contribute to the wise stewardship of our natural resources.

Finally, I'll finish with one of the most important lessons I learned: Two heads are better than one, and two hearts are better than one.

Value Orientations and Conflict Resolution: Using the Kluckhohn Value Orientations Model

Thomas J. Gallagher

Introduction

Differences in values underlie most conflicts, whether between individuals or groups. Appropriately, most conflict resolution processes strive to identify value differences between the competing parties. Successful conflict resolution efforts typically involve finding some common ground where the solution satisfies the values of both parties. Indeed, in conflict resolution a "solution" is that alternative which both parties accept—in which some package of values is satisfied for each.

What is not often well articulated in conflict resolution is that values occur at various levels, often in a hierarchy of surficial, intermediate, and foundation values. The surficial values are those expressed visibly in day-to-day activities; it is this group of values that are most often the immediate subject of conflict. The intermediate values are those we discover after some effort in conflict resolution. These values may have to do with larger issues, such as the value of education or the amount of tolerable risk. The foundation values include those identified in the Kluckhohn value orientations model: Human Nature, Person-Nature, Time, Activity, and Human Relations—and probably others yet to be discovered. One of the great contributions of the Kluckhohn model has been to provide a set of useful, core foundation values to support conflict resolution.

I propose that the Kluckhohn value orientation model has utility in conflict resolution by helping participants to recognize and use foundation values as part of a hierarchy of values and in exposing to participants their own value set, opening them to deeper reflection on the source of conflict.

Conflict Resolution Method

The "rational method" of problem solving underlies most if not all conflict resolution methods. The rational method involves five essential activities, often collapsed into as few as two or expanded to as many as twelve steps: (1) identify the problem, often stated as a goal or a value to be protected or achieved; (2) identify, gather, and analyze relevant information to help understand the situation; (3) creatively generate alternative ways to solve the problem; (4) analyze the alternate ways and select the best; and (5) develop the best alternative into a plan and implement it.

In conflict resolution this rational process is executed using methods that encourage people to explore Step 1—identify the problem—at length. A great deal of effort may be spent in identifying the values held by each stakeholder. Specific methods may be used to encourage participants to explore and understand the problem as seen by their opponent. A good conflict resolution process identifies what values are held by each side and how these values relate to the conflict at hand.

Before proceeding, however, it is important for me to note that not all conflict concerns values. The rational process is useful in reminding us that conflict can also be about information or alternatives. For example, from my own experience, two academics agreed on the value of statistics in a degree program but disagreed completely on how to achieve that value. One argued for a class in statistics, while the other argued for integrating statistics into several classes, as is done in writing classes. Such conflicts concern means more than ends and lend themselves to the classic rational method approach.

Conversely, many value-based problems are erroneously thought to be about information or alternatives. It is common to hear "If they knew all the facts, they would agree with us." Or "If they would just study this alternative, they would agree with us." In these situations one group assumes that the other has the same values but just differs on means. For many subtle cultural values, such as those identified by the Kluckhohn model, the assumption that there is agreement may be false. The first need, then, in conflict resolution is to identify if, indeed, there is a real or expressed difference in values.

To do this—to identify whether there is a difference in values—one's initial task is to separate values from supporting beliefs, norms, and behaviors. Most often values are not as visible or tangible as the beliefs and norms that support them. For example, I strongly value my relatives but find the norm of sending holiday greeting cards to be a hallmark of irrelevance. I much prefer to express my feelings through a timely call, visit, or gift. Some of my relatives may feel that since I don't share in their normative behavior, that is, sending greeting cards, I also don't share their value. A conflict resolution process would explore their and my behaviors, norms, and beliefs to get past incorrect assumptions—and bring greater joy to the family during the holidays.

This simple example captures the essence of conflict resolution—to get beyond specific behaviors and to discover where values are shared or not shared. The need is relevant at all levels of conflict, from interpersonal to intercultural. For the interpersonal scale, the Myers-Briggs Type Indicator (MBTI) provides a way to understand values that shape our individual norms and behaviors. For many people the MBTI instrument provides their first exposure to their own hidden values, which they have assumed, erroneously, others share. As one professor exclaimed on taking the test, "I thought it (the MBTI) was a true/false test! What an eye-opener to realize how different we all are. No wonder we get into conflicts when we assume others are like us."

The range of possible differences increases severalfold when we jump from interpersonal to cross-cultural conflict. Cultural differences have a much greater span of potentials than do interpersonal differences identified by the MBTI. Thus, the range of incorrect assumptions and misunderstandings is even greater. For example, in Alaska traditional Inupiak children are taught to divert their eyes when addressed by or addressing an elder or person of rank. This "looking away" behavior runs contrary to the norm in the remainder of the mainstream United States, where it is said, "You can tell a person is lying if he or she doesn't look you in the eye." This difference in normative behavior has been linked to Native children faring poorly in school and to the very high rate of conviction of Native youth in courts of law.

Whereas the MBTI provides insight into individual differences within the United States (and possibly only among Anglos), the

Kluckhohn model provides insight into differences between cultures. As with the MBTI, the Kluckhohn model provides insight into how misinterpretations of the meaning of a behavior—the value that it expresses—occurs across cultures. Just as some people are surprised that the MBTI is not a true/false test for personality, others are surprised that the Kluckhohn instrument is not a true/false test for culture.

Uncovering the Values Hierarchy

Much of conflict resolution involves getting people to think and talk and listen. For many people thinking and talking about their concerns is not easy, particularly when the conflict has already escalated and become heated. Of course, listening is always hard. Yet it is essential to get people to move beyond their positions to explore the root causes of their differences and the information and alternatives that may give rise to a solution. Getting people below the surface, to the underlying values, is essential, particularly when the values are confused with behaviors or hidden within the culture.

It is common to confuse behaviors with values. For example, the old adage "I climbed the mountain because it was there!" doesn't tell us much about motive or values. Similarly, a statement of values such as "I like open space" doesn't tell us much that might help in conflict resolution. Much "acquired taste" fits into this category; we learned the behavior while growing up and now find that it suits us.

Extending this idea, many of our values are hidden within our culture. This situation is expressed in a comment such as "That's the way we do things around here." Again, the comment doesn't tell us much about underlying values.

A strategy for digging below behaviors to values is to ask, gently, "Why?" This childlike question drives the discussion deeper—toward motives, which are deeper values. Although difficult at times, a series of "why" questions can be used to develop a hierarchical, integrated set of values. This set of values will have a "cat-in-the-hat" character, where at each level there are higher- and lower-level values. Many modern vision statements of corporations and institutions are developed from this process. The five Kluckhohn value dimensions are often discovered, either explicitly or implicitly, at the deepest levels.

This questioning of deeper values, or motives, can make conflict resolution difficult. In much conflict resolution individuals and groups are only willing to defend their positions, not explore their values. Such exploration may lead an individual or group to discover that its "enemies" have reasons for their behaviors that are built on values, too. Or, such exploration could lead people or groups to discover that their own value set is not internally consistent. The five Kluckhohn dimensions help to make this questioning easier by showing that it is not a matter of right or wrong, true or false. The Kluckhohn values provide insight into the fundamental differences that separate us as individuals and peoples. For example, the value of Doing versus Being is something we all quickly understand after exposure to the Kluckhohn model, but few of us think about this value as a foundation for assessing ourselves and others. Just the awareness that we can vary on such fundamental ideas opens the discussion to analysis of values. The Kluckhohn model provides a way to adjust attitudes in the process and to educate participants about the possible range of causes and solutions. It is an excellent means of encouraging curiosity about cultural differences.

Values Hierarchy and Process

The conflict resolution process must accurately identify value conflict when it exists. This conflict may be surficial or deep. The process must lead to the development of an understanding of the value structure, or hierarchy, as it relates to the conflict. It must do so effectively (accurately), efficiently (with reasonable time, energy, and money), and equitably (with all stakeholders involved). Such a process does not just happen; the search to understand values requires concentrated effort.

The rational process provides insight into the different elements of a problem: values, information, and alternatives. It is not, however, an effective conflict resolution process. Its weakness is that it passes through the five steps only once. It begins with the question "What is the problem (or goals or values?)" and then moves to information and alternatives. While each completed step serves the next step, there is no way for later steps to inform earlier ones. People learn about the conflict during the information and alternatives steps and need the opportunity to go back and change their values. People don't know their values so well that they can express them in one sitting; they need several efforts, and time between, to reflect. The process of creating and selecting an alternative, in particular, helps people to sort out their values.

To deal with this feedback between the steps, a good conflict resolution process requires several cycles through each of the steps, each time adjusting and correcting the problem statement and clarifying values. In conflict resolution it is typically best to plan for several iterations (I use three to five depending on the complexity of the issue) than to have them happen unplanned.

In addition to iterations, it is useful in the process to examine values both from the general to the specific and the specific to the general. Some people prefer starting with the big picture and then refining; others prefer starting with the specific. One strategy when working with a group is to go through the process with one group exploring foundation values while another group explores the problem (surficial values) first. The two groups need to compare notes during each iteration so that by the end of the process they have a fully integrated set of values. A skilled facilitator will ensure that each group makes incremental progress toward understanding the value structure.

This incremental nature of a cyclical process has another benefit in conflict resolution. It helps participants to relax. It is not necessary to have perfect understanding the first or even the second time through the steps. If there is an information gap in the first cycle, it can be filled in the next. Similarly, there is more time to explore alternatives with some brainstorming possible in each cycle. The use of cycles or iterations is useful in working with hierarchies, structures, or systems. Each cycle can focus incrementally on building part of the structure, or explore a different level in a values hierarchy.

The rational process, without cycles or iterations, has proven ineffective and sometimes highly offensive in many cross-cultural settings. Used by federal and state land management agencies in Alaska, the once-through rational process (required by federal and state law) has created deep animosity between agencies and Native people. Cyclical forms of the process, however, have proven far more useful in developing the depth of understanding and the cross-cultural trust needed for cooperative land management.

The Department of Natural Resources of the State of Alaska, for example, used a nine-iteration process to prepare the Northwest Area Plan. This plan identifies acceptable land uses on millions of acres of state land in Alaska's northwest region. The entire landscape is used extensively by local Native people for subsistence activities, primarily fishing and hunting. State lands, however, which have a checkerboard pattern throughout the region, are for use by all people, Native and non-Native alike. Land-use designations for these lands determine whether such facilities as public cabins can be built. For Native people such cabins are a threat, as they encourage more non-Native hunters who compete for the limited fish and game.

To develop the plan, Natural Resources staff outlined a cyclical process that involved all interested parties, including Native people as well as fishing and hunting guides. In each cycle, agency staff set a target for the five steps: understanding of goals (values), gathering of information, development of alternatives, analysis of alternatives, and selection of the best course of action. At the end of each cycle they made a "go/no go" decision. If they had not made sufficient forward progress in the steps, they repeated the cycle. In this way they kept a balance in the steps and they refrained from moving ahead without agreement among participants that the process was worth the effort.

The Kluckhohn model was not formally integrated into this process but rather served as a frame of reference used by staff to understand foundation values and how they can influence more visible norms, behaviors, and expectations. As experience with the Kluckhohn model has grown over the years, it is apparent it can be formally incorporated into a cyclical process. This might involve, in part, identifying different levels of values in each cycle, thus developing a hierarchy of values with the Kluckhohn group establishing the foundation.

The cycle process suits the Kluckhohn method well as it provides the time necessary for participants and agency personnel to understand values, which takes time, and what they mean to the final plan and eventual action. The Alaska process described above took longer than the traditional linear process, but along the way opposing groups began to understand (and sometimes accept) each other's values, to share information, and to work together to find creative alternatives. Staff wisely forced participants to "sign off" on the process after each of the cycles, in this way assuring that participants were supportive and ready to move forward. The final plan is considered a model of cross-cultural conflict resolution and remains in effect today because it is supported by both Native and non-Native people of the region. Perhaps the ultimate indicator of the success of the plan is that there have been no legal challenges.

Conclusion

The Kluckhohn model is not itself a conflict resolution model. It is, however, a valuable tool for conflict resolution efforts. Most important, the model establishes the foundation values, which may be the ultimate source of the conflict. The model has exceptional value in conflict resolution related to cross-cultural issues; it also has value for interpersonal conflict. Even if the model does not address the values central to the conflict, the insight provided by the model creates a deeper awareness of and appreciation for the complexity and subtlety of personal and cultural differences. Through this insight the Kluckhohn model has the potential to defuse cross-cultural conflicts, to diminish the "we're right and you're wrong" mentality.

In the challenge of conflict resolution the Kluckhohn value orientation model is a major tool. It does not sufficiently address other aspects of problems, such as information and alternatives, to be a stand-alone conflict resolution method. The greater opportunity lies with integrating the model into a cyclical process in which the foundation values can be incrementally and rigorously linked to the conflict and its resolution.

Selected Readings

Gallagher, Thomas J. "Language, Native People, and Land Management in Alaska." In *Culture, Conflict, and Communication in the Wildland-Urban Interface,* edited by A. W. Ewert, D. J Chavez, and A. W. Magill. Boulder, CO: Westview Press, 1993.

———. "Native Participation in Land Management Planning in Alaska." *Arctic* 41, no. 2 (1988): 91–98.

———. *Problem Solving—With People: The Cycle Process*. Lanham, MD: University Press, 1987.

Noland, L. J., and Thomas J. Gallagher. "Cross-Cultural Communication for Land Managers and Planners in Alaska." *Agroborealis* 21, no. 1 (1989): 18–23.

Appendices

Appendix A

Value Orientations Survey

The Kluckhohn Value Orientations Survey provides an instrument for eliciting value orientations and for gauging intra- and intergroup perceptions. The survey consists of twenty-three items distributed among the four value dimensions of Activity, Person-Nature, Human Relations, and Time. Situations for the fifth dimension, Human Nature, are still under development by Kluckhohn Center staff.

In each survey item, respondents are asked to pick what they believe is the best, or ideal, solution to a general life situation. The survey items in the dimensions of Person-Nature, Human Relations, and Time include three possible choices, requiring the respondents to also select what they believe to be the "next best" solution to the situation. In certain instances they are also asked to pick which of the alternatives best represents how they would *actually* behave in such situations. The letter (*A* or *B* or *C*) following each choice, or "solution," is shorthand notation for a value orientation. Thus, in the Activity situations, *A* always stands for the Doing orientation and *B* for Being. The respondents are asked to *pick the number* beside their choice; the letter is later used by the analyst to determine the orientation.

In each situation respondents are also asked to select what they believe "most others" in their own group (their family, organization, or community) would say is best. In order to gauge intergroup perceptions, they are asked to guess what most people in "the other" group (organization, culture, or community) would say is best. Readers are referred to the first article ("Value Orientations Method: The Conceptual Framework") for a detailed discussion of the survey.

You are encouraged to complete the survey to assess your own value orientations. Simply place *the number* of your first (and, when asked, second) choice in the space provided. A user's key is included at the end of the survey to assist in profiling your value orientations. To be most accurate, you should complete *all* of the items before referring to the key, and you should answer all of the situations in the order presented. You are also encouraged to be aware of how and why you arrived at your choices.

Activity 1: Job Choice

A person needed a job and had the chance to work for two people. The two bosses were different. Listen to what they were like and say which you think would be the best one to work for.

1. One boss was fair enough and gave somewhat higher pay than most but was the kind of boss who insisted that people work hard and stick to the job. This boss did not like it at all when a worker sometimes knocked off work for a while to go on a trip or to have a day or so of fun and thought it was right not to take such a worker back on the job. [A]
2. The other paid just average wages but was not so firm. This boss understood that a worker would sometimes just not turn up—would be off on a trip or having a little fun for a day or two. When this boss's workers did this, the boss would take them back without saying too much. [B]

Which kind of boss do you think it is *better to have* in most cases?
[Your answer:]

Which kind of boss do you think most other people in ______ (your family, group, or community) would say is best?
[Your answer:]

Which kind of boss do you think most ________ (people in another group, community, or cultural group) would say is the better boss?
[Your answer:]

Activity 2: Job Choice

A person needed a job and had a chance to work for two different kinds of people. The two bosses were different. Listen to what they were like and say which you think would *be the best kind to be*.

1. One boss was fair enough and gave somewhat higher pay than most but was the kind of boss who insisted that people

work hard and stick to the job. This boss did not like it at all when a worker sometimes just knocked off work for a while to go on a trip or to have a day or so of fun, and thought it was right not to take such a worker back on the job. [A]

2. The other paid just average wages but was not so firm. This boss understood that a worker would sometimes just not turn up—would be off on a trip or having a little fun for a day or two. When this boss's workers did this, the boss would take them back without saying too much. [B]

Which kind of boss do you believe it would be better to be in most cases?

[Your answer:]

Which kind of boss do you believe most other people in ________ (your family, group, or community) would think it is better to be?

[Your answer:]

Which kind of boss do you believe most ________ (people in another group, community, or cultural group) would think it is better to be?

[Your answer:]

Human Relations 1: Well Arrangements

When a community has to make arrangements for water, such as drilling a well, there are three different ways they can decide to arrange things like location and who is going to do the work.

1. There are some communities where it is mainly the older or recognized leaders of the important families who decide the plans. Everyone usually accepts what they say without much discussion, since they are the ones who are used to deciding such things and are the ones who have had the most experience. [A]
2. There are some communities where most people in the group have a part in making the plans. Lots of different people talk, but nothing is done until almost everyone comes to agree as to what is best to be done. [B]
3. There are some communities where everyone holds to his [or her] own opinion, and they decide the matter by vote. They do what the largest number wants, even though there are still a great many people who disagree and object to the action. [C]

Which way do you think is usually best in such cases?
[Your answer:]

Which way do you think is second best?
[Your answer:]

Which of the three ways do you think you, yourself, would follow?
[Your answer:]

Which of the three ways do you think most others in ________ (your family, group, or community) would usually think is best?
[Your answer:]

Which of the three ways do you think most ________ (people in another group, community, or cultural group) would say is best?
[Your answer:]

Time 1: Child Training

Some people were talking about the way that children should be brought up.
Here are three different ideas.

1. Some people say that children should always be taught the traditions of the past. They believe the old ways are best, and it is when children do not follow them that things go wrong. [A]
2. Some people say that children should be taught some of the old traditions, but it is wrong to insist that they stick to these ways. These people believe that it is necessary for children to always learn about and take on whatever of the new ways will best help them get along in the world of today. [B]
3. Some people do not believe children should be taught much about the past traditions at all, except as an interesting story of what has gone before. These people believe that the world goes along best when children are taught the things that will make them want to find out for themselves new ways of doing things to replace the old. [C]

Which of these people has the best idea about how children should be taught?
[Your answer:]

Which of these people has the next best idea?
[Your answer:]

Which of the three ways would most other people in ________ (your family, group, or community) say is best?
[Your answer:]

Which of the three ways would most ________ (people in another group, community, or cultural group) say is best?
[Your answer:]

Person-Nature 1: Livestock Dying

One time a person had a lot of livestock. Most of them died off in different ways. People talked about this and said different things.

1. Some people said you just can't blame a person when things like this happen, and a person can do almost nothing to prevent such losses when they come. We all have to learn to take the bad with the good. [A]
2. Some people said that it was probably the person's own fault that he or she lost so many. The person didn't think to prevent the losses. They said that it is usually the case that people who keep up on new ways of doing things, and really set themselves to it, almost always find a way to keep out of such trouble. [B]
3. Some people said that it was probably because the person has not lived right—has not done things in the right way to keep harmony with the forces of nature (i.e., the ways of nature like the rain, wind, snow, etc.). [C]

Which of these reasons do you think is most usually true?
[Your answer:]

Which of the other two reasons do you think is more true? Which of these reasons do you think most other people in ________ (your family, group, or community) would say is most usually true?
[Your answer:]

Which of these reasons do you think most ________ (people in another group, community, or cultural group) would say is most usually true?
[Your answer:]

Time 2: Expectations about Change

Three young people were talking about what they thought their families would have one day as compared with their fathers and mothers. They each said different things.

1. The first said, "I expect my family to be better off in the future than the family of my father and mother or relatives, if we work hard and plan right. Things in this country usually get better for people who try." [C]
2. The second said, "I don't know whether my family will be better off, the same, or worse off than the family of my father and mother or relatives. Things always go up and down, even if people work hard. So one can never really tell how things will be." [B]
3. The third said, "I expect my family to be about the same as the family of my father and mother or relatives. The best way is to work hard and plan ways to keep up things as they have been in the past." [A]

Which of these people do you think had the best idea?
[Your answer:]

Which of these people do you think had the second best idea?
[Your answer:]

Which of these people do you think most other people in _________ (your family, group, or community) say has the best idea?
[Your answer:]

Which of these people do you think most _________ (people in another group, community, or cultural group) would say had the best idea?
[Your answer:]

Person-Nature 2: Facing Conditions

There are different ways of thinking about how God (or the Gods) is (are) related to people and to weather and all other natural conditions that make the crops and animals live or die. Here are three possible ways.

1. God (or the Gods) and people work together all the time. Whether the conditions that make the crops and animals grow are good or bad depends upon whether people themselves do all the proper things to keep themselves in harmony with their God(s) and with the forces of nature. [C]
2. God (or the Gods) does (do) not directly control all the conditions that affect the growth of crops or animals. It is up to the people themselves to figure out the ways conditions change and to try hard to find ways of controlling them. [B]

3. Just how God (or the Gods) will use power over all the conditions that affect the growth of crops and animals cannot be known. It is useless for people to think they can change conditions very much for very long. The best way is to take conditions as they come and do as well as one can. [A]

Which way of thinking do you think is best? Which of the other two ways do you think is second best?
[Your answer:]

Which of the three ways best describes how you really are?
[Your answer:]

Which of these three ways do you think most other people in ________ (your family, group, or community) would say is best?
[Your answer:]

Which of these three ways do you think most ________ (people in another group, community, or cultural group) would say is best?
[Your answer:]

Human Relations 2: Help in Misfortune

A family had a crop failure or, let us say, lost most of their sheep or cattle. The family had to have help from someone if they were going to get through the winter. There are different ways of getting help. Which of these three ways would be best?

1. Would it be best if they depended mostly on brothers and sisters or other relatives to help out as much as each one could? [B]
2. Would it be best for them to try to raise the money on their own outside the community from people who are neither relatives nor employers? [C]
3. Would it be best to go to a boss or an older important relative who is used to managing things and ask that person to help out until things get better? [A]

Which way of getting help do you think would usually be best?
[Your answer:]

Which of the other two ways would you say is next best?
[Your answer:]

Which of the three ways do you think you, yourself, would follow?
[Your answer:]

Which of the three ways do you think most other people in ________ (your family, group, or community) would say is best?
[Your answer:]

Which of the three ways do you think most ________ (people in another group, community, or cultural group) would say is best?
[Your answer:]

Human Relations 3: Family Work Relations

I'm going to tell you about three different ways families can arrange work. These families are related and they live close together.

1. In some groups or communities it is usually expected that each of the separate families (husband, wife, and children) will look after its own business separate from all others and not be responsible for the others. [C]
2. In some groups or communities it is usually expected that close relatives in the families will work together and talk over among themselves the way to take care of whatever problems come up. When a boss is needed, they usually choose one person, not necessarily the oldest able person, to manage things. [B]
3. In some groups or communities it is usually expected that the families that are closely related to each other will work together and have the oldest able person be responsible for and take charge of the most important things. [A]

Which of these ways do you think is usually best in most cases?
[Your answer:]

Which of the other two ways do you think is second best?
[Your answer:]

Which of the three ways do you think you, yourself, would follow?
[Your answer:]

Which of the three ways do you think that most other people in ________ (your family, group, or community) would say is best?
[Your answer:]

Which of the three ways do you think most ________ (people in another group, community, or cultural group) would say is best?
[Your answer:]

Human Relations 4: Choice of a Delegate

A community like yours is going to send a delegate—a representative—to a meeting. (This can be any sort of meeting.) How should the delegate be chosen?

1. Is it best that a meeting be called and everyone discuss things until almost everyone agrees so that when a vote is taken almost all people will agree on the same person? [B]
2. Is it best that the older, important leaders take the main responsibility for deciding who should represent the people, since they are the ones who have had the most experience in such matters? [A]
3. Is it best that a meeting be called, names be put up, a vote taken, then the person sent who gets the majority of votes even if there are many people who are still against this person? [C]

Which of these ways of choosing a delegate is usually best in cases like this?
[Your answer:]

Which of these ways do you think is second best?
[Your answer:]

Which of the three ways do you think you, yourself, would follow?
[Your answer:]

Which of these ways do you think most other people in ________ (your family, group, or community) would say is best?
[Your answer:]

Which of these ways do you think most ________ (people in another group, community, or cultural group) would say is best?
[Your answer:]

Person-Nature 3: Use of Fields

There were three people who were farmers. The three people had quite different ways of planting and taking care of crops.

1. One put in crops, worked hard, and also tried to live in right and proper ways. This first person felt that it is the way a person works and tries to keep harmony with the forces of nature that has the most effect on conditions and the way crops turn out. [C]

2. One put in crops and afterward worked on them sufficiently but did no more than was necessary to keep them going along. This person felt that how they would turn out depended mainly on weather conditions and that nothing extra that people do could change things much. [A]
3. One put in crops and then worked on them a lot of the time and made use of all the new scientific ideas that were available. This person felt that by doing so, many of the effects of bad conditions could be prevented. [B]

Which of these ways do you believe is usually best?
[Your answer:]

Which of the other two ways do you believe is second best?
[Your answer:]

Which of these ways best describes how you really are?
[Your answer:]

Which of the three ways would most other people in _______ (your family, group, or community) say is best?
[Your answer:]

Which of the three ways would most _______ (people in another group, community, or cultural group) believe is best?
[Your answer:]

Time 3: Philosophy of Life

People often have very different ideas about what has gone before and what we can expect from life. Here are three ways of thinking about these things.

1. Some people believe it is best to give most attention to what is happening now, in the present. They say that the past has gone and the future is much too uncertain to count on. Things do change, but it is sometimes for the better and sometimes for the worse, so in the long run it is about the same. These people believe the best way to live is to keep those of the old ways that one can—or that one likes—but be ready to accept the new ways, which will help to make life easier and better as we live from year to year. [B]
2. Some people think that the ways of the past (the traditional ways) were right and the best and as changes come, things get worse. These people think the best way to live is to work

hard to keep up the old ways and try to bring them back when they are lost. [A]

3. Some people believe that it is almost always the ways of the future—the ways that are still to come—that will be best, and they say that even though there are sometimes small setbacks, changes bring improvements in the long run. These people believe that the best way to live is to look a long time ahead, work hard, and give up many things now so that the future will be better. [C]

Which of these ways of looking at life do you think is best?
[Your answer:]

Which of these ways do you think is second best?
[Your answer:]

Which of these three ways best describes how you really think?
[Your answer:]

Which of these three ways do you think most others in ________ (your family, group, or community) would say is best?
[Your answer:]

Which of these three ways do you think most ________ (people in another group, community, or cultural group) would say is best?
[Your answer:]

Human Relations 5: Wage Work

There are three ways that people who do not themselves hire others (people who do not have any employees) may work.

1. One way is working on one's own as an individual. In this case, people are pretty much their own boss. They decide most things on their own, and how they get along is their own business. They only have to take care of themselves, and don't expect others to look out for them. [C]
2. One way is working in a group where everyone has something to say in the decisions that are made, and everyone can count on each other. [B]
3. One way is working for an owner—a big boss—or someone who has been running things for a long time. In this case, people do not take a part in deciding how the business will be run, but they know they can depend on the boss to help them out in many ways. [A]

Which of these ways is usually best for someone who does not hire others?
[Your answer:]

Which of these ways do you think is second best?
[Your answer:]

Which of the three ways do you think you, yourself, would follow?
[Your answer:]

Which of these ways do you think most other people in ________ (your family, group, or community) would say is best?
[Your answer:]

Which of these ways do you think most ________ (people in another group, community, or cultural group) would say is best?
[Your answer:]

Person-Nature 4: Belief in Control

Three people from different areas were talking about the things that control the weather and other conditions. Here is what they each said:

1. One said, "My people have never controlled the rain, wind, and other natural conditions and probably never will. There have always been good years and bad years. That is the way it is, and, if you are wise, you will take it as it comes and do the best you can." [A]
2. The second said, "My people believe that it is our job to find ways to overcome weather and other conditions just as they have overcome so many things. They believe they will one day succeed in doing this and may even overcome drought and floods." [B]
3. The third said, "My people help conditions and keep things going by working to keep in touch with all the forces which make the rain, the snow, and other conditions. It is when we do the right things—live in the proper way and keep all that we have (the land, the stock, and the water) in good condition—that all goes along well." [C]

Which of these people do you think had the best idea?
[Your answer:]

Which of the people do you think had the second best idea?
[Your answer:]

Which of these three ways best describes how you really are?
[Your answer:]

Which of these people do you think most other people in _______ (your family, group, or community) would say had the best idea?
[Your answer:]

Which of these people do you think most _______ (people in another group, community, or cultural group) would say had the best idea?
[Your answer:]

Time 4: Ceremonial Innovation

Some people in a community like your own saw that the religious ceremonies were changing from what they used to be.

1. Some people were really pleased because of the changes in religious ceremonies. They felt that new ways are usually better than old ones, and they like to keep everything—even ceremonies—moving ahead. [C]
2. Some people were unhappy because of the change. They felt that religious ceremonies should be kept exactly—in every way—as they have been in the past. [A]
3. Some people felt that the old ways for religious ceremonies were best but that you just can't hang on to them. It makes life easier just to accept some changes as they come along. [B]

Which of these three felt most nearly what you believe is right?
[Your answer:]

Which of the other two do you think is most right?
[Your answer:]

Which of the three ways do you think most other people in ________ (your family, group, or community) would say is most right?
[Your answer:]

Which of the three ways do you think most ________ (people in another group, community, or cultural group) would say is most right?
[Your answer:]

Activity 3: Ways of Living

There were two people talking about how they liked to live. They had different ideas.

1. One said, "What I care about most is accomplishing things, getting things done just as well or better than other people do them. I like to see results and think they are worth working for." [A]
2. The other said, "What I care most about is to be left alone to think and act in the ways that best suit the way I really am. If I don't always get much done but can enjoy life as I go along, that is the best way." [B]

Which of these two people do you think has the better way of thinking?
[Your answer:]

Which of these two people are you really most like?
[Your answer:]

Which of these two people do you think most other people in _________ (your family, group, or community) would think has the better idea?
[Your answer:]

Human Relations 6: Livestock Inheritance

Some sons and daughters have been left some livestock (sheep or cattle) by a father or mother who has died. All these sons and daughters are grown up and live near each other. There are three different ways they can run the livestock.

1. In some groups of people it is usually expected that the oldest able person (son or daughter) will take charge of, or manage, all the livestock held by that person and the other sons and daughters. [A]
2. In some groups of people it is usually expected that each of the sons and daughters will prefer to take his or her own share of the stock and run his or her own business completely separate from all the others. [C]
3. In some groups of people it is usually expected that all the sons and daughters will keep all their cattle and sheep together and work together and decide among themselves who is best able to take charge of things (not necessarily the oldest) when a boss is needed. [B]

Which way do you think is usually best in most cases?
[Your answer:]

Which of the other two ways do you think is second best?
[Your answer:]

Which of the three ways do you think you, yourself, would follow?
[Your answer:]

Which way do you think most other people in ________ (your family, group, or community) would say is best?
[Your answer:]

Which way do you think most ________ (people in another group, community, or cultural group) would say is best?
[Your answer:]

Human Relations 7: Land Inheritance

Now I want to ask a similar question concerning farmland. Some sons and daughters have been left farmland by a mother or father who has died. All these sons and daughters are grown and live near each other. There are three ways they can handle the property.

1. In some groups of people it is usually expected that the oldest son or daughter will take charge of, or manage, the land for him- or herself and all of the other sons and daughters, even if they all share it. [A]
2. In some groups of people it is usually expected that each son or daughter will take his or her own share of the land and do with it what he or she wants—separate from all the others. [C]
3. In some groups of people it is usually expected that all of the sons and daughters will make use of the land together. When a boss is needed, they get together and agree to choose one of the group (not necessarily the oldest) to take charge of things. [B]

Which of these ways do you think is usually best in most cases?
[Your answer:]

Which of these ways do you think is second best?
[Your answer:]

Which of the three ways do you think you, yourself, would follow?

[Your answer:]

Which of the three ways do you think most other people in ________ (your family, group, or community) would say is best?
[Your answer:]

Which of the three ways do you think most ________ (people in another group, community, or cultural group) would say is best?
[Your answer:]

Activity 4: Care of Fields

There were farmers who lived differently.

1. One farmer kept the crops growing all right but didn't work on them more than was necessary. This farmer wanted to have extra time to visit with friends, go on trips, and enjoy life. This was the way this person liked best. [B]
2. The other farmer liked to work with the fields and was always putting in extra time keeping them clean of weeds and in fine condition. Because of this extra work, this person did not have much time left to be with friends, to go on trips, or to enjoy life in other ways. But this was the way this person really liked best. [A]

Which person do you believe it is better to be?
[Your answer:]

Which person do you believe you are really most like?
[Your answer:]

Which person do you think most other people in ________ (your family, group, or community) would say it is better to be?
[Your answer:]

Which person do you think most ________ (people in another group, community, or cultural group) would say it is better to be?
[Your answer:]

Person-Nature 5: Length of Life

Three people were talking about whether people themselves can do anything to make the lives of men and women longer. Here is what each said:

1. One said, "It is already true that people like doctors and others are finding the way to add many years to the lives of most men and women by discovering (finding) new medi-

cines, by studying foods, and by introducing such things as vaccinations. If people will pay attention to all these new things, they will almost always live longer." [B]

2. The second one said, "I really do not believe that there is much that human beings themselves can do to make the lives of men and women longer. It is my belief that every person has a set time to live, and when that time comes, it just comes." [A]
3. The third one said, "I believe that there is a plan to life that works to keep all living things moving together, and if people will learn to live their whole lives in accord with that plan, they will live longer than other men and women." [C]

Which of these ways do you think is usually best?
[Your answer:]

Which of the other ways do you believe is second best?
[Your answer:]

Which of these three ways best describes how you really are?
[Your answer:]

Which of the three ways would most other people in ________ (your family, group, or community) say is best?
[Your answer:]

Which of the three ways would most ________ (people in another group, community, or cultural group) believe is best?
[Your answer:]

Time 5: Water Allocation

The government is going to help a community to get more water by redrilling and cleaning out a community well. The government officials suggest that the community have a plan for dividing the extra water, but they don't say what kind of plan. Since the amount of extra water that may be available is not known, people feel differently about planning.

1. Some say that whatever water becomes available should be divided just about like water in the past was always divided. [A]
2. Others want to work out a really good plan ahead of time for dividing whatever water becomes available. [C]
3. Still others want to just wait until water becomes available

before deciding how it will be divided. [B]

Which of these ways do you think is usually best in cases like this?
[Your answer:]

Which of the other ways do you think is second best?
[Your answer:]

Which of the three ways do you think most others in ________ (your family, group, or community) would say is best?
[Your answer:]

Which of the three ways do you think most ________ (people in another group, community, or cultural group) would say is best?
[Your answer:]

Activity 5: Housework

There were two women talking about the way they liked to live.

1. One said that she was willing to work as hard as the average woman, but that she didn't like to spend a lot of time doing extra things in her house or taking up extra work outside. Instead, she liked to have time free to enjoy visiting with people, to go on trips, or to just talk with whoever was around. [B]
2. The other woman said she liked best of all to find extra things to work on that would interest her. She said she was happiest when kept busy and getting lots done. [A]

Which of these two ways do you think is usually better for women to live?
[Your answer:]

Which of these two women do you think most other people in ________ (your family, group, or community) would say had the better idea?
[Your answer:]

Which of these two women do you think most ________ (people in another group, community, or cultural group) would think had the better idea?
[Your answer:]

Activity 6: Nonworking Time

Two men spend their time in different ways when they have no work to do (when they are not at work).

1. One man spends most of this time learning or trying out things that will help him in his work. [A]
2. The other man spends most of this time talking, telling stories, singing, and so on with friends. [B]

Which man has the better way of living?
[Your answer:]

Which of these two men do you think most other people in _______ (your family, group, or community) would say had the better idea?
[Your answer:]

Which of these two people do you think most _______ (people in another group, community, or cultural group) would say had the better idea?
[Your answer:]

*** End of Survey ***

User's Key

Activity

A = Doing orientation
B = Being orientation

Human Relations

A = Lineal orientation
B = Collateral orientation
C = Individualistic orientation

Time

A = Lineal orientation
B = Collateral orientation
C = Individualistic orientation

Person-Nature

A = Lineal orientation
B = Collateral orientation
C = Individualistic orientation

Appendix B

Analysis of Value Orientations

Introduction

A review of the various applications of the value orientations method reveals many different approaches to analyzing value orientations. In certain instances, researchers have focused on the dominant (first-order) orientations for each of the four value spheres of Time, Person-Nature, Human Relations, and Activity. In other cases they may concentrate on the general sums for each of these dimensions. In the work conducted by the Kluckhohn Center, however, we have taken the analysis further and have attempted to tease out the more subtle meanings by examining the full range of variations beginning with the overall sums and then combining this with a detailed analysis of the variations within, as well as between, the four value spheres.

Our approach is based on the assumption that the general sums for the four dimensions are merely the point of departure. We believe that in order to understand the full meaning of these sums it is necessary to work through the full range of data in a manner that responds to the interdependency of the survey situations and of the four value spheres. Two groups, or two subgroups within one sampled population, may share a Doing orientation but differ in their orientation to Person-Nature. In order to understand the meaning of what they have in common, it is important to appreciate the nature, extent, and consequence(s) of their differences. In addition, we believe that in order to understand the overall sum for any given dimension, it is necessary to analyze variations in orientations in each of the situations within the dimension.

What follows is a brief description of how we have analyzed information generated by the Kluckhohn survey. In addition, we have provided some guidelines for involving the participants in a sampled population as observers. This process of feedback has been useful not only in deepening our understanding of the results but also in determining how best to utilize the information within the participating group or groups.

Principles of Analysis

An analysis of value orientations is greatly enhanced by adherence to several principles. First, it is important to have an understanding of the philosophical foundations and theoretical assumptions of the Kluckhohn method. An understanding of such concepts as "value orientations," "variations," and "value spheres" (also referred to as "value dimensions"), among others, is critical to any credible analysis. Next, it is important to understand the linkage between the survey situations and the theory of value orientations. Third, the analyst must have an appreciation of the interrelationship between situations within each dimension *and* the interdependence of these value spheres. Also, the analyst should have a working understanding of the statistical methods used for purposes of analysis. Finally, it is always advisable for the analyst to predict, prior to conducting any Kluckhohn interviews, the situational as well as cumulative patterns for the participating group or groups. Completing the Value Orientations Survey with the participating group in mind will provide the researcher with a portrait of his or her own assumptions relative to the participating group(s), which will assist him or her in the effort to approach the research in an objective manner. In the same vein, we believe it is important for each interviewer to first be interviewed with the Value Orientations Survey and to be familiar with his or her own orientations before utilizing the survey.

Analyzing the Data

Eight steps for analyzing the data have been followed by Kluckhohn Center staff:

Step 1: Examine the overall sums and the statistical significance of each value dimension.

Step 2: Examine results for each situation within each dimension.
Step 3: Analyze variations in orientations within each dimension and between or among groups.
Step 4: Examine role-related situations across dimensions.
Step 5: Analyze the results of self "actual" versus self "ideal."
Step 6: Analyze variations across dimensions between or among groups.
Step 7: Examine the results of intra- and intergroup perceptions.
Step 8: Complete a cumulative analysis.

As a first step, the analyst should review, and think through, the overall sums and the statistical significance of each of the value dimensions. If the project includes two or more groups, attention should be given to those dimensions in which the groups are most similar, or where they differ significantly. These overall sums should be kept in mind as the analyst proceeds through each step of the analysis. It should be remembered, however, that the ultimate meaning of the sums cannot be determined without a close examination of each of the situations in all four of the value dimensions.

The second step involves working through each of the value dimensions. Once again, if the analyst is working with two or more groups, he or she will want to give close attention to situations where the two groups are either very similar or markedly different, either in first- or second-order rankings. For example, consider the Time dimension. What is the orientation pattern for the group, or groups, in T1: Child Training? What is the rank ordering and the strength (the statistical significance) of the pattern? Next, what are the first-order percentages in Child Training and how does this compare to the overall pattern for this situation? Finally, the analyst should compare the pattern for this situation with the overall pattern for the dimension. This type of analysis explores the deeper meaning of the order of choice in terms of both the dominant orientation and, just as important, the variation in orientations in the situation. The analyst should proceed in this manner through each of the situations in the Time dimension.

The third step consists of an examination of variations within each dimension and between or among groups. You may find, for example, in the Time dimension that the Present and the Future shift from first- to second-order ranking. In which situations, and to what extent, do the patterns shift? If you are considering two or more groups, how do they differ in their variation within the dimension? What might be the significance of these variations for relations within the group or between two or more participating groups? This examination can be accomplished by the analyst looking at the overall patterns as well as the first-order percentages. The analyst should combine an examination of these variations with a careful reading of the appropriate survey situation. It is also important to keep in mind at every level of analysis the statistical significance of the pattern. These three steps should be followed in examining each of the remaining value spheres.

In the fourth step it is especially important for the analyst to keep in mind the overall goal or intent of the analysis. The analyst should now look across the dimensions and select situations that (1) are closely related to each other, (2) reveal the greatest degree of variation within or between the participating group(s), and (3) may have the greatest importance for purposes of the overall goal of the project.

Dr. Fremont J. Lyden associates roles that are implied in each of the situations. Looking across the value spheres, he points out that situations in Time (Child Training, Expectations about Change), Activity (Nonworking Time), and Human Relations (Well Arrangements, Help in Misfortune, Family Work Relations, Livestock Inheritance, and Land Inheritance) all imply family roles. The analyst should look across dimensions comparing patterns in situations that describe similar roles or share a central focus. This type of integrated analysis will provide added insight as he or she searches for subtle or hidden meanings beneath the surface of the data.

Once again, if the analysis includes two or more groups, the analyst should look for outstanding variations in the rank ordering of the value orientations. In which situations are the two groups similar? To what extent do they differ? What might these similarities and differences suggest about the groups? The analyst should utilize the example of roles, discussed above, while keeping in mind the overall purpose of the analysis.

Another key to a successful analysis is to combine a creative approach with discretion in assigning meaning to the data. The challenge is to maintain a critical and creative awareness of the trends and tendencies while methodically exploring the data. The genius of the method presumes the ability to hold in mind the *whole* while examining each of its *parts.*

The fifth step of the analysis consists of comparing how the group scored on the "ideal" versus "actual" measurements. In many of the Activity situations, and two of the situations in Human Relations, the schedule asks the respondents to answer what they believe is best ("ideal") and how they actually behave ("actual"). Center staff has expanded this measurement to other situations as well. A review of this information for a group is important at this point to determine whether there is variation within a group or between groups in terms of this measurement. The analyst should give closest attention to where there is, or is not, a sharp division between the actual and the ideal.

The sixth step is to analyze variations in value orientations *across* the value dimensions and between or among groups. Prior to this step in the analysis, the process is confined to looking *within* each dimension for key variations within and between the participating groups. For example, we may find that one group is primarily Present-oriented in the Time dimension and Being-oriented in the dimension of Activity. In a second group, the Present-orientation may also be dominant, but they may prefer the Doing-orientation in the Activity dimension. In this instance, the broader meaning of what the two groups have in common (the Present-orientation) can best be understood by taking into account this variation in the Activity dimension.

The seventh step considers intra- and intergroup perceptions. The researcher may want to add a question to each situation that asks respondents to pick what they think others in their own group, or individuals in another group, believe is best, right, or most true in each situation. In the former case, this provides a profile of the "shadow" group or organization; that is, how the group as a whole is perceived by its members. In the latter instance, the results provide information on the field of intergroup or cross-cultural perceptions.

The eighth step, the cumulative analysis, is the most challenging and rewarding step in the process. The intellectual challenge is for the analyst to master and keep in mind hundreds of bits of information accumulated in steps 1–7 while revisiting and thinking through what appear to be the most important trends and tendencies. It is the most time-consuming step in the process and requires the analyst to focus on individual trends, ever mindful of the accumulated knowledge gained in each of the previous steps. The process itself is, however, deeply rewarding. This cumulative analysis illuminates unexpected connections and hidden meanings and deepens the analyst's understanding of the nature, and importance, of the value orientations method.

This information can be helpful, but it must be used with great care. The analyst should devote special attention to the situations that magnify how well or how poorly two groups understand their similarities as well as their differences in orientations. The orientation matrix presented below may assist in this portion of the analysis.

Orientation Matrix

	Know	Don't Know
Similar	**A**	**B**
Different	**C**	**D**

In Box A the respondents have similar dominant (first-order) orientations and know it. In Box B they have similar orientations but are not aware of the fact. In Box C they display variations in orientations in the situation and know it. In Box D they vary in their orientations but do not know it. This information can be used to look into a range of communication issues between different groups or cultures.

Descriptive Analysis: Rules of the Road

There is a fine line between describing the survey results and investing the results with meaning. In the descriptive analysis, the analyst conducts a straightforward examination of the orientation profiles. The results, for example, might suggest that a group is highly Collateral, favoring decisions based on the participation of the whole community. However, in the situation R4: Choice of a Delegate, they shift to first-order Individualistic. What meaning can the analyst assign to this variation? Our assumption is that we must limit our discussion to meanings that are inherent in the data and implied in the method.

The analysis can be complemented by additional research into the group, through open-ended interviews that address the current issues in depth or by way of a *home review* process within the group or community. In fact, the firsthand experience of the group or organization is important if, for example, we are to understand the social and cultural context of the orientations. One approach taken by Kluckhohn Center staff is to communicate the results to the group or community. This includes not only providing a descriptive analysis of the results but also some tentative meanings brought out in the course of the analysis. An example may help to illustrate this point.

One group was interviewed utilizing the Kluckhohn method and the results were analyzed. Center staff found that the group was very Doing-oriented. The data also revealed that most people in the group felt that others around them were Being-oriented. Clearly, this was a situation similar to that which is captured in Box B in the Orientation Matrix above.

This information was then presented to the group for their comments. What did it mean that people felt they were Doing-oriented while they believed others around them to be Being-oriented? What might cause such perceptions? What were some of the symptoms of this misunderstanding? What might be done to address it? Center staff found, in the course of the discussion, that the group had its own ideas about what the results might mean (e.g., the causes and consequences). This type of home review, whereby the participants become observers to the data, deepens the analyst's understanding of the subjective meaning of the data. It is also crucial for understanding how to best apply the results in a manner that is meaningful to the participating group(s).

Interpreting the Data

One of the most difficult challenges faced by the analyst is how to describe the results without merely referring to the technical language of value orientations. Over the years the Kluckhohn Center staff has developed an approach that might be useful for others evaluating and attempting to describe orientation patterns. In this approach, we are ever mindful of the fact that value orientations are the foundation for a group's worldview and reach far beneath the surface of values, attitudes, or opinions.

In the Time dimension, for example, we have identified the subject of change as the common denominator for all of the situations in this dimension. What does the group's pattern tell us about their relationship to change? How does the meaning of change differ from situation to situation? We developed a scale which might be useful for others evaluating the results in this dimension.

Continuum of Change

Resist Change <——> Accommodate Change <——> Seek Change
(Past) *(Present)* *(Future)*

We found that describing actual orientations in terms of this Continuum of Change, rather than referring to the orientations themselves, helped to communicate the meaning of the results to the participating group(s). While the subject of change does not capture the entire meaning of the results of the Time dimension, it does touch upon a common theme in most of the situations in this dimension. It is, we found, also a subject that groups are both able and willing to discuss.

In the Person-Nature dimension we used the data to help us understand issues of control. How much control do we, or should we, have? Does our belief in control vary with the scale of natural *forces* within and around us? Certainly, the situations PN2: Belief in Control and PN4: Facing Conditions are concerned with forces on a larger scale than are the other situations in this dimension. We developed a continuum to help us understand the data in these terms.

Continuum of Control

No Control <——> Partial Control <——> Total Control
(Subject to) *(Harmony with)* *(Mastery over)*

Once again, the issue of control does not capture the entire meaning of this dimension; it is, however, a central theme that permeates all of the situations. It is an important element of a group's specific view of the world and its relationship to large- and small-scale forces in it.

In the Activity dimension we have described the results in terms of a group's relationship to internal as opposed to external rewards. In this sense, Being is no more "active" or "passive" than Doing; rather, the two orientations indicate whether a group assigns meaning to activity through internal as opposed to external systems of reward and gratification.

Continuum of Rewards

Internal <——> External
(Being) *(Doing)*

The locus of meaning is an important element in understanding what motivates behavior. Where the two orientations differ is in their reference to internal as opposed to external standards of value and the degree to which they favor intrinsic versus extrinsic rewards and gratification.

A Sample Analysis

The data presented in Tables 1 and 2 represent the orientations data in the Time and Activity dimensions for two different groups, here labeled *A* and *B*. The title of each table includes the overall preference pattern for the group for a dimension. The first column lists the names of the situations in the dimension, followed, in the second column, by the group's pattern of rank ordering of orientations. The third column, labeled *P*, contains the level of statistical significance of the pattern.[1] The remaining columns tabulate the actual preference data for each of the named situations. For sake of comparison the listed values are *first-order percentages only;* that is, simply the percentage of the group that selected the respective orientation as "best" for themselves, for others in their own group, and for people in the other group, rather than the "deeper" second-order values usually derived for the Self responses but not for Perceived Others responses.

[1] The displayed "P-value" can range from .000, meaning a highly significant pattern, to .999, meaning a near-random or nonsignificant pattern. The term *statistically significant* does not necessarily imply significance in the everyday sense of "importance." A survey result that possesses no statistically significant pattern may be of as much research importance as one that does. This statistical measure is described as the probability that a given group of responses could have simply occurred by chance if no actual consensus of preference existed in that group, and it is based on the statistical variance of the data relative to the hypothetical null mean. On first encounter it can be difficult adapting to the fact that this traditional statistical gauge of a data-set's "reality" seems to have an inverse relationship to our intuitive assessments, in the sense that "P = zero" means "definitely yes, a pattern; no possibility of chance occurrence," while "P = maximum" means "most surely *not* a pattern; nearly 100 percent probability of no actual consensus," but this is what we must keep in mind when using this descriptor. Mathematically, the P-value can equal 1.000 but does not actually reach the certitude level of 0.000, as it is an asymptomatic exponential function ranging to infinity both positively and negatively, but, due to computational and display round-off, the value of zero sometimes does appear in these tables.

Table 1: Time Dimension Comparison

Group A, Overall Pattern: PR>FU>PA

		P	Self			Others in A, Perceived			Perceived B		
			PA	PR	FU	PA	PR	FU	PA	PR	FU
Child Training	PR>FU>PA	.000	00	91	09	00	94	06	26	71	03
Expectations Change	FU>PR>PA	.092	09	34	57	11	14	74	17	49	34
Philosophy of Life	PR>FU>PA	.031	00	69	31	00	66	34	29	63	09
Ceremonial Innovation	PR>FU>PA	.690	14	63	23	14	74	11	37	49	14
Water Allocation	FU>PR>PA	.001	00	11	89	03	06	89	27	23	51

Group B, Overall Pattern: PR=PA>FU

		P	Self			Others in B, Perceived			Perceived A		
			PA	PR	FU	PA	PR	FU	PA	PR	FU
Child Training	PR>PA>FU	.025	38	61	02	28	63	09	05	35	60
Expectations Change	FU=PR>PA	.915	38	31	32	37	26	37	00	40	60
Philosophy of Life	PR>PA>FU	.326	26	54	19	32	54	19	15	13	72
Ceremonial Innovation	PA>PR>FU	.002	72	27	01	47	36	17	02	32	66
Water Allocation	FU>PA>PR	.310	20	25	55	25	51	25	00	37	63

Table 2: Activity Dimension Comparison

Group A, Overall Pattern: DO>BE

		P	Self		Others in A, Perceived		Perceived B	
			DO	BE	DO	BE	DO	BE
Job Choice (1a)	DO>BE	.013	69	31	58	40	29	71
Job Choice (1b)	DO>BE	.043	60	40	69	31	34	66
Ways of Living	DO>BE	.000	89	11	94	06	34	66
[Actual]			[86]	[14]				
Care of Fields	BE>DO	.022	34	66	57	43	17	83
[Actual]			[75]	[25]				
Housework	DO>BE	.038	66	34	83	17	40	60
Nonworking Time	BE>DO	.038	34	66	60	40	20	80

Table 2: Activity Dimension Comparison (cont.)

Group B, Overall Pattern: DO>BE

		P	Self		Others in B, Perceived		Perceived A	
			DO	BE	DO	BE	DO	BE
Job Choice (1a)	DO>BE	.028	76	24	70	30	65	35
Job Choice (1b)	DO>BE	.001	82	18	38	62	70	30
Ways of Living	DO>BE	.038	66	34	40	60	75	25
[Actual]			[54]	[46]				
Care of Fields	DO>BE	.038	66	34	40	60	55	45
[Actual]			[45]	[55]				
Housework	DO>BE	.034	61	39	34	66	55	45
Nonworking Time	DO>BE	.272	57	43	35	65	50	50

Step 1: Examine Overall Sums

We begin with a review of how the two groups compare in their overall patterns. Here we can see that they differ significantly in the Time dimension. In very general terms we can describe Group A as rooted in the present and willing to accommodate change, even if this means modifying or leaving behind past beliefs or traditions. Group B differs significantly in its view of how the past influences the present. The pattern describes a group that places equal emphasis on the past and the present and is generally unwilling to seek change if it means leaving behind lessons, traditions, or beliefs that come from the past.

In the Activity dimension we find that the two groups are very similar. Both groups generally prefer the Doing orientation and can be characterized as being made up of individuals who prefer to keep active and busy, doing things that result in tangible rewards valued by others around them.

Step 2: Examine Results for Each Situation

Looking first at Group A we can see that the Present orientation is preferred in three of the five situations and that, in each case, the levels of statistical significance are very high, with the notable exception of Ceremonial Innovation. In their general life philosophy and in those situations that implicate family teachings (Ceremonial Innovation and Child Training), what is most important is what is "happening now." If forced to choose they would rather look to the future and seek change than preserve the "old ways." We should also take note of those situations when the Future orientation is first-order. Most people (89 percent) agree that the future belongs to those who plan ahead (Water Allocation). A majority (57 percent) would also agree that progress means change, and change brings improvement for those who are willing to make sacrifices (Expectations about Change).

In Group B, we find a pronounced variation in orientations in the Time dimension. In some cases (Child Training and Philosophy of Life) the Present orientation is most preferred. In another situation (Ceremonial Innovation) the Past orientation clearly dominates the pattern. The Future, however, also plays a role in two other situations (Expectations about Change and Water Allocation). This wide range of variation is, in itself, an important element to keep in mind during the analysis.

We can also see that in Group B, the closer the situations touch upon family or community traditions, the more prominent the Past orientation becomes (e.g., Ceremonial Innovation and Child Training). In the group's general life philosophy, they are rooted in the present and "paying attention to what is happening now." Looking at Group B's Philosophy of Life item, we can see that 54 percent of the respondents selected Present as compared to 26 percent who picked Past. When the subject turns to planning (Water Allocation), however, or what they think their families will have "compared with [their] fathers and mothers" (Expectations about Change), this group turned with increasing frequency to the Future orientation.

Turning to the Activity dimension, we find that Group A is Doing-oriented in four of six situations. What, we might ask, caused them to shift to Being-oriented in the other two (Care of Fields and Nonworking Time)? Looking more closely at these two situations, we find that they both implicate leisure time. We might describe this group as one that believes it is important to do work that is meaningful to the group around them, but that it is also important to cultivate leisure-time activities.

Group B has less variation than Group A in the Activity dimension, preferring the Doing orientation by a wide margin in all but one of the situations. Group B clearly emphasizes the work ethic and activities that are meaningful both to the individual and to the group as a whole.

Step 3: Analyze Variations within Dimensions and between or among Groups

It is now time to look at how the groups vary or are similar in different situations in each dimension. For purposes of this illustration, we will look at the Time dimension. Here we find that the groups differ from each other in all five situations. Although both groups generally prefer the Present orientation (e.g., Philosophy of Life), there is significant variation between them in the importance they assign to the Past and the Future (e.g., Ceremonial Innovation). We should also note that the patterns for the two groups most resemble each other in the situation Expectations about Change. However, the pattern for Group A has a much higher level of statistical significance than that of Group B in this situation.

Step 4: Examine Role-Related Situations across Dimensions

The analyst should now turn to examining variations across dimensions based on role relations. We have identified two situations for Group B from the Activity (Ways of Living) and Time (Ceremonial Innovation) dimensions. In Ways of Living, two-thirds of Group B prefer staying busy accomplishing things with clear results, even if this means sacrificing leisure-time activities. At the same time, the group has a strong Past orientation in the situation Ceremonial Innovation, with 72 percent of the sample preferring to keep religious ceremonies "exactly, in every way, as they had been in the past." There may be some crossover effects of these two orientations. Work-related responsibilities, for example, may require sacrificing the family time required to maintain family religious practices.

Step 5: Analyze Results of Self "Actual" versus Self "Ideal"

The analyst should now compare the response of "actual" versus "ideal." Here we will look at the Activity dimension. We can see for Group A that there is a notable variation between these two measures in the situation Care of Fields. In this situation, two-thirds felt that the Being orientation, with its emphasis on cultivating leisure time, was the "better" way to live. When asked which kind of person they were "actually more like," three-quarters portrayed themselves as Doing-oriented. In other words, approximately four out of ten of the respondents believe they are doing more and working harder than they believe is best. A similar, though less pronounced reversal is found in this situation for Group B.

Step 6: Analyze Variations across Dimensions between Groups

To illustrate analyzing variations across dimensions we have selected one situation from the Time dimension (Expectations about Change) and another from Activity (Ways of Living). In the former situation, the orientation of Group A suggests a faith in the future and that "things in this country usually get better for people who try" (e.g., those who work hard and plan right). At the same time, their Doing orientation in the situation Ways of Living tells us that they will look to the results of their labor to determine whether or not "things are improving." This linkage suggests that for this group, diminished opportunities for "getting things done" could have a dramatic effect on their belief in the future. By contrast, Group B is more conservative in what it expects from the future (FU = PR on Expectations about Change) and is slightly less Doing-oriented in the situation Ways of Living. Declining opportunities, while problematic, would not be as traumatic for most members of this group.

Step 7: Examine the Results of Intra- and Intergroup Perceptions

Looking first at intragroup perceptions in Group A, we find that in the Activity dimension they are reasonably accurate in their perceptions of the first-order choices of others around them. Two notable exceptions are Care of Fields and Nonworking Time. In both situations, many respondents mistakenly perceived that others around them would think that the Doing orientation was "best." We see a tendency that is different in both degree and kind in Group B, where intragroup perceptions are far less accurate. Here we find that most people, regardless of the situation, believe that Doing is best, while describing others around them in terms of the Being orientation.

Most people in Group A are generally correct in their perceptions of others around them in the Time dimension. The notable exception to this is the situation Expectations about Change. Interestingly, approximately one in five respondents believes that others around them are more optimistic about the future than they themselves are. We find a reversed tendency in Group B, where many respondents picture others around them as more pessimistic about the future than they are. On the whole, Group B is less accurate in its perceptions of its group than is Group A. This misunderstanding is evident, for example, in the situation Ceremonial Innovation, where only 47 percent of the sampled population picked for "most people" the orientation that was actually most preferred by the group.

How well do the two groups understand each other? In the Activity dimension, we can see a serious misunderstanding in how Group B is perceived by Group A. In each situation, Group B is perceived as Being-oriented, when in fact, they are strongly Doing-oriented. Looking at the Time dimension, we find that Group B generally underestimates the importance of the present to Group A's orientation while overestimating the role of the future.

Step 8: Combine Data in Cumulative Analysis

This is the most complex and demanding step in the process of analysis. The analyst has, by this point, worked through the data and must keep the earlier findings in mind as he or she combines the data in a cumulative analysis. Once again we must return to the general intent and purpose of the analysis. If, for example, the main objective is to improve communication between groups, we may pull out certain data items and combine them. The analyst should consider not only how the groups compare in their overall sums but also how these variations and similarities manifest themselves in key situations. The Orientation Matrix (page 220) can be employed to take a closer look at intergroup perceptions, mixing in data from the measurements of "actual" versus "ideal" in the Activity and Human Relations dimensions. Some of the questions the analyst might consider include the following:

- How would the variations in orientations influence relations between the two groups?
- What does the data tell us about the meaning the two groups give to such issues as control, change, and quality of life?
- How might intergroup perceptions affect interaction between them?
- Do the variations in orientations help to explain how the two groups perceive each other?
- Which situations most closely resemble those actually encountered by the two groups?
- What does the data tell us about the most effective ways to communicate the results of the research within the group?
- How might the data be used to structure critical cultural incidents that can be used in a workshop setting?

Step 9: Apply the Information in a Workshop Setting

We felt it important to offer a few thoughts about applying this information in a (cross-cultural) workshop setting. First, workshops provide an excellent opportunity to present the results of the Value Orientations Survey. It is often best to simply *describe* the results of the interviews and ask the participants to discuss what the results *mean* for them and their group. Second, it is important for the individuals designing these sessions to understand the variations in value orientations of the workshop participants *and* their parent organization. Collaterally oriented groups, for example, may respond to large-group discussion, where everyone can participate; groups with an Individualistic orientation may feel more comfortable in a small-group (one-on-one) format. Lineal groups may expect a more formal, lecture-type presentation, followed by a structured discussion period. Finally, the survey information can be applied in the development of critical cultural incidents. These incidents should be designed to evoke similarities or differences between the participating groups and allow the participants to be exposed to, and have ample opportunity to discuss, perceptual diversity. The incidents should be hypothetical and nonthreatening in nature but relevant to actual issues of mutual interest to the participating groups.

Appendix C

Administering and Modifying the Kluckhohn Survey

Interview Protocol

The interview protocols set forth in this appendix promote comparability of values research based on the Kluckhohn method to the benefit of both the researchers and their respondents or study groups.

A one-on-one oral interview, where time and personnel constraints allow, is the best method for administering the Kluckhohn survey. This interview format has several important advantages. First, it encourages respondents to answer all of the questions without skipping over any of the alternatives. Second, it allows the researcher to exercise some discretion regarding the inclusion of "suspect" interviews in the final analysis of results (in some cases, for example, it may be evident that the respondent is being disingenuous and therefore his or her answers must be carefully considered). Third, oral interviews permit the interviewer to record the subject's comments during the interview, which may prove very useful in the development of workshops or discussions. Lastly, oral interviews ensure that the respondent has understood the content of the situation and has not changed any of his or her previous answers.

Ideally, interviewers should be thoroughly familiar with the survey and have a good working understanding of the theoretical foundations of the Kluckhohn method and its relationship to the survey. The respondents, however, should know as little as possible about the mechanics of the method until after completion of all the interviews in the group.

The original survey as designed by Dr. Kluckhohn requires approximately one hour to complete. Before beginning the interview, the interviewers will want to briefly outline the interview process and provide a few simple guidelines. They will typically:

- inform the interviewee that the interview will take approximately an hour to complete;
- give a brief history of the method;
- stress that there are no "right" answers other than whatever the respondent most honestly feels to be the "best," "right," or "most true" answer;
- ask the respondents to answer all questions;
- tell the respondents they may take as long as they wish in answering each question but that they will not be allowed to ask to change any answers to previous questions;
- explain that the interviewer will read the situation aloud as many times as necessary but cannot explain or interpret the situations; and
- assure respondents of the confidentiality and anonymity of their answers.

In the event that individual oral interviews are not possible, there are several other possible formats. First, one interviewer may interview several subjects simultaneously. This approach has been utilized by Kluckhohn Center staff and, while it produces reliable results, it does not allow for confidential comments by the subjects during the course of the interview. Second, respondents may also use a computerized version of the Kluckhohn survey, such as the Computer Assisted Data Collection program developed by the Kluckhohn Center.[1]

The least preferred option is to provide the respondent with a written questionnaire to be completed without the assistance of the researcher. Interviewers who choose this format must strongly discourage respondents from returning to previous situations in order to change their answers. They may also want to ask interviewees to take notes on what they thought and felt during the survey.

---

[1] For copies of the survey, write to the Florence R. Kluckhohn Center, 119 N. Commercial, Room 820, Bellingham, WA 98225. The Center can make available scoring sheets for the Kluckhohn survey. In addition, the Center can provide a computerized "Value Orientation Data Analyzer" for processing the results.

Modifying the Kluckhohn Survey

Since 1960 researchers working with many different cultural groups around the world have chosen independently to use the Kluckhohn method. At the Center we have started to collect and catalogue these studies. One of the basic strengths of the method is the comparability of the cultural value orientations profiles it produces. We wish to provide workers in the field with the opportunity to compare results from different studies, but that ability rests almost entirely on the consistency of the schedules used. Substantially modified surveys may not be credible extensions of the Kluckhohn model, and results obtained may only apply to the group(s) tested with the same survey. We strongly encourage the use of the original survey as the "gold standard" for Kluckhohn research.

Over the years, some researchers have chosen to modify the original schedule to suit the immediate purpose and cultural context of their research. Without wishing to detract from the considerable independent value of the studies performed using nonstandard schedules, we suggest the use of some general validity tests, which allow researchers to make minor modifications without sacrificing the ability to compare results. We encourage researchers, wherever possible, to use the schedule as is, because its imperfections are outweighed by its worth as a "fixed variable" in the complicated equation of values comparison.

Anyone who works closely with the instrument will notice its imperfections. It lacks, for example, situations that tap into the Human Nature dimension. Also, the Activity dimension has only a two-point range; a way to measure Being-in-Becoming has not been developed. However, the method continues to be widely used. It is truly a pioneering effort into a very complex and delicate arena, one that attempts to get at the heart of values and their complexity.

As more and more people use the method, they will generate critiques and suggestions. Connections with and comparisons between large bodies of experience and observation will gradually give shape to the hazy cross-cultural territory the method attempts to navigate. But such a rich exploration and inquiry will not be possible unless a high degree of correspondence among different versions of the instrument is maintained.

Alternate Survey Schedules

One of the distinguishing features of a substantially changed schedule is that the standard statistical manipulations used with the original schedule cannot sensibly be applied to the new schedule. Such new schedules are structurally changed enough to be considered alternate value instruments. Important examples of these are discussed briefly below.

Probably the most substantially revised and also arguably the most robust alternate version is the Inter-cultural Values Inventory (ICV) developed by Robert T. Carter and Janet E. Helms.[2] The format of the ICV consists of 150 short idiomatic statements such as "Work is a virtue in and of itself" and "Hard work never hurt anyone," to which the interviewee answers yes or no.[3] These questions can be classified according to dimensional content, although in some sense they represent explicit values rather than the orientations that underlie those values. For example, "Any society that does not allow individuals to voice their dissent is not a free society" expresses an explicit social value. Carter and Helms have completed a large number of interviews with their schedule and found the results very interesting and useful. However, it is not possible to compare data from their version with data from the original Kluckhohn survey.

In 1974 Logan L. Green and Michael Haymes developed a schedule called "My Feelings about Life." This schedule may be useful as a scale on which to measure personal value orientations as opposed to cultural profiles. The Green and Haymes questions recast the story situations of the Kluckhohn method in the form of statements starting with the phrase, "By my own standards" (e.g., "By my own standards, I feel that what I am doing should always prepare me for the future"). There are forty-nine statements in the schedule, and, unlike the Kluckhohn survey, it includes the Human Nature category. Respondents mark a scale of 0–5, where 0–2 is a range of *Disagree*, and 3–5, of *Agree*. This type of response differs from the choice of one alternative over another in the story situations of the original survey in terms of both statistical content and theoretical approach. The story situations are designed to tap un-

---

[2] The ICV can be obtained by writing to Dr. Robert T. Carter, Teachers College, Columbia University, 525 W. 120th Street, Box 102, New York, NY 10027.

[3] So far only an English-language version of the ICV has been developed.

conscious systems of meanings by allowing interviewees to project their own orientations onto the actors of the stories, whereas the Green and Haymes questions are cast as deliberate statements of personal belief. It is not clear exactly how such a difference may affect responses.

Some researchers have completely rewritten the original instrument to serve an immediate and specific research need. William B. Clifford and Thomas R. Ford (1974) studied fertility among farm women in Kentucky. They wished to test for "attitude toward sex," so their alternate version of the schedule included questions on the Person-Nature dimension refigured as the Nature of Sex. Again, like Green and Haymes, interviewees answer a series of statements, *Agree-Disagree*, on a scale of 0-4. Since respondents do not choose among three alternatives, the statistical calculations for internal consistency are quite different from the original Kluckhohn survey. In addition, these kinds of binary choice surveys, in contrast with the original schedule, do not provide second-order patterns of responses.

The schedule Danilo E. Ponce uses in his work at a psychiatric center for juveniles in Hawaii falls somewhere between a fully alternate version and a modified version. Dr. Ponce, in the interests of time and the necessity for information about the Person-Nature dimension, uses an abbreviated and revised version of the schedule containing two original situations from each dimension, plus one additional story-format question of his own design on Person-Nature. Dr. Ponce's abbreviated schedule is derived almost entirely from the original schedule, but the information it generates cannot be treated in the same statistical fashion as that deriving from the longer interview because it contains too few questions in each dimension.

Modified Survey Schedules

It is possible to change the language and/or content of particular story situations without losing the character and intent of the original survey. One of the most extensively changed versions, which still qualifies as a "modified" and not "alternate" version, is Sharon Ogden-Burke and Rita Maloney's "Women's Value Orientation Questionnaire" (WVOQ). Ogden-Burke and Maloney maintained the story format of the original but changed six of the situations in order to adapt the schedule for use with women, with particular regard to issues of health care. For example, the team substituted for the relational question called "Well Arrangements" a story about a new prenatal and well-baby clinic.

Ogden-Burke and Maloney provide an excellent model for content changes to the schedule. After developing new story situations, the team tested them for face validity and criterion validity. In the face-validity testing, they tried to answer the questions: Is the question appropriate and sensitive? How does it strike the interviewees? Ogden-Burke and Maloney consulted child-care experts and members of the cultural group they planned to interview and, on their advice, made minor changes; for example, "God or gods," became "God, god, gods, or the Creator." During the criterion-validity testing, they asked themselves: Does the question accurately reflect value orientation constructs and is it congruent with the original schedule? To find out, they administered both the original Value Orientations Survey and the WVOQ to ten women and analyzed the results of both tests for comparability. On the basis of this analysis, they dropped two of their new situations and edited a third.

Another extensively revised schedule is the "Urban Value Orientations Schedule," used by Pamela J. Brink, Diane DeMay, and others. This schedule follows the same format as the Kluckhohn method schedule except that many of the story situations are adapted to fit an urban context. Research is needed to determine whether or not this schedule meets the face- and criterion-validity tests.

We recommend that any substantial story content change(s) be tested for face and criterion validity. However, some very minor changes have been made (without such testing) that probably do not deeply affect the structural integrity of the schedule. Janice Egeland, for instance, noticed that among the Amish, R6 and R7 always produced the same response, so she eliminated one of them. Brink noticed the same thing among the Annang. Terry Gushiuliak, when interviewing Hutterian women, found it useful to add a question about inheritance. In addition to questions about land and cattle, she asked a question concerning the inheritance of personal belongings "such as a chest containing one's own things." Saul Arbess, interviewing among the George River Inuit peoples, changed R1: Well Arrangements into a question about a fishing project. And the standard schedule used by the Kluckhohn staff has been slightly changed to reflect gender-neutral constructions. For example, "A person" now replaces "a man."

****

Thoughts and criticisms about the Kluckhohn method deserve to be as widely communicated within the field of cultural studies as possible. The Kluckhohn Center hopes to stimulate and circulate active criticism of the method by its users. We appeal to all users of the Kluckhohn method to communicate to us your creative innovations or suggestions so that we may distribute them to other practitioners in the field. In this way we hope to promote conversation about the changes necessary to create a better survey and at the same time allow for the unique opportunity to compare results from different studies.

We especially appeal to all practitioners to send the Center the results of their work. We are interested in small and large projects and in research. This networking will provide everyone with a tapestry of results from other groups to compare with their own group's data. These shared results will increase the meaning and interest of every survey performed.

References

Carter, Robert T., and Janet E. Helms. "The Intercultural Values Inventory (ICV)." In *Tests in Microfiche Test Collection.* Princeton, NJ: Educational Testing Service, 1990.

Clifford, William B., and Thomas R. Ford. "Variations in Value Orientations in Fertility Behavior." *Social Biology* 21, no. 2, 1974.

Ogden-Burke, Sharon, and Rita Maloney. "The Women's Value Orientation Questionnaire: An Instrument Revision Study." *Nursing Papers* 18, no. 1 (1986): 32–44.

Selective Bibliography of Value Orientations Research

Adinolfi, Allen A., and Robert E. Klein. "The Value Orientations of Guatemalan Subsistence Farmers: Measurement and Implications." *Journal of Social Psychology* 87 (1972): 13–20.

Bachtold, Louise M., and Karin L. Eckvall. "Current Value Orientations of American Indians in Northern California: The Hupa." *Journal of Cross-Cultural Psychology* 9, no. 3 (September 1978): 367–75.

Brink, Pamela J. "Value Orientations as an Assessment Tool in Cultural Diversity." *Nursing Research* 33, no. 4 (1984): 198–203.

Carter, Robert T. "Cultural Value Differences between African Americans and White Americans." *Journal of College Student Development* 31 (1990): 71–79.

Carter, Robert T., and Janet E. Helms. "White Cultural Values and Racial Identity Attitudes." In *Black and White Racial Identity Attitudes: Theory, Research and Practice,* edited by Janet E. Helms. Westport, CT: Greenwood Press, 1990.

———. "The Relationship of Black Value Orientations to Racial Identity Attitudes." *Journal of Measurement and Evaluation in Counseling and Development* 19, no. 4 (1987): 185–95.

Carter, Robert T., and Elizabeth Parks. "White Ethnic Group Membership and Cultural Value Preferences." *Journal of College Student Development* 33 (1992): 499–505.

Caudell, William, and Harry A. Scarr. "Japanese Value Orientations and Culture Change." *Ethnology* 1, no. 1 (1962): 53–91.

Chandler, C. R. "Traditionalism in a Modern Setting: A Comparison of Anglo and Mexican American Value Orientations." *Human Organization* 38, no. 2 (1979): 153–59.

———. "Value Orientations among Mexican Americans in a Southwestern City." *Sociology and Social Research* 58 (1971): 262–71.

Danielian, Jack. "Development of Construct-Relevant and Cultural Non-Biased Criteria for Measuring Judging Accuracy." *International Journal of Psychology* 4, no. 2 (1969): 129–34.

Druckman, Daniel, Benjamin J. Broome, and Susan H. Karper. "Value Differences and Conflict Resolution: Facilitation or Delinking?" *Journal of Conflict Resolution* 32, no. 3 (1988): 489–510.

Gallagher, Thomas J. "Language, Native People, and Land Management in Alaska." *Arctic* 45, no. 2 (1992): 146–49.

———. "Native Participants in Land Management Planning in Alaska." *Arctic* 41, no. 2 (1988): 91–98.

Gallagher, Thomas J., and Laura J. Noland. "Cross-Cultural Communication for Land Managers and Planners in Alaska." *Argoborealis* 21, no. 1 (1989): 18–23.

Khoury, R. M., and G. T. Thurmond. "Ethnic Differences in Time Perception: A Comparison of Anglo and Mexican Americans." *Perceptual and Motor Skills* 47 (1978): 1183–88.

Kluckhohn, Florence R., and Fred L. Strodtbeck. *Variations in Value Orientations.* Evanston, IL: Row, Peterson, 1961.

Lyden, Fremont J. "Value Orientations in Public Decision Making." *Policy Studies Journal* 16, no. 4 (1988): 843–56.

Lyden, Fremont J., Ben W. Twight, and E. Thomas Tuchmann. "Citizen Participation in Long-Range Planning: The RPA Experience." *Natural Resources Journal* 30 (1990): 123–38.

Menon, D. K., N. N. Wig, Verma Jain, and Sudha Jain. "Preliminary Experience with PGI Achievement Value Index." *Indian Journal of Clinical Psychology* 2 (1975): 177–78.

Mestenhauser, Josef A. "Travelling the Unpaved Road to Democracy from Communism: A Cross-Cultural Perspective on Change." *Higher Education in Europe* 23, no. 1 (1998): 83–137.

Ogden-Burke, Sharon, Barbara Kisilevsky, and Rita Maloney. "Time Orientations of Indian Mothers and White Nurses." *Canadian Journal of Nursing Research* 29, no. 4 (1989): 5–19.

Ortuño, Marian M. "Cross-Cultural Awareness in the Foreign Language Class: The Kluckhohn Model." *Modern Language Journal* 75, no. 4 (1991): 449–59.

Papajohn, John, and John P. Spiegel. *Transactions in Families: A Modern Approach to Resolving Cultural and Generational Conflicts*. San Fransisco: Jossey-Bass, 1975.

———. "The Relationship of Culture Value Orientation Change and Rorschach Indices of Psychological Development." *Journal of Cross-Cultural Psychology* 2, no. 3 (1971): 257–72.

Ponce, Danilo E. "Value Orientation: Clinical Applications in a Multi-Cultural Residential Treatment Center for Children and Youth." *Residential Group Care and Treatment* 2, no. 4 (1985): 71–83.

Remer, Rory, and Pamela A. Remer. "A Study of the Discrepancies among the Values Orderings of Twelve Counseling Tribes: The Quantification of Values Differences." *Counseling and Values* (1982).

Russo, Kurt W., and Steven Zubalik. "Squa'di'lich, Board Feet and the Cedar Tree." In *Native Americans and Public Policy*, edited by Fremont J. Lyden and Lyman Legters. Pittsburgh: University of Pittsburgh Press, 1988.

Schwarzweller, Harry K. "Value Orientations in Educational and Occupational Choices." *Rural Sociology* 24 (1959): 246–56.

Trimble, Joseph E. "Value Differences among American Indians: Concerns for the Concerned Counselor." In *Counseling across Cultures*, edited by Paul Pedersen, Walter J. Lonner, and Juris G. Draguns. Honolulu: The University Press of Hawaii, 1976.

Twight, Ben W., Fremont J. Lyden, and E. Thomas Tuchmann. "Constituency Bias in a Federal Career System? A Study of District Rangers of the U.S. Forest Service." *Administration and Society* 22, no. 3 (1990): 358–89.

———. "Measuring Forest Service Bias." *Journal of Forestry* 87, no. 5 (1989): 35–41.

Twight, Ben W., and John J. Paterson. "Conflict and Public Involvement: Measuring Consensus." *Society of American Foresters* (1979): 771–76.

Valdez, Ramiro. "Chicano Value Orientations and Mental Health Policy." Ph.D. diss., Brandeis University, 1980.

Wagner, Eric A., and Lawrence G. Hald. "Sport as a Reflector of Change: Football, Wilderness Sport and Dominant American Values." *Arena Review* 10, no. 1 (1986): 43–55.

Zaharna, Rhonda S. "Understanding Cultural Preferences of Arab Communication Patterns." *Public Relations Review* 21, no. 3 (1995): 241–55.

Zern, David. "The Relevance of Family Cohesiveness as a Determinant of Premarital Sexual Behavior in a Cross-Cultural Sample." *Journal of Social Psychology* 78 (1969): 3–9.

About the Contributors

Contributor and Editor

Kurt W. Russo: M.S., University of Washington, College of Forestry, executive director and cofounder of the Florence R. Kluckhohn Center for the Study of Values. Mr. Russo began working with the value orientations method in 1982 under the supervision of Dr. Florence Kluckhohn and has directed research and training programs utilizing the method in tribal communities and public- and private-sector groups in Washington State and in the Republic of South Africa. He has been employed by the Lummi Nation since 1978, focusing on treaty rights and environmental issues. In addition, he has served as coordinator for the International Indigenous Exchange Program at Northwest Indian College since 1989.

Contributors

Pamela J. Brink: Ph.D. in cultural anthropology, Boston University, professor and associate dean, University of Alberta. Dr. Brink is the founder and executive editor of the *Western Journal of Nursing Research* and associate editor of *Medical Anthropology*. Dr. Brink's research topics include childhood socialization of the Northern Paiute Indians, ethnography of a southeastern Kentucky community, and value orientations. Her publications include articles on these topics as well as three books: *Transcultural Nursing: A Book of Readings*

(1976), *Basic Steps in Planning Nursing Research* (1988), *and Advanced Design in Nursing Research* (1989).

Dorothy Caplow: B.A. in literature from Yale University. After moving to Washington State, she conducted research for the University of Washington Friday Harbor Laboratories prior to her two-year association with the Kluckhohn Center. During her tenure with the Center she organized and coordinated the Values Symposium, which provided much of the material for the present volume, and participated in the design of a series of Center cross-cultural conflict resolution projects. She resigned her position with the Center in 1998 to undertake graduate studies in physics at the Univeristy of Washington and to parent her five-year-old son.

Ann D. Chapman: Ph.D. in educational psychology, associate professor of educational psychology and counseling at Eastern Kentucky University and a licensed psychologist in the Commonwealth of Kentucky. Dr. Chapman was the past president of the Kentucky Association for Counselor Education and Supervision from 1992–1993. Her publications include numerous articles and conference presentations on educational psychology and counseling, including "Value Orientation Analysis: The Adaptation of an Anthropological Model for Counseling Research" (*The Personnel and Guidance Journal*, 1981).

Thomas J. Gallagher: Ph.D. in natural resources, University of Michigan. Dr. Gallagher is leadership specialist and associate professor with the Extension Service at Oregon State University. Prior to that he was professor of public administration, natural resources, at the University of Alaska, where he researched cross-cultural aspects of land management and public involvement in government planning. He is a Kellogg Leadership Fellow and a Phi Theta Kappa Certified Leadership Trainer. His present research and consultation is in cross-cultural aspects of leadership and decision making.

L. Robert Kohls: Ph.D. in cultural history, New York University. Dr. Kohls has provided intercultural training for mid- and upper-level executives in more than seventy-five of the Fortune 500 companies. He has served as senior cross-cultural trainer with the Business Council for International Understanding, the American Management Association, and the National Training Labs, and for such independent consulting firms as The East West Group and Global Dynamics. He was a human resource development officer for seven years with Westinghouse and Time Inc., and he served for more than a decade with the U.S. Foreign Service. He has lived and worked in Korea, Japan, Brazil, Libya, Tunisia, and Spain. His *Survival Kit for Overseas Living* is one of the best-selling cross-cultural books ever published, and his *Training Know-How for Cross-Cultural and Diversity Trainers,* coauthored with Herbert L. Brussow, is also a current best-seller.

Alexander H. Leighton: M.D., Johns Hopkins University. Following psychiatric training at Johns Hopkins and after serving in the Navy during World War II, Dr. Leighton was appointed professor of sociology and anthropology and also professor of psychiatry at Cornell University from 1946 to 1966. In 1966 he moved to the Harvard School of Public Health until his retirement in 1975, at which time he was professor of social psychiatry and head of the Department of Behavioral Sciences. Currently he holds postretirement positions as professor of psychiatry and professor of community health and epidemiology at Dalhousie University in Nova Scotia. He has served on a number of advisory committees for the governments of the United States and Canada and for the World Health Organization.

Marian M. Ortuño: Ph.D., University of Michigan, assistant professor, Baylor University, Texas. Dr. Ortuño teaches Spanish literature and culture courses at Baylor. Her Ph.D. specialization is in Spanish literature of the sixteenth and seventeenth centuries. She has been using the Kluckhohn model in the classroom since the late 1980s to raise awareness among her students of how cultural differences may influence the ways people from different cultures interact with and perceive one another. Some of her publications include "Cross-Cultural Awareness in the Foreign Language Class: The Kluckhohn Model," *The Modern Language Journal* (1991) and "Teaching Language Skills and Cultural Awareness with Spanish Painting," *Hispania* (1994).

John Papajohn: Ph.D., lecturer in psychology in the Department of Psychiatry, Harvard Medical School, and attending psychologist, McLean Hospital, Belmont, Massachusetts. Dr. Papajohn began his professional career at Harvard University, where he joined Florence Kluckhohn and John P. Spiegel in their continuing studies on acculturation stress in American ethnic groups. He has written several books on behavior therapy. With J. Spiegel: *Transactions: The Interplay between Individual, Family, and Society* (1971) and *Transactions* *in Families: Ethnic Families and Culture Change* (1975). In progress: *The Hyphenated American: The Hidden Injuries of Culture* (Free Press). In addition, he has published several articles on value orientations.

Danilo E. Ponce: M.D., professor of psychiatry at John A. Burns School of Medicine, University of Hawaii. Dr. Ponce has been interested in the cross-cultural clinical applications of the value orientations model for more than twenty-five years and has used it extensively in individual, group, and family counseling and psychotherapy. He has also found the model particularly useful in supervision, consultation, mediation and conflict resolution, systems analysis, and program planning. Through the years, Dr. Ponce has been invited to present the clinical applications of the model at various local (Hawaii), national, and international scientific conferences, most notably in the Philippines, Indonesia, Singapore, Malaysia, Thailand, Taiwan, China, and Canada.

Richard D. Robinson: Ph.D., Massachusetts Institute of Technology; Jewett Distinguished Professor of Business, University of Puget Sound; and Professor Emeritus of Management, School of Management, MIT. Dr. Robinson resided in Turkey for several years and acted as a staff specialist for the American Universities Field Staff and was a correspondent for the *Chicago Daily News* foreign service. He has authored numerous books and articles that largely focus on various aspects of international management. Such publications include *The International Communication of Technology* (1991); *Cases on International Technology Transfer* (1988); *The Japan Syndrome—Is There One? Japanese Management in the United States* (1985); and *International Business Management, A Guide to Decision Making* (1978).

John P. Spiegel: M.D., professor emeritus, Florence Heller School for Advanced Studies in Social Welfare, Brandeis University. At Harvard University the late Dr. Spiegel was a pioneer in the study of culture change and mental health in American ethnic groups. He also served as president of the American Psychiatric Association. He published widely in the area of culture and mental health. Such publications include *Transactions in Families* (1975), coauthored with John Papajohn, and *Transactions, The Interplay of the Individual, Society and Culture* (1971), edited by John Papajohn.

George E. Taylor: Litt. D. in history and politics, University of Birmingham. In 1928 Dr. Taylor came to the United States to study at Johns Hopkins University and Harvard University respectively. Shortly after his foray in the United States, he moved to China, where he was a professor at the Central Policy Institute in Nanjing. He lived in China and traveled extensively in East Asia from 1930–1939. In 1939 he moved to Seattle, Washington, where he taught at the University of Washington and became the director of the Far Eastern and Russian Institute. He retired from the university in 1976 and served as president of the Washington Council on International Trade until 1987. Dr. Taylor has published several articles and books on East Asian history and politics, which include *The Philippines and the United States: Problems of Partnership* (1964) and, with Franz Michael, *The Far East in the Modern World* (1956).

Bill Wallace currently serves as northwest regional manager for the Department of Natural Resources of Washington State. He has worked with the department for twenty-two years, eleven of which were spent in the Northwest. While implementing land management and fire control programs, he has had the opportunity to interact with numerous Indian Nations in Washington. In 1988 he participated in a values project coordinated by the Florence R. Kluckhohn Center for the Study of Values.

Index

A

B

C

D

E

F

G

H

I

J

K

W